ABOUT THE AUTHOR

Valerie Helps was born in London and grew up in East Africa. Widely travelled, she has lived in Australia, Greece and France where she established herself as a successful travel writer and illustrator. Her short stories, poetry and children's books have been published in major newspapers and journals worldwide. She now lives in Sydney close to her family.

THE SILENT TOWERS SPEAK

SECRETS OF THE DEEP MANI

Valerie Helps

THE SILENT TOWERS SPEAK

Artwork Valerie Helps and Geoffrey Bull
Cover painting Valerie Helps

Vanguard Press

VANGUARD PAPERBACK

© Copyright 2021
Valerie Helps

The right of Valerie Helps to be identified as author of
this work has been asserted by her in accordance with the
Copyright, Designs and Patents Act 1988.

All Rights Reserved

No reproduction, copy or transmission of this publication
may be made without written permission.
No paragraph of this publication may be reproduced,
copied or transmitted save with the written permission of the publisher, or in
accordance with the provisions
of the Copyright Act 1956 (as amended).

Any person who commits any unauthorised act in relation to
this publication may be liable to criminal
prosecution and civil claims for damages.

A CIP catalogue record for this title is
available from the British Library.

ISBN 978 1 784659 77 6

*Vanguard Press is an imprint of
Pegasus Elliot MacKenzie Publishers Ltd.*
www.pegasuspublishers.com

First Published in 2021

**Vanguard Press
Sheraton House Castle Park
Cambridge England**

Printed & Bound in Great Britain

Dedication

To the people of the Mani for the friendship given to us during our sojourn in their fascinating and memorable land of towers.

Acknowledgements

The Greeks have dreamt the dream of life best

Johann Wolfgang von Goethe

My gratitude to Melissa for her proof reading skills and to Don for his invaluable advice with the Greek language and for their friendship.

Other works by Valerie Helps

The Voyages of de Villehardouin Cruising French Waterways
Vanguard Press (2018)
ISBN 9781784654542

A Third of a Pond
Vanguard Press (2020)
ISBN 9781784656812

Berrywine
A book of poems by Valerie Helps and Laura Murray
The Magpie Press (1977)
ISBN 0 9596518 0 2

Acknowledgements by The Magpie Press in the slim volume read:

"Many of Valerie's poems first appeared in the *Canberra Times* whose permission to publish them was gratefully acknowledged. Other poems have appeared previously in *The Saturday Club Poetry Magazine*, *Canberra Poetry*, the *Golden Eagle Book of Golden Verse*, and the *Bungendore Mirror*."

Reviews for *A Third of a Pond*

Valerie Helps has given us another delightful insight into her very special world of flora and fauna in the slice of Paradise she and Geoff created in Central France. She describes her pleasure in each season and discovering characteristics of formerly unfamiliar plants and introduces us to her increasing family of charmingly named creatures who visit their pond. References to some of the earlier events in her multi-faceted life add piquancy.

I look forward to her next book.

Patricia Manfredi, Italian Literary Translations

CONTENTS

CHAPTER ONE Return to the Deep Mani 17

CHAPTER TWO Will we live in a tower? 35

CHAPTER THREE Profitis Elias and beautiful sad Mystras 63

CHAPTER FOUR On buying a car in Sparta 93

CHAPTER FIVE Ruins and a secret grotto 107

CHAPTER SIX Tigani peninsula and Crete revisited 125

CHAPTER SEVEN A winter world and Christmas 153

CHAPTER EIGHT Halcyon days and Olympia at last 167

CHAPTER NINE Chasing castles and King Nestor's Palace 189

CHAPTER TEN A wild rock garden and the Amazons of Dirou 207

CHAPTER ELEVEN A hidden Byzantine gem 223

CHAPTER TWELVE Greek Orthodox Easter 233

CHAPTER THIRTEEN Have I eaten Helen of Troy? 239

CHAPTER FOURTEEN In Homer's footsteps 249

CHAPTER FIFTEEN Zagori land behind the mountains 255

CHAPTER SIXTEEN Bryon hero of the Greeks 263

CHAPTER SEVENTEEN An evening with Sophocles 273

CHAPTER EIGHTEEN Kindred spirits 283

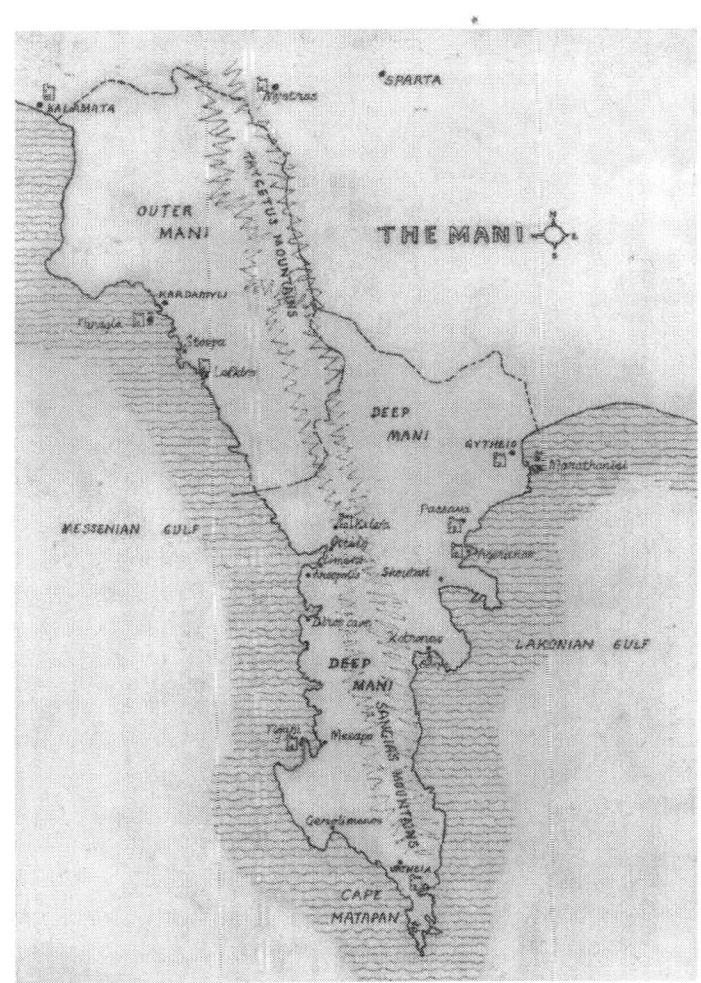

CHAPTER ONE

RETURN TO THE DEEP MANI

I had dreamed of returning since my first fleeting visit and now here I am. And no longer alone. I awoke this morning just before dawn. Geoff was still asleep as I stood at the window and leaned my arms on the cool marble sill of the stone house. Above the mountains a sickle moon lay sideways in a pale sky filled with feathery clouds and to the south the unruffled sea was sleeping. This was the way all days should begin, with a sense of calm and in a landscape that is pleasing to the soul, although I am certain these barren rock and thistle-filled fields which surround this old stone house would not appeal to everyone. The sparse uncluttered shapes of these feudal watchtowers in the Deep Mani hold a special kind of fascination for me; this stark landscape of austere soaring towers rising from the ground locked in by a forbidding mountain range, has a beauty all its own. I love the solid, square strength of them, the curved turrets at the corners and the stern face they turn to the rocky terrain and I wonder about my passion for this wild and decidedly inhospitable place. I also prefer black-and-white photography for in my opinion, texture, light and shade add a depth often lacking in colour photography—however the simple lines of these two-tone towers with little other than the interjection of royal purple from the occasional bougainvillea or the geranium's pillar-box red, please me greatly. So I do favour a hint of colour as well.

We have found a rocky inlet with a strip of soft sand where we swim each day in the shining waters of the Messenian Gulf. Bright green seaweed that feeds darting shoals of translucent fish lies like a necklace around the sharp edges of rock where sea urchins, malevolent black stars, cover the rocks and we have to tread carefully. Oddly, in this land of angular shapes, the remains of two round windmill towers stand at the entrance of the arm of land that stretches out into the sea; swimming in the cold water and gasping for breath I feel content within their gaze. Protectors from another age. Indestructible. Three massive square watchtowers, our own private castles, stand on either side of the cove and a miniature church, always locked, faces seawards; one of the towers has been converted into a house that stands with shuttered eyes as if waiting for a blue painted boat to use the slipway. Some thirty head of cattle graze on the dry grassy slopes of the mountain flanking the stone house and in the late afternoon they are brought to one of the crumbling ruins by the bay, the pungency of sage and thyme and the earthy smell of dung rise into the cooling air as the animals assemble in the walled enclosure. We sit on the hot stones and dream our dreams holding hands, silent with the wonderment of it all—at the transformation of our lives. Two people discovering a new world together, a new exciting world especially for Geoff who has not lived in Greece before. How did it all happen? It doesn't matter. It has.

*

Nothing is by chance, if you look with care you will discover there is always a pattern, but you may not find it at first.

*

Our new acquaintances are Yiannis, a middle-aged taverna-hotel owner and his identical brother Theo, who live in the little fishing port of Gerolimenas a few kilometres down the road from our small house. Yiannis is a droll man, an ex-sea captain who has returned to his roots to care for his parents and to run the family hotel and taverna. The brothers look to me like accountants with their serious, somewhat uncompromising demeanour, fair of skin, short in stature with grey hair and pale eyes behind steel-rimmed spectacles. I think they must be twins. Their sister who does most of the cooking is short and stumpy, dark-skinned and low-browed; very Maniot looking. Both men have the same tired body language and make no attempt to hide their irascibility at the stupidity, real or imagined, of the very few tourists who call in. Initially we christened them "The Grumpy Brothers". On the other hand, as soon as they discovered we were not itinerants but planned to actually stay in the Mani—and this raised some incredulity—the brothers warmed to us. Having broken the ice, Yiannis took every opportunity to talk to us between serving the occasional customers—it was never busy—we covered many subjects and when the quality of tourists who visited the Mani was discussed he became heated, mainly about the Germans whom he loathed. He said they were all rude and all the men were "Hitlers"! I protested vehemently but he raised his eyes showing the heavily veined whites and continued with some insistence to his other pet hate which was motorcyclists whom he referred to as "those bastards"! He found the summer quite exhausting and was not looking forward to it. When we told him we were looking for somewhere to live for the entire season, his attempts to find accommodation for us became quite embarrassing. As we sat at his taverna on the seafront for our evening meal he would amble up and regale us of yet another place he had found or of more rooms in his hotel which he could convert for us. He even offered to complete a partly built balcony to give us a view of the sea which we had said was essential. We began to feel bad turning down his kind efforts but none of them were quite right; he seemed to understand, though his shoulders slumped just a fraction more.

Each time we mentioned we wanted to stay at least until the winter, the locals, including Kostas from whom we were renting the room in the stone house, went into a state of astonishment, *yia toso kairo?* for so long?—they echoed and became excited and quarrelsome, argued loudly amongst themselves and, when we gave them a rough figure of how much we were prepared to pay, their reactions were such that we realised we were offering far too much, seeing it was in the Peloponnese and a non-tourist area. The arguments became so heated it often seemed as if they might come to blows. I noticed both in Gerolimenas and subsequently, that there was always one dissenter in the group, one person who did not want us there; but the others prevailed and the discussions continued. Where could they put us? Was Eleni's apartment free this summer? No, her cousin was coming from America, *po, po poli makria*, so far away, with one hand gesticulating in a circular movement, eyes rolling. Then they would warn us against certain rent rooms as being *pio akrivo*, very expensive, and not too clean. The top priority required of a place was that it was *katharos*, clean. Again, the expansive gestures with the hand. It was like a game as they tried to outdo one another and we found it most entertaining, although as the pace heightened and they spoke faster and faster, I found it quite exhausting keeping up with translations to Geoff.

Then a breakthrough as they racked their brains. Maybe the taxi driver would be interested. They called him. Yes, he was interested. He had an apartment above his house that he said was *konda*, close, which was always a worry because it never was, indicating with the flat of his hand as they all do. We were bundled into his taxi and driven up a steep road to a smart villa surrounded by an award-winning garden. Nice surroundings we thought, but a bit far from the sea. He called rudely for his wife to bring the keys; she didn't respond immediately and he became angry. When she appeared, he shouted at her again. No, I could not live here and observe this careworn woman being bullied by her husband. In any case the apartment was at the rear of the building and had no view, the front ones were taken for the summer, of course. So, he drove us back, and Yiannis looked suddenly tired, finding us difficult to please yet for some reason felt duty-bound to locate a place for us. More discussion.

*

We went south this June morning, nudged seawards by brooding limestone peaks past clusters of deserted towers, seemingly the only product of this unproductive soil. The terrain becoming more barren and inhospitable as we passed abandoned village after village of fortified stone watchtowers; tall, square, grey, blending so perfectly with the stony ground they seemed like an extension of the land itself, their crenellated shapes resembling the bare bones of a dinosaur punctuating the skyline along the crest of the hills. They rose out of bleak slopes where ancient terraces clung on tenaciously down to the wintry sea. No trees in this rugged land. The Deep Mani was once inhabited by a hundred and seventeen fortified hamlets and villages yet I was still amazed by the number of settlements we passed, so many centuries later. As the land opened up into yet another bay in south-eastern Laconia, we spied the gaunt fingers of the substantial village of Vatheia lying along a hilltop, the silent towers beckoning. In the eighties, the Greek National Tourist Organisation took over the abandoned settlement and began to restore some of the towers as guest houses, paying careful attention to tradition and detail; wisely they left a scattering of ruins amongst the restorations to ensure the settlement did not look too new. Vatheia, first mentioned by a Venetian diplomatic mission in 1571 as Casale di Vathia, is now allegedly the most photographed village in the Peloponnese. The staggering abundance of wildflowers across the nearby hills and the views over the ocean made our visit worthwhile, and I had to introduce Geoff to this slightly eerie place and to the ghosts of the long-distant past.

The Mani is the middle finger and the southernmost part of the three-fingered Peloponnesian peninsula. It is divided into two—in the north it is known as 'the Outer Mani' and the southern half 'the Deep Mani' or 'the Inner Mani'. This mountainous region is dominated by the North and Central Taygetus range which, on reaching the Deep Mani division, changes its name to the Sangias mountains. The peninsula is located in western Laconia and eastern Messenia in the southern Peloponnese.

Hiking and guided mountain tours offer marvellous experiences such as "traversing the long and narrow razor-like ridge which is suspended between Messenia and Laconia and between earth and sky". I am not sure about traversing the razor-sharp ridge but wish I were fitter and could be suspended between earth and sky on the Taygetus range; the distribution of rare alpine plants on the heights is also a huge attraction for me.

The history of this peninsula so carefully guarded by the barrier of the Taygetus mountain range, reeks of bloodshed and fearful battles and now, these silent obelisk villages stand as sentries and retain their warring ghosts. The Maniots are described as being the descendants of the ancient Dorian people of the Peloponnese and, as such, are related to the ancient Spartans.

*

I was last in Vatheia some years ago with Amanda, one of my daughters and Tom Forge a young friend, when I fulfilled one of my improbable dreams; to sleep in a Maniot watchtower. We stayed the night in one of the converted towers high above the sloping hillside overlooking the ocean after a pleasant meal in one of the village towers, designed by the GNTO the Greek National Tourism Organisation to accommodate visitors. The project seemed to be doing well at the time and we were impressed by the management's efficient yet relaxed standard of comfort offered to us. It was a rewarding experience, surreal and almost spiritual, redolent of the past as we watched silent bats fly through the rainy night sky past the narrow, barred windows of our seventy-foot tower. I could almost hear the grunts and sighs of neighbouring feuding Maniots as they elevated their towers through the darkness in order to gain superiority in height before the dawn; I understand these clan wars continued well into the nineteenth century—and was it one of the Mani dirges I heard drifting around the silent towers?

It was following this visit that I was certain I would return to the Deep Mani to live in a Maniot tower and write a book. It has taken a while for that to materialise but here I am, back in the village of the silent towers of Vatheia with my sketchbook; I climb the hill above the towers and frantically sketch the many aspects and views of this intriguing and now ghost-ridden settlement. I *knew* I would be back, and I am never surprised when my dreams come true; just delighted to greet them when they do.

*

Above the pale stony beach of Vatheia bay Geoff found a perfect picnic spot in the shade of an olive tree against an old stone wall. Pressing down the grasses we lunched on fresh bread, sardines with lemon juice, succulent tomatoes, crisp cucumbers and the saltiness of fat, black Kalamata olives; cool retsina, sharp against the palate reduced us to a catatonic state and we lay dreaming as insects droned and the afternoon slumbered. A white butterfly sat on my hand. The hillsides seemingly so barren from afar were starry with myriad patches of wildflowers: tall, swaying cow parsley with flowers as large as dinner plates, pink cistus, also known as rockrose smothered in blossom; and two-metre-high hollyhocks. The still air sweet with the perfume of wild stock combined with crushed thyme and in the wall crevices, long stalks of oregano grew upwards towards the sun; we sprinkled some on our tomatoes. Below us in the bay round grey pebbles clicked together rhythmically as the waves approached and receded on the beach; the colour and tone of the shallows was astonishing. I have never been able to find the words to describe the translucence nor the changing shades of the shallow waters of Greece. Is it turquoise or some other magical combination? And the blue-black of the deep—what colour is that? One cannot write about the seas of Greece—they have to be experienced.

Following our siesta, we drove further south and stopped by a magnificent, though dilapidated tower sporting a large Greek flag.

"I have to get a photograph," said my eager-beaver photographer, ever on the lookout for wonderful views and this was superb, a panorama of sea and swirling bare mountains falling away steeply from a solitary and proud tower that stood on the crest of a rock like an eagle's nest. He was away for a while as I sat in the car and soaked in the drama around me and when he returned, he was quite elated.

"I met an architect and his wife, also an architect," he explained.

"They own the tower and are going to restore it and they told me of someone who might lease us a tower house in Areopolis. His name is Iakovos and he runs a guest house called Londas just off the old square."

And so links are forged and I am sure I have said this before: In *Illusions* my bedside reading, Richard Bach my long-time guru tells us that every person and all the events in one's life are there because we have invited them to be there, and he warns us that it is our choice what we do with them.

*

We have decided to take a rest from exploring for a spell and remain in our somewhat spartan room in the stone house; it is quiet, totally isolated and sits in the middle of a stony, thorny field against towering mountains. I like the sheer indifference of our surroundings. Earlier this year we spent a fortnight in eastern Crete packing up my daughter Francesca's belongings and shipping them back to Australia, plus sorting and repacking my possessions for storage and seeing old friends. It had been enjoyable if somewhat tiring. Prior to that, leaving Australia after my three-month visit to see our separate families made my departure emotionally draining and I realised I needed an extended change and rest far away from pressures—away from everyone—even loved ones. I longed for silence and space and I knew it could be found in this wilderness of mountain, sea and sky.

*

A world of blue from my journal:

It is a week since we left Kissamos in western Crete on the inter-island ferry heading for Neapolis in the southern Peloponnese. I sit in the sun with my back to the rough stone wall of the stone house and recall how we stayed on deck for a while watching the mountains of western Crete fade, and then, wind-blown and tangled, sought relief in the saloon which had comfortable lounge chairs and couches. The corner that we had reserved, indeed where we had left our belongings, had been taken over by the gypsies we had seen driving into the bowels of the ferry in their trucks bright with decorative hangings. They had commandeered 'our' corner and were already asleep on blankets on the floor between or languishing in the leather armchairs with children tumbling over them like puppies. Others were spreadeagled in all the leather armchairs. Loud and colourful are the gypsies and happy with themselves in their bright flowing dresses and voluminous skirts, brown wrists a-jangle with bracelets, gaudy necklaces and spectacular earrings submerged by blue-black hair, oily and curling as it falls about their faces and they really do have flashing eyes with a boldness totally lacking in their Greek counterparts.

Their dark-eyed children were beautifully dressed and as joyous as their mothers as they raced along on top of the tables bringing scowls from the man behind the bar. But he said nothing. Both the women and men were overweight, the women voluptuous with smooth shapely bosoms which they displayed with obvious pride. A breed unto themselves these attractive people. The men sat in groups, never with the women and children and a lot of back-slapping and hearty laughter issuing from beneath their curling moustaches. Someone told me that the Cretan gypsies ply to and from the mainland in their huge trucks where they pick up factory 'seconds' in Athens and sell them in the markets of Crete; I gather the drivers get special dispensation on the ferries for tickets and meals.

We could not escape the popular music even on deck where the speakers followed us relentlessly; skilakia, dog music, the Greeks call it. The plink-plunk of the bouzouki accompanied the popular song of the moment, 'S'agapore', 'I love you', and other versions on the same theme. Occasionally the mournful love songs were interspersed with the fussy sound of lyre music from Crete and I realised that though at first, I couldn't stand it, I had grown used to it after seven years, and now missed it.

I have always loved Greek ferries and the sensation that I am living in a world of many shades of blue. It is like living in a blue *bubble, the sky wider and higher than any other, a lighter shade than the sea and the demarcation line where horizon and sky meet though barely discernible, has been pencilled in, in blue. The decks on the ferry-boat are blue. Even the frames of the deckchairs are blue. The Greek flag is blue and white and around me the sea that dominates this land which produces the world's best sailors—hardly surprising as no piece of land in Greece is further than fifty kilometres from the coast—is blue! The blue of the deep has black in it. Indigo? In contrast, pale biscuit-coloured atolls rise jaggedly out of the sea. Austere, treeless. I am thrilled to be back in the Mediterranean after six months' absence in Australia and thrilled to again be part of this seascape with its harsh islands, turtle-backed and barren as they materialise in the distance and even more thrilled to be sharing it with Geoff for the first time.*

*

Today we explored silent Alikas—a sprawling hamlet of crumbling towers and barrel-vaulted stone houses that amble along the hillside. The overgrown courtyards are filled with *Frangosyka,* Frankish figs or prickly pear, now in yellow flower, and wild figs fill crumbling nooks and crannies dropping sweet fruit on the narrow flagstone paths that curve in and around the many towers. It is as if their fingers are reaching for the heavens, metamorphosing from the stony earth to a place above, but they are fixed forever in the Maniot soil and gradually return to it as they fall. A few towers have been restored; they remain true to tradition, the reconstruction neat and the stones paler. The hamlet appeared to be deserted until we saw a woman shaking a scarlet rug from the balcony of a house at the top of the path. She smiled at us. A little later we met an elderly man pushing a wheelbarrow up the steep hill and asked him if any of the towers were either for lease or for sale. He seemed amazed and slightly suspicious then, after pushing the barrow into the curved doorway of a tower which he said he was using as a storeroom, showed us round another disintegrating tower which he said was his. He pointed out the rotting timbers beneath the upper storey and described how much work would have to be done to restore it, and how much it would cost. At least a million drachmas he said, rolling his eyes. Anyway, no one would sell their towers, they belonged to the family and that was the most important thing. Could we rent one in the village we asked? No, he replied firmly and wished us *kalo taxithi*, good journey, as we left.

*

Out early to greet another shining morning. Noticing a rough track leading towards an inviting bay, we drove down and reached a ramshackle fishing village which we later discovered to be Mesapo. A steep approach with tight corners led to a tiny port that seemed to be abandoned but for a skeletal and aimless young man who was coming up the hill, looking for the next 'fix' I figured. We parked the Blue Girl, my ancient and rust-ridden Fiat, close to the rim of an extraordinary harbour; it was deep with immensely high overhanging cliffs of a sulphurous yellow that closed in on three sides leaving a narrow entrance to the sea. Centuries of rough seas had gouged out the walls that looked as if they might cave in at any moment and bright *caiques*, traditional fishing boats, lay at anchor in water so calm and so clear it had the clarity of glass; Geoff thought it looked as if they were sailing on air above the clean, sandy bottom. In the bay, a sleek cruiser did a slow turn, flag fluttering idly and radar rotating, and then silently steamed away. The skeleton of a ruined tower with archways invaded by figs stood above the jetty adding to the sense of desolation which surrounded the place. The heat was blistering and the air very still, almost as if it was waiting for something to happen—the atmosphere was strange but the tiny village's proximity to the sea, its isolation and lack of people attracted us. It was exactly what we were looking for so we went into the only taverna. The elderly owner, who was not only very deaf but also extremely dirty, had a wayward eye. We sat on his terrace from which we could see an enticing cove and pale peppermint sea and at the far end, the dark mouth of a cave. I had a difficult and tiring conversation in Greek with the old man as he shouted incomprehensibly at the top of his voice and waved his arms around excitedly.

"You want an apartment for five months?" he yelled in Greek with incredulity. "*Po po*—no one stays here for that long. Only July and August."

But he was intrigued and wanted to be helpful. Then his two sons returned from fishing and joined us, stretching out horizontally on the rickety chairs, laughing and joking with their father. I could not help thinking it was a good thing my three blonde daughters were not with me as they might have come to blows over the brothers. They were so different yet so attractive, each in his way. The younger of the two had a sensitive face with tightly curling hair and deep khaki eyes identical to those of his ravaged and toothless old mother who sat in a world of her own, barely able to comprehend what was going on around her. His features were superbly chiselled, clean-cut, the clichés come pouring out but they *were* chiselled and clean-cut. He was also clean-shaven with a strong firm body. His renegade brother might win Amanda's wild heart I thought, being a bit of a renegade herself. Stubbly chin which nowadays is the fashion, seriously bloodshot eyes and a knowing, somehow intimate demeanour. Moody too I would think. Difficult I was sure, but exciting. It was he who was negative about our enquiries while the other brother and his father yelled *Scase!* Shut up! at him and continued to discuss various possibilities for us. Another villager joined them, an obese and grubby man and the conversation grew livelier with angry interjections from the anti-brother. Eventually we unglued ourselves from the plastic chairs and stood up, dripping with perspiration; it was obvious there were no places for rental. We would return we promised, to swim and to photograph the amazing enclosed harbour, and we would consider hiring his boat to take us across the bay to the intriguing rock known as *Tigani*, frying-pan, that stretched out into the sea to the south. We knew it held the remains of a fortress built by Frankish crusaders and as soon as the summer heat diminished, we would explore the famous frying pan!

Towards the end of our short stay in Gerolimenas, we visited Areopolis several times and decided to make it our centre while we explored the northern coastline to find somewhere to spend the summer. However, once ensconced in the small town we found ourselves being lackadaisical about exploring further so we are going to stay here. I believe the decision was made partly by Geoff whilst we were still in Crete as he liked the sound of Areopolis and asked me if I had visited it when I was last in the Deep Mani with Amanda, seven years earlier. We had, in fact, virtually bypassed the town which was barely a town, having driven round the large and ugly square, admired the magnificent statue of the leader of the revolution, Petrobey Mavromichalis then drove on southwards lured by the beckoning watchtowers in the peninsula. No, I did not know what Areopolis was like. We put out the word which was met by the same incredulity as in Gerolimenas, little old ladies in black with rickety legs like Chippendale chairs stopped us in the street asking, in Greek of course:

"You want a *spiti*, house, for all the summer? *Po po*, no one stays here so long!" They all say this!

Then after a summing up of our appearance and demeanour they would shuffle ahead, letting out a piercing screech to "Yianni" or "Georgio" at which some long-suffering son or brother appeared, and negotiations would commence once again.

*

Areopolis has been settled for aeons and until the end of the last century was known as Tzimova, its seventh-century Slavic name meaning "City of the Devil." Around the area are indications of habitation during the Palaeolithic period. The tower village of seven hundred and fifty inhabitants was re-named in honour of its fighting hero, Petrobey Mavromichalis, whose family's towers dominate the town and surrounding countryside. The Greek flag was first raised in Taxiarches Square on the seventeenth of March 1821 and signified the commencement of the revolution led by Mavromichalis. The name Areopolis is a combination of two words: *Ares* the god of war and *polis*, city, although some say it is derived from the Greek *aeros*, wind, as it is renowned for the violent winter north-easterly that comes howling through the gap in the Sangias mountains, not an enticing prospect I murmured but was ignored.

Areopolis is a protected settlement and efforts to retain the past architecturally continue, with cobbled streets and stone restoration a priority. Stone houses, modest dwellings and mansions, many with massive wooden doors always closed, lead into secret gardens a-blaze with flowers the air heady with perfume on a hot afternoon; high-walled lanes, primitive churches and Maniot watchtowers mostly unoccupied and crumbling. The town has retained its traditional shops a-clutter with dust-covered tins and jars, mostly with the use-by date well past. One of the three bakers, a friendly middle-aged woman called Milya, that translates into 'apple tree' still uses the traditional olivewood fired oven where piles of hewn logs lie neatly stacked outside her tiny *foúrnos*, bakery, oven, as the tantalising aroma of freshly baked country bread, called *horiatiki psomi,* fills the old cobbled square. We are unable to go past without purchasing a pulsating loaf of bread or two of her delicious *spanakopita,* spinach and cheese pies. She uses sourdough for her loaves and the double-baked rusks called *paximathia* are prepared with wholewheat, chickpea or barley flour. There are mercifully only two new shops here, one is an upmarket chemist with heavily barred windows and the other a *zaharoplasteio* that sells a variety of honeyed, nut-filled and irresistible pastries and sweets. The post office is tiny and the bank only opens twice a week for half a day.

The town is known as the entrance to the Deep or Inner Mani from the Outer Mani and is therefore of some importance. It stands on a plateau, one of several that gradually peter out through walled fields and rough paths to precipitous cliffs a hundred metres above the sea—thus making it well placed to catch summer breezes and to be several degrees cooler than the coastal villages

A winding escarpment leads several kilometres down to the inlet of the Bay of Limeni where we are assured the swimming is perfect. The next bay Nea Oitylo, New Itilo has a sandy beach, several *psarotaverna*, fish tavernas and was once known as 'Little Algiers' as the slave trade flourished there. On the opposite hillside the massive walls of the late seventeenth-century Kelefa fortress, the Ottoman's frontier built to defend the invading Venetians can be seen standing high on a plateau; a stern reminder to the Maniots of the Turkish presence. The deep gorge that separates Pano Oitylo and Nea Oitylo is where the Deep and Outer Mani meet and where the waterless, tower-filled villages of the Deep Mani are gradually replaced by the gentler landscape to the north, with softer contours and fertile vegetation on the lower slopes of the Taygetus whose austere heights follow the coastline and look as if they are trying to push the fishing villages into the ocean.

We have moved into a quaint, two-hundred-year-old converted tower house called Tzimova. Our room leads onto a tiny paved courtyard where we sit amongst a profusion of roses of every shade, gladioli, geraniums, ferns, fuchsia, two lemon trees and vines that tumble over rooftops above a stone wall. Outside the front door in painted tins, two flowering gardenias welcome one into the cool dark room that Poppy, the friendly and somewhat lumpy daughter, quaintly calls 'the common-room'. Her elderly parents are Georgios and his quarrelsome and highly vocal wife Thea. The three of them run the guest house that sports the GNTO badge which means it has won the approval of the Greek National Tourist Organisation. We can order breakfast each morning if we choose though we normally make a fruit salad that we have with yoghurt and honey while we brew our own fresh coffee. Our spacious room in the old house has an arched timbered ceiling, old, old pictures and heavy dark furniture and is supremely comfortable. It is also the first even faintly luxurious living we have experienced since leaving Bangkok where we had four marvellous days in the honeymoon suite where our evening meals, when we so wished, were wheeled into our suite with great aplomb, silver lids lifted off to be dazzled by delicious Thai food. A feast for eye and palate.

Gytheio, our nearest centre is twenty-six kilometres away

through the gap in the Taygetus mountains on the east coast of the Deep Mani. It is a lively and picturesque port at the top of the Gulf of Lakonia which was once the main port for Sparta; first settled in prehistoric times, it was a Phoenician trading station known for the collection of murex shells for their purple dye—and for its ancient theatre. A few Roman remains can still be seen to the north of the town but most of them now lie beneath the sea. The waterfront is closely flanked by elegant neoclassical houses that have been faithfully restored; a central square faces the harbour and we have our coffee and *spanakopita* at a taverna festooned with drying octopus. Behind me, the town climbs in steep tiers to Koumaro Hill that overlooks the islet of ancient Kranae—now called Marathonisi—which is connected by causeway to the mainland. This, according to Homer, is where Helen and Paris spent their first night following their elopement from Sparta, thus sparking off the Trojan War. We spent hours in the pictorial museum dedicated to the history of the Mani which is now housed in the ungainly building on the island, once the stronghold of the Grigorakis clan. In summer, ferries from the Athens port of Piraeus and Crete call in frequently and the harbour is alive with cruise ships and visiting yachts. The local shops resound with foreign tongues and the tills ring with joy at their purchases while rent rooms, hotels and tavernas jostle for customers and there are several sandy beaches nearby, the longest being Mavrovouni which is said to be four kilometres in length. I wonder about that.

Geoff is keen to find out where he can buy artists' materials and we are told there is a shop called Hasanakos with an art gallery upstairs in Gytheio, it should not be hard to find as there is only one street along the port towards the older part of the town. And it was there that we found it, though there was no indication from the outside that anything remotely serious occurred behind the touristy frontage of the usual postcards, posters, bric-a-brac, icons, bad pottery but quite striking jewellery. We met a young man with a look of Byron and the eyes of a dreamer who turned out to be Petros, son of Georgios, the owner. When I asked Petros if he painted, he said no then added rather bashfully, that he was a poet.

I congratulated him and murmured that we had something in common. He smiled and took us upstairs to an extensive gallery where some excellent artwork was on display. When Geoff showed him his paintings, he was obviously impressed and asked us to call back when his father was there. We returned several days later and met Georgios, a bearded and handsome man who was exhausted and agreed with me that high summer and the tourist season was the worst time of the year. He liked Geoff's work and was preparing to negotiate but as they were already ear-marked for a shop in Pyrgos Dirou, we said we would return when we had more to show him. We went home happy and elated with visions of becoming rich and famous overnight—hum!

*

Books are the treasured wealth of the world and the fit inheritance of generations and nations.
(Henry David Thoreau)

My father owned a leather-bound copy of Henry David Thoreau's book 'Walden,' it was almost his bible and could be found on the handsome wooden desk in his study. He used to read passages and quotes to me so I felt I knew the poet, philosopher, naturalist and dreamer quite well by the time I grew up. The attraction Thoreau had for my father and for me were his need for solitude, to live in a place away from it all. This he found in 1854 and spent a decidedly isolated existence for two years 'living the simple life' by Walden Pond in Concord, Massachusetts. During these years he wrote what is now called his masterpiece *Walden: or, Life in the Woods* and his philosophical musings are quoted worldwide.

If a man does not keep pace with his companions, perhaps it is because he hears a different drummer. Let him step to the music he hears, however measured or far away.

*

CHAPTER TWO

WILL WE LIVE IN A TOWER?

We are still looking for somewhere to settle and have seen a couple of apartments and even a hotel where the owner was prepared to offer us several rooms with a bathroom and kitchen facilities. The problem remains, it is the high season and although we want to rent from now through to November when they are empty it doesn't seem to make much difference. During the height of summer, they are able to fleece the willing holidaymakers for large sums of money per night. All of a sudden, we have several irons in the fire with regard to long-term accommodation, including, unbelievably, two tower houses—another of my wild dreams coming true? The first is a luxurious and very spacious three storey tower mansion, far too big for us but most enticing with its private courtyard, upper terrace and is aesthetically pleasing and comfortable. It belongs to a Swiss called Hans, mid-forties who leases it out long or short-term. He was about to visit Athens to see the dentist and after we had seen over it and made the appropriate comments such as, "we'd love it but surely it is too expensive?" he suggested we should discuss the rental on his return, but also suggested that we contact one Stephanos Koronaios who had a newly restored tower house just down the lane.

"The one with the blue doors and windows," he said.
I liked the sound of that; it echoed my children's stories titled *"The Chanky Tales"* which are about a little girl whose little house in Africa had 'blue doors and windows'. A good omen. Hans's tower was a little too big, heating costs in the winter would be astronomical, but it was grand and we do love space. I phoned Stephanos's father Yiannis again and again, but no reply; eventually I heard his gruff voice at the end of the line. Yes, he

would tell Stephanos and I should ring again the next day or come to see him the following evening at six o'clock.

Six o'clock came and we found the tower house standing back from the laneway between two churches; it was smaller and more squat than I had envisaged and looked brand new. Areopolis has several huge tower mansions and this one looked somewhat stunted, not aesthetically pleasing to the eye, but cute nonetheless. Yiannis was waiting for us, a heavy, slow-moving man, very deaf and not at all friendly. Stephanos was not to be seen he announced, we should come again the next day.

I liked Stephanos the moment I set eyes on him. A shambling bear of a man in his late thirties with a big nose and a ready bright smile. His deep bass voice was the most striking thing about him, I will have to ask if he sings. Somehow, I doubt it, he would never find the time. He exuded a restless energy as he showed us round the two levels of the tower house with great enthusiasm. It was not quite ready he said, but it would be "very soon". This is Greece I reminded Geoff later as he began to get excited about the possibility of moving in immediately, expect nothing and you will not be disappointed. So, we wait to hear from Stephanos and have not made any decisions, but it seems we are to live in a tower house for the foreseeable future and that is sooner than expected. Another dream comes true. Am I surprised? Not really.

*

Georgios, of the Tzimova Guest House, sports a captain's hat and is a very natty dresser with blue blazer and well-cut trousers, however, the pale cream shoes are bizarre and look like old-fashioned spats. I thought he told us he was in the navy but his daughter said he 'minded a school in Areopolis' however, he was certainly active during the war as many proud portraits in the common room proclaim. He wants us to take his quarters in the guest house but his wife will not let him; he says all the problems of the world are due to women and he made the remark in the presence of his wife with a twinkle in his pale blue eyes. They bicker all the time and as the day lengthens her voice gets higher and shriller except during siesta when, praise the lord, she sinks into some sort of blissful immobility and silence reigns until five o'clock. This guest house is noisy, but it is Greek noise which I don't mind. They always have visitors sitting in the common room quaffing *kafés* and *glika*, sweet things, sticky, nutty chunks of mouth-watering cakes, and bottles with interesting looking labels invariably cover the central table among the artificial hibiscus flowers. On the walls faded portraits and hand-tinted photos stand around an old radio and a wooden HMV wind-up gramophone beside a pin-up shot of busty Sophia Loren! Too bizarre for words.

It is lunchtime and Geoff has wandered off to buy some bread for our picnic lunch. He has taken to the Mani like a duck to water and is also learning Greek very quickly; I guess his musical ear helps as his accent is normally good. My Greek is also coming on in leaps and bounds and to my delight, few people speak English although I must admit that after hours of negotiating prices and rooms and apartments my brain is tired. But elated.

The aroma of beans and tomatoes is filling the air from Tzimova's small kitchen and my gastric juices are driving me mad but they do not cater for meals, other than breakfast. We have found the food to be excellent in the few tavernas in the town but for the pizza place, which, for some strange reason does not serve wine so we moved on. We tend to eat out most nights and sometimes at midday as well—the fish dishes are superb and in the market seafood prices per kilo are less than they were in Crete. Nikos's taverna is on the ugly main square where the children play football on hot nights. He caters for the few tourists in the season and has a fantastic selection of *mezethes* which have always been our favourite choice in Greek tavernas. If really hungry one is able to order up to a dozen different small dishes of Greek and Turkish appetisers, though the Greeks would prefer not to mention the Turks! The table becomes so overwhelmed with delectable offerings that it becomes difficult to decide where to begin. Should we start with *octapodi*, octopus, *calamari*, squid, *keftedes*, meatball patties, *loukaniko*, spiced sausage, *dolmades*, stuffed vine leaves, *saganaki*, grilled *kefalograviera* cheese, *manitaria*, stuffed mushrooms or *spanakopita*, *phyllo* parcels of feta and spinach, or various pulses such as *gigantes*, a type of large white bean soaked in herbs, olive oil and tomatoes so sweet they make my mouth water. The list goes on and on and on and we accompany these dishes with chunks of hot grilled village bread soaked in oil and herbs, Nikos's *psomi tost* is utterly divine! The Greek words μεζέ—μεζέδες in English—are pronounced *meze* in the singular and the plural *mezethes*, were originally borrowed from the Persian *mazze*, which means 'taste' or 'snack'. It also means 'many little dishes' or 'to graze' according to my research. Its roots have been traced back in antiquity to the Middle East and Eastern Mediterranean region. Our meals are invariably accompanied by cool village wine from the barrel which is almost always acceptable. Dionysus the god of wine seldom lets us down.

Nikos's grill also serves main meals of *horta*, a generic term for any wild green vegetable often resembling spinach, in oil, stuffed eggplant, tomatoes and courgette, *briam*, a traditional dish prepared with baked vegetables that is close to the French *ratatouille*, as well as roasts including lamb in egg and lemon sauce and grilled chicken from the spit. Salads are plentiful and crisp with more generous portions than anywhere else I've lived in Greece. I could go on forever there are so many choices. I find the dishes are tastier than in Crete, perhaps they use more herbs or different herbs? The prices are much the same. Greece is no longer a cheap country to live in; most commodities in the supermarket are almost identical to those in the UK and Australia, however, strangely enough dining out is a very real possibility whereas during the six months we spent in Sydney, we seldom ventured into good restaurants, they were simply too expensive. *Hima*, village wine, literally 'on draught', both the resinated white and the rosé – which is a rather nasty brown colour – is usually acceptable; our local supermarket sells it from the barrel and a kilo and a half is so affordable we could happily turn into cheap drunks this summer if the heat gets too much for us.

*

What I like about the Peloponnese especially the Deep Mani, is that it is unspoiled by tourism. The shopkeepers go about their daily business in the normal way, and although polite but a little aloof initially, they are now beginning to treat us like locals. It feels so good. Those excessively bright, tourist-orientated smiles that sadly, many Cretans have now adopted, do not exist in the Deep Mani and we have already made a few friendly acquaintants. The visitors are mostly Maniot families returning home for their summer break; they are pleasant, courteous people, cautiously welcoming. No skinheads and hardly a German in sight although we did come across twelve beautifully restored Morgan sports cars parked in the square. Their owners were all German; several wore old-style goggles and flying caps from the war and looked the part. We found them to be extremely aloof which was disappointing as we both would like to have talked with them; I sensed a bit of a story but was not prepared to risk a snub. There have been a few British travellers, walkers, nature lovers and birdwatchers and on rare occasions I hear their muted tones as they wander around in their extraordinary gear and funny hats looking at buildings, churches and wildflowers; a few Dutch and one or two Australians drift in and out of the guest house but mostly we are surrounded by Greeks which is why we came to this remote region of Greece.

*

I am content. Mahler's *Fifth Symphony* is in the air and all's well with the world. I have not been able to share my passion for Mahler with anyone before except with Amanda, my musician daughter who introduced this giant of a composer to me, and I find this sharing to be so important at this stage of my life. Mahler challenges the intellect and outside the music scene I have not met many people who like his music, although interestingly, Jonathan—mostly known as J.D. and is Amanda's husband—is as hooked on the composer as we are and his favourite Mahler symphony is also the *Fifth*. Shostakovich rates high on his list as well—what brilliance these two musicians shared. On meeting J.D. for the first time, we instantly established a rapport of depth in music, the love of it forges a strong link. We also quite often enjoy the same authors. As soon as we find somewhere to unpack our belongings, we are going to buy a CD player but for the moment, the cassettes on my old machine will have to suffice.

*

I am writing many words each day; they pour out of my brain and Geoff has already designed the restoration of the two ruined towers that jut out into the sea at Limeni one of which he says he wants to buy for us; being an architect with building acumen every ruin challenges him and he spends hours sketching and planning. Georgios took us to the spot and showed us the twin towers which he says belong to his family. They want ten million drachmas for the ruins and the surrounding land, of which there is precious little as the towers stand precariously on a small rocky promontory, the sea on three sides. It is certainly an invaluable site with tiny sandy bays on either side, but restoration would cost even more millions.

Limeni is our closest fishing village though barely a village, more a hamlet with a collection of stone houses, some being beautifully restored with a few collapsing towers in between. Georgios pointed out Mavromichalis's family tower that has been restored and is now a museum although it looks more like a Norman church to me. The little cove has several fish tavernas and a *kafenion* that look out into the narrow inlet where caiques rock in crystal clear water. We found only one open; it was lined with painted pots filled with brilliant flowers including orange cannas and giant sunflowers. The place was deserted but for several cats and we sat in the sun and had a Greek coffee and talked rentals and purchase prices. Georgios is hard to understand, the Maniots have a dialect which I cannot describe and find difficult to follow. Geoff thinks he will not buy yet, of course it remains to be seen whether we would want to stay here for good. But it is so wonderful to be free as he keeps remarking. And I agree, naturally.

*

We were enjoying a foaming *café frappe*, Greek iced coffee, in the grubby corner taverna at Pyrgos Dirou where the road forks down to the famous caves, when I saw a youngish woman sitting by the window. She appeared to be distressed and was being comforted by a tall man in smart casual clothes and I was about to whisper to Geoff "I think they want some help" when the man came to our table, introduced himself as Herman and after apologising for the intrusion sat down to explain their problem. He and Hendrickje, his wife had just arrived from Holland and had discovered the 'medieval tower' they had leased online for two weeks had turned out to be just that. Medieval in every way and totally unacceptable. He had brought her out for a late lunch only to discover the taverna they had chosen was unusually filthy and run by a bad-tempered and hugely fat old woman; his wife had burst into tears and could not be comforted. He guided her to our table and we cheered her up by assuring her that not all tavernas were like this, and that there were many attractive places to eat, swim, and explore. Once she had dried her tears, we said our farewells, told them where we were staying and hoped we would meet soon in town or on the beach at Oitylo where the swimming was so enjoyable.

A few days later while walking along the beach at Oitylo we found them reading on the sand and our friendship established itself there and then. We lunched in a *psarotaverna*, fish taverna overlooking the sea, besieged by kittens with which Hendrickje had already made friends and had a thoroughly entertaining afternoon. Herman is a professor of philosophy and inclined to be academic but open to argument even from an ignoramus like me. He is a humorous man, very ready to laugh. Hendrickje is a well-published novelist so we talked literature and writing until our eyes began to close and siesta called. Our new friends are an enchanting, intelligent and entertaining couple.

*

Thea and Poppy have asked us to lunch and the aromas emanating from the kitchen are making my mouth water. They are so generous and have showered us with gifts of food, including bunches of red, red tomatoes and juicy oranges. Fortunately, Poppy speaks English—neither of her parents do—and we are getting to know her well. She is a bit scatty, excitable and exceedingly demonstrative given to stroking and touching, much to Geoff's continual embarrassment. In her mid-thirties I would consider her a handsome woman, but she is fast running to fat. Her real name is Calliope but, like all Greek women called Calliope she prefers to be called Poppy; I've never figured out the reason for their aversion to the name Calliope but there is one. Something historical maybe? She has offered to teach Geoff Greek and is sitting in the courtyard with him giving him a lesson while I have hysterics quietly. She says briskly:

"Very well Meester Tzef," when he gets something right. Stroking commences in her charming and innocent way.

Then: "Continue Meester Tzef," when he hesitates. And then: "Bravo Meester Tzef," loudly and emphatically. More stroking, I am *so* fond of Poppy.

His accent is accurate although he tends to ignore the emphasis on the vowel which is so important in this difficult language, he complains that his memory is decidedly marred but it is not as bad as he believes it to be.

*

Following an enormous lunch at Nikos's taverna of absolutely delectable kid, spaghetti with cheese and delicious sauce, salad and then watermelon washed down with ice-cold retsina, I can feel a siesta coming on; the sensation creeps over my limbs and I am compelled to lie down before catalepsy overtakes me completely. I have no idea why we decided to have our main meal at mid-day, but we did. Geoff has gone to collect the Blue Girl from the auto-electrician just down the road, the gear stick is wobbling rather nastily. The problem with having a twenty-year-old Fiat is that things continually go wrong with her and we knew this would be the case. However, it is a lot cheaper than hiring a vehicle on a permanent basis which we will have to do very soon unless we purchase another car since she is due to give up the ghost any day. Right now, however, the engine is going very sweetly though the body is fragile with rust and has been for years. A bit like me really.

*

Sunday in June and the church bells have blasted us out of bed. The din is deafening as the guest house is next to the beautiful Church of Taxiarches and, as all services in Greek churches are amplified as soon as the priest begins intoning his morning prayers, all conversation has to cease. Even switching on our radio fails as our own music is drowned by his monotonous and sometimes agreeable chanting. An elderly and rather weary looking spaniel with white hairs on his face sets up a wolf-like howling every time the bells ring—often carrying on long after the bells have stopped. Occasionally another dog joins in, his howl is about a third of a note higher in tone, quite a pleasant descant. Geoff thinks the spaniel is always tired because he spends his life waiting for the bells. I should think he would go quite crazy at Easter. During the evening sessions we have heard a woman's voice joining in with the priest's, it would have been bearable had she been able to sing in the same key but she could not, and their ill-matched voices amplified by the inevitable microphone was blasted out all over the village until we were quite literally deafened. I had no idea that women were permitted to accompany the priests when they were chanting. Something warned me that the voice might be Poppy's and when she invited us proudly to come to the church and listen to her, we procrastinated politely and made sure that we were out of sight before she could collar us for evensong.

We have been swimming again with Hendrickje and Herman with whom we dined last night at Nico's tavern in the square. They, unlike us, take swimming very seriously. Both wear goggles, and he swims with a smooth crawl, his long arms and hands cutting into the water at a steady pace, and she bobs up and down a bit like a cork in a determined breaststroke. There are two white houses at the end of the bay and they told us they always swim to the last one. We managed the distance at a slower speed but I had to stop several times as my shoulders ached; they always tend to when I do my fast, strong crawl for some reason. So I turn over and do more backstroke. The sea temperatures are so changeable along this coastline due to the many underground springs; ice-cold patches unexpectedly surround one, lower legs become rapidly numb and one is forced to swim away at speed. Later we lay on the silky sand until hunger drove us once again to our *psarotaverna* on the beach. The others had fresh crayfish chosen from the tank and I, being allergic to crustaceans, ordered crunchy squid, together with a crisp Greek salad. Ice-cold retsina as usual was the order of the day and we talked incessantly on every subject under the sun until we drove ourselves up the escarpment to our cool, airy bedroom. As soon as we collapsed on the bed Geoff began to feel nauseous and spent the remainder of the afternoon regurgitating his lunch. I was fine and I checked the next day when we saw our friends again; they had had no nasty reactions. Strange. Too much sun plus the crayfish perhaps? He was better, although a little pale, the next day.

*

Today we headed south to find the road to the curiously shaped rock at the end of a long approach aptly called Tigani, frying pan, that stretches out into the sea and can be seen from many vantage points along the coast road. I had read about Tigani in Patrick Leigh Fermor's book *Mani*, many years ago when my plans were to live in Greece. Friends have told us about the great fortresses established by Guillaume II Villehardouin, the Frankish Prince of the Morea, which is the old name for the Peloponnese. There were three fortresses—Mystras in Sparta, once known as "the wonder of the Morea" built as an amphitheatre around the town in the thirteenth century, and he captured the medieval rocky fortress of

Monemvasia off the eastern shores of the Peloponnese and the ruined fortress of the Maina on Tigani. Guillaume took over power after Geoffroi de Villehardouin I died and I was interested to read that Geoffroi was "also a humane prince, benevolent and just, solicitous for the condition of the common people". Evidently a good man. The Villehardouin dynasty was most notable as the ruling house of the Principality of Achaea, a Frankish Crusader state in the Peloponnese peninsula of Greece.

We simply must explore the fortresses soon but research, although easy to find nowadays, is often contradictory—sometimes a fortress is called a castle—a Mani tower is called a watchtower, a tower house and even a house tower and as for determining which is the correct spelling of Greek castles, towns, rivers, mountains, monuments etc I give up! I record current spelling as I write my journal and don't intend to alter a thing when a new spelling comes into fashion—plus I am going to write a trilogy about Guillaume's three kingdoms and I shall call it *Chasing Castles*.

Unable to find any signposts of any kind we took to narrow side roads and explored around olive groves, past old churches, through scattered tower settlements mostly in ruins and unable to withstand the invasion of prickly pear. There were few indications of life. The odd dog on a chain, chickens, a cat lying comatose in the shade and an occasional Maniot woman dressed in black with a huge, pointed straw hat on her head and a black scarf tied round her head, knotted beneath her chin. The Maniots wear these curious hats that hide their faces; at first glance they could be mistaken for Chinese field workers in the paddy fields until one sees a face prematurely aged by hardship and the unrelenting sun—and a cool, straight look of indifference. When I wave and greet them, on rare occasions a faint smile plays around their lips as they acknowledge my presence. It is as if we have stepped back in time; the villages look untouched by this century and where restoration is taking place it is executed with the past in mind, by artists in stonework. The only things to remind us of the present are the ubiquitous telephone and electricity pylons and the occasional television antennae.

Whenever we came to a high point in the road where we could see the ocean, the Tigani rock was obscured and we were unsure as to which bay we were overlooking, so we pressed on in the heat which was becoming uncomfortable as the temperature climbed to its predicted zenith of forty degrees. Finally, the road ran out and we stopped high above the coast on a promontory with a tower mansion and a church, nothing more. As we walked down the side of the secretive stone walls the rock again came into view, its 'handle' jutting out into the sea ending in the 'pan'—a lump of rock with little evidence of the grand castle it once was. Standing there with the midday sun blazing down I found it hard to believe the stories of beautiful princesses held captive in glorious splendour, of chandeliers and crystal, of duels fought and lost. It was far too hot, and we were too hungry to contemplate the long trek to the rock, so we headed north on a rough dirt road through a valley and up the other side and found ourselves at the little swimming cove at Mesapo. A grey pebble beach lay at the bottom of steep cliffs full of dark caves but when we climbed down, we found the stones to be covered in thick black tar from passing ships. The water was as clear as glass, so inviting. We negotiated our way around the rocks to the next cove where there was less tar and dived gratefully into the cool depth washing away the heat and dust of our travels.

We picnicked on bread and chunks of sharp feta cheese, cucumbers and sun-ripe tomatoes and as the day sizzled around us with no sea breeze to relieve the heat, we decided it was time to head for home All I could think about was a cool shower, the smoothness of the pearly marble floor, our room darkened by aquamarine shutters and the bed with crisp clean sheets and the sledge-hammer variety of sleep that afternoon siestas induce. But when Geoff turned the key in the ignition, nothing happened.

"Try again!" I urged, my heart sinking. My life has been blighted by unreliable cars and I knew for certain this was one of those times.

"I can't believe it." I spluttered furiously. "It was at the garage this morning for heaven's sake!" Geoff opened the bonnet and tried to look intelligent but he has always insisted that he knows nothing about engines. "We'll have to phone the rescue service," he said in a dull tone, a bleak expression in his eyes, so we made our way up the hill in the pulsating heat through the sleeping houses to the only taverna. I silently thanked Manolis, my mechanic friend in Crete, who had insisted I took out the extra insurance on the Fiat.

"I will not be there to rescue you when it breaks down again. I cannot come from Crete to the Peloponnese!" he had said laughingly.

We had parked the car at the bottom of a steep slope on the edge of a gully as near to the bay as we could, so we realised it was going to be extremely difficult for a tow truck to make its way down to rescue us. We reached the taverna where the still grubby owner greeted us like long-lost friends; had we found a house yet? I was surprised he remembered us but perhaps it is not so common for two people in their sixties to be looking for accommodation for five months or longer in these remote parts.

"Could we phone?" I asked after telling him my car had broken down.

"Of course," he said. Then warily, "where to?"

"Athens," I said, brightly. "I will pay."

He grunted and grumbled and insisted on making the call himself and bellowed down the phone, deafening me and most certainly the unfortunate woman on the other end. It took a good five minutes before she could understand his shouted instructions on how to get to the taverna at Mesapo. Then followed a three-cornered conversation with the Greek Rescue Service in Sparta who also could not understand his instructions. It took two hours before he reached us and then he could not get down the slope to the car since there was a vehicle blocking the road and, of course, it was sacred siesta time. It took him twenty minutes to find the sleepy driver who moved it with ill grace, and another twenty for him to negotiate the narrow strip of road and get into position to pick up my car. Finally, amid cheers from us and a helpful young man who had been poking around in the engine, he winched my old heap onto his huge truck and took it and us to the garage which we had left that morning. The look of despair on the mechanic's face caused us great merriment. Our driver spoke to him and together they isolated the problem within a second—the timing belt had been stripped. The long and the short of it was it could not be fixed until Wednesday. Monday was a religious feast day and he would not be working, and the spare belt had to come from Sparta; most things seem to come from Sparta I have discovered. On the Tuesday maybe, and we could phone and collect it on Wednesday maybe! Our obliging rescuer took us to Areopolis at hair-raising speed and we limped back to the tower house, totally exhausted and carless.

*

I am re-reading Tim Severin's marvellous adventure *The Ulysses Voyage* in which he and his crew in a replica of a Bronze Age galleon constructed by Severin and his team, attempt to retrace Odysseus's voyage as described by Homer. Severin postulates most convincingly that Mesapo is the rounded cove with the narrow entrance where Ulysses lost eleven of his fleet of twelve ships; his was saved only because he had wisely anchored outside the tiny harbour. The cannibalistic Laestrygonian giants hurled down rocks from the enclosing arms of the high overhanging cliffs, attacked and then devoured the wounded men. The scene in front of us seems to match Homer's description perfectly. I have no idea how his findings were accepted by historians but for me, it was convincing enough and I derived some consolation in the thought that if we had to break down—at least it was in an ancient place possibly described by Homer where Ulysses and his fleet also had what one might loosely call—a maritime break down! I could write a short story titled *Not only Ulysses*!

*

We have managed to find some raki at last, although the first bottle we purchased from the shop on the corner was labelled raki but turned out to be ouzo which we both dislike; so we gave it to Georgios who accepted it with alacrity. Then we found another brand and the helpful young man in the shop who, like almost everyone else in the village, is related to the Koronaios family, assures us it was real raki. Unlike the Cretan fiery brew, it is very expensive so we will have to be more prudent with our evening drink which is always accompanied by *mezethes* of sliced apple, crisp pear, cucumber and chunks of tomato sprinkled with fresh oregano from the garden. Stephanos tells us we can find the real home-made stuff up in a mountain village called Arna so we will explore this source with our empty bottles.

*

It is mid-June and we have clinched our deal with the smaller of the two tower houses and move in tomorrow; Hans is not back from Athens so obviously we are not meant to have his tower house. I can always accept disappointment because there is invariably a good reason for it, like something better is waiting around the corner, whatever the situation may be. Stephanos is a structural engineer who specialises in restoring Maniot towers; his business is based in Gytheio and he comes to Areopolis most days. He employs only Polish workmen who he says are refined and reputed to be the best in stone and marble work—and infinitely more hard-working than the Maniots or Albanians. He appears to be pleased at the prospect of us living there and we've negotiated a price for six months and/or twelve months which is not cheap but is affordable, or so my treasure of a treasurer tells me. Stephanos's father, Yiannis, who lives across the garden from us in a triple-storied stone villa, has a washing machine which we may use, as well as a fixed phone. Wow! After eight years of mostly handwashing in Crete this is a luxury beyond my wildest dreams, but there is one major snag that is somewhat off-putting though we are determined to overcome it. Yiannis has a guard dog called

Azore, a colossal Alsatian, jet black and very ferocious. On his first meeting with Geoff, he attacked him and tore his trousers and the next time went for me, despite being restrained by Yiannis most ineffectually. He drew blood on both my wrists and really gave me a fright, yet we are neither of us scared of dogs. The compound has a garden and trees, includes our tower house, Yiannis's villa and another small edifice which is the workshop and store for their building materials. Azore certainly is a most effective watchdog but he is also dangerous because unless he knows one, he literally charges with fangs showing and then uses them. We will attempt to befriend him; that has always been my philosophy as it's the only way in life when confronted with an adversity.

Finally, we have *finally* met the reclusive Iakovos, a shy and rather handsome Greek who is Hans's partner. I gather he paints and we are keen to see his work. But he refuses to comply; I found him to be most likeable. They run the guest house Londas, just off the old square and after Hans returned from the dentist and found that in his absence, we had taken Stephanos's tower house, we spent some time with them. They came to supper the other evening but were so terrified of the dog they threatened never to visit again at night when it roams free. I must admit the first time Geoff and I went out to dinner we were a little nervous of opening the gate in case Azore was patrolling the property so we snuck in like thieves, fortunately he didn't hear us as we hot-footed it to our front door.

'Our' tower house, built from the original stones from Stephanos's family tower that stood on the same spot and collapsed some sixty years ago, has been completed for two years but has remained empty. We are the first people to live in the restored version and I like that idea, especially as it is our first home together. Stephanos said we can move in any time and has promised to complete the alterations and additions as soon as possible. We don't feel like waiting another minute. It stands at the entrance to his extensive family property that is also his builder's yard—not quite what we envisaged for our 'ivory tower'—but again he has promised to clear all the rubble, the marble, planks of timber, old fridges, cement mixers and will move his workshop up the hill behind his father's house and build a car port. One can only hope he will. The house is barely visible behind a screen of eucalyptus, olives and mulberry trees and, above the treetops and the turrets of crumbling Maniot towers and the spires of many churches, the great barrier of the Sangias mountain range rises above our small town and runs southwards as far as the eye can see. The nearby crest known as *Agios Elias*, St Elijah blocks out the sky, the white chapel a miniature speck on the highest point; it also prevents the early morning sun from reaching us until several hours after dawn which will be a blessing during the long summer, but not as welcome in the winter obviously. The highest mountain in the Outer Mani of the Peloponnese is Mount Taygetus, the summit reaching two thousand, four hundred and four metres, or seven thousand, eight hundred and eighty-eight feet. Also known as *Profitis Elias* or Prophet Elias, the name appears in Homer's *Odyssey* and is one of the oldest recorded in Europe; it was associated with the nymph Taygete in classical mythology.

The reconstructed tower is quite modest in size with thick walls and small windows with shutters which, like the doors are painted a pleasing shade of deep turquoise. I had visions of living in one of the traditional, seventy-foot Maniot towers of old, but our future home cannot by any stretch of the imagination, be called graceful or even traditional. It is a tower house nonetheless, so I am not grumbling. Within its thick walls I feel a sense of solidity, of history somehow, yet the interior is modern and bright and has little resemblance to the other traditional towers we have seen. It consists of two rooms, one up and one down. On the ground floor the living room has an air-conditioner and a generous fireplace, medieval in concept and a tiny kitchen alcove at one end, and a bathroom with shower and loo. The upper level is the small bedroom leading onto an open terrace with a vista of untidy trees, a few scattered houses with fences and further still, small farms housing various animals, bored looking; I cannot wait to meet and make friends with them. A wide terrace flanks the ground floor and runs the length of the tower house and looks onto a forest of Frankish figs, I plan to cover the low rough walls with pot plants.

The floors inside are marble of a pearly-grey colour, cool and silky-smooth as are the dining table and kitchen shelf surfaces. The walls are off-white with little niches of warm ochre, the curving wall above the tiny kitchen where the marble stairs lead to the upper level, is painted a lighter shade of ochre and the door surrounds are sky blue. The settee, which is actually a single bed has outsize cushions and there are two cane chairs covered in a most attractive Jacobean design of mustard on navy blue.

Geoff, with some input from Stephanos, has designed a workspace for us; a double- desk about five metres long is to be fitted along the end wall of the living-room-cum-kitchen. It will have marble shelves and be made of pale pine to be varnished not painted. I have never before worked side by side with anyone, but I am looking forward to it. The marble stairs lead up to the small tower itself and our bright bedroom with its cinnamon-coloured quarry tiles and a second bathroom. A door opens onto the upper terrace that faces west and we will be able to watch the sun setting across the treetops. There is a third, rooftop terrace that can only be reached by climbing up clamps on the bedroom wall that have yet to be fixed, but I have decided that two terraces are quite sufficient and I will not be investigating that hatch in the ceiling. I expect Geoff will climb up for the finer view but an Ugly House, not of stone but of white concrete, partially blocks our view of the sea. Eventually it will be hidden by future bamboo screens which will give the terrace a familiar touch – and we already have basil and geranium cuttings in pots on the stone walls.

*

Our first night was a bit of a disappointment. The bedroom looks out seawards across fields criss-crossed by stone walls, olive trees and a few scattered buildings and the odd stone tower, a short walk past the fields and animal enclosures the land comes to a sudden stop where a cliff plunges down deep into the sea. A rural scene on the edge of the village and positively tranquil we thought. However, our tower house is next to a steep and very narrow laneway leading from the centre to the outskirts and it is busy, especially at night, when youths on motorbikes career round the tight corners and rev their horrid little engines to get back up the hill and the Polish workmen drive right past our door up to the workshop a dozen or more times a day. This is not the quiet haven we had hoped for. The property is fenced and has an enormous sliding iron gate which protests and groans and clangs when Yiannis closes it at midnight and opens it early in the morning. It is a bit like living in a medieval village I suppose, as it sounds like a portcullis clanging shut, not that I have ever heard one I have to admit; so a satisfying sense of isolation from the rest of the world drifts over me after I hear the gates crash to a close. This, combined with the knowledge that the black wolf Azore is patrolling the property, completes this sensation then the angry buzz of a motorbike interrupts the mood and I am brought back to the noisy twentieth century.

"Oh, woe is me," says this young maiden as she wipes her hands on her grubby shorts and suggests to her dear friend that a little drop of mead might be a good idea!

*

I have finally 'cracked' it with the greengrocer Georgios—yes, another Georgios, it is a very common name in these parts. Sons and grandsons are named after one another which is why the same masculine first names turn up all over the Greek world. Confusing to put it mildly. Georgios is an untidy, bulky man with tightly curling blonde hair and baleful eyes who has been abrupt to the point of rudeness. I have ignored his unfriendly behaviour and have been excessively polite when purchasing groceries from his ramshackle shop that bursts out onto the narrow main street where his long-suffering and elderly mother sits all day, but for the few hours of siesta, removing old leaves from green vegetables. She has a sweet face. Today, having greeted him in Greek as usual and on receiving his reluctant grunt in response, I asked him brightly if he spoke English. To my amazement he looked up, which he never does and said "yes" in English and then continued:

"Your Greek is good; your accent is pure!"

Swallowing my surprise I congratulated him on his grasp of English and he actually smiled then went on chatting most amicably. Finally, the ice was broken. It transpired he is an occasional actor and loves to talk about the films he has been in and when I said I had never met a "real film-star" before, he blushed and looked quite shy. Why was he so hostile initially? I know not—nor I suspect, does he.

The three white mulberry trees in the garden around us are heavy with fruit that drop like pale green bobbles onto the ground. Yiannis has a long table beneath the tree in front of his house that every few days, becomes covered with a thick tablecloth of mostly overripe and rotting mulberries which he sweeps away. The locals do not appear to eat these berries though the delightful Polish workmen Christos and his brother Michal do. We do too, and they are deliciously sweet.

I read somewhere that the spelling of the name 'Michael' that obviously varies depending on the individual's nationality means "Who is like God" and is derived from Mikha'el the Hebrew name. I can just picture my brother Michael's reaction—his wide grin, green eyes creasing and his deep-throated laugh had I told him the meaning of his name! I was six years younger and he was a perpetual tease, he called me "Freckleface" and we did love one another but often fought with gentle fisticuffs.

My brother died three years ago in South Africa. Sadly, I never really knew him; we were at different boarding schools and during the holidays in Dar es Salaam he spent his days skippering his yacht 'Umeme'—which means 'Lightning' in Swahili—with his friends across the warm waters of the Indian Ocean. He lived in another world from me but every now and then I was invited with his small dog 'Montmorency' to come aboard and go skimming and dancing across the waves to the nearby islands, spinnaker billowing, the hoarse laughter of young men carried on the wind with the bright, light voices of several young and attractive girls. One was Danish, I remember her. What fun we had. I still get a thrill when I recall those days of sun-tight skin and hair prickly and stiff with salt. He used to say, 'You've collected even more freckles today Freckleface!' and I loved that.

The name is recognised and used by Jews, Muslims and Christians alike and is allegedly the most world's most popular name for a man.

*

Yesterday was summer solstice. The moon was full as she rose over the Taygetus at ten o'clock—lighting our terrace table as we dined on chicken in lemon and garlic, flavoured with thyme freshly picked from the mountain-side, potatoes and onions cooked in the large oven tray under the grill and *horta,* that added colour and a wonderful earthy flavour to our palates. We drank village wine, *kokkino,* which means red but looks more like a rosé and finished up with juicy slices of pink watermelon. What more could anybody want? A slight breeze cooled the still air and when we went upstairs, we needed a sheet over our legs, a welcome change from the two previous nights which had been so abominably hot; I was so uncomfortable that I had begun privately to question our decision to live here.

Later, and we are now sleeping outside on the upper terrace, armed with mosquito coils and drenched in citronella on our extremities as we lie on two mattresses beneath the stars. Even on the stillest nights, the temperature is at least ten degrees cooler than in the adjoining bedroom which collects the day's heat and harbours it, as though saving it for our poor tired bodies when we finally stumble up the curved marble stairs to a bed almost too warm to lie upon. I have noticed as I rest looking up at the sky, that as the moon waxes it steals the light from the stars and floods the terrace with a luminous whiteness, criss-crossed by dark shadows thrown by the wooden trellis that hides the Ugly House from our view. I have planted several roots of the wild vine in painted pots and one of them is doing well; its eager fingers are gradually seeking out the corners of the trellis while the other seems to be sulking a bit and is going nowhere after an initially eager start. We have dug cow manure into all the pots and already the leaves are greener, those on the downstairs terrace are thriving, the maidenhair fern is so delicate. A tiny root I brought from a cliff-face in the mountains has sent out a bright green frond; it has grown so fast we could hardly believe our eyes; I could swear it grew about half an inch between our going out for a morning swim and our return home. The geranium cuttings I brought from Crete last year have been in full flower for months, the snowy white and the shocking pink variety are heavy with enormous blooms; they like it here. The lavender is definitely not happy, although to my surprise it flowered profusely shortly after we transplanted it from the rocky hillside in the spring, maybe it is too hot here. We already have a show of petunias of various shades varying from palest lilac to deep royal purple, one of them is striped purple and white, a harlequin hybrid, positively exotic.

Stephanos called in the other day and we told him about the mosquitoes and the need to keep the outer doors open on summer evenings; he promised to put mosquito screens downstairs and off the bedroom so we could feel the night breeze when it sweeps across the land, usually after midnight. I hope he does it before winter sets in! Shortly after, Yiannis came over with a small fan that made a big difference, it was such a thoughtful gesture; it seems everything we ask for is supplied—we are so lucky.

It remains uncomfortably hot and we spend a lot of time in the sea, we have found an ideal swimming spot off the rocks at Limeni. It takes a good fifteen minutes to drive from the town to the shores of the bay, all the way round the bay then up the other side in a series of looping bends and there, tucked into the bottom of a steep valley some two kilometres further on is the Bay of Limeni. Two sloping grey rocks lead out in a shallow, sandy channel to deep water and we dive in and swim along the rocky shoreline towards the tiny white church on the point—and the graveyard where Petrobey Mavromichalis is buried—past moored fishing boats and bobbing buoys to a smooth boulder that juts out of the water, and there we rest and day-dream, lulled by the sound of the waves, feeling the sun on our salty skins. It is our special rock, perfectly designed for lovers in search of privacy, peace and quiet and we seldom see anyone though Hans and Iakovos tell us they also swim off the same rock. We are warned that in July and August this place goes mad with hundreds of Maniot families returning home for the summer holidays but for now, we have the rocks of Limeni and the cove to ourselves.

Sitting on a plateau of smooth sun-warmed rock the other afternoon fresh from our swim, we saw what initially looked like a flying fish skimming at great speed towards us; it flew across the surface of the water and leapt into the air several times, twisting and contorting its gleaming body, the cause of this propulsion out of its natural element and very close to its tail we saw a large, tuna-shaped fish moving like a dark torpedo through the water. The intended victim—a small fish, not a flying fish but flying nevertheless—kept swerving and turning in a frantic effort to evade its pursuer as it came closer to us and disappeared transitorily from view beneath our rock; within a second the predator had swirled around and sped out to the depth once again. Thwarted. I wouldn't be surprised if the smaller fish died of fright after its terrifying escape.

Did I say we had the sea to ourselves? Well nearly, but for the German invasion over the summer, just above the beach at Nea Oitylo which is a few kilometres along the bay where they cluster in their campervans along a grassy strip. I sense they must feel insecure since they travel around in groups and park in a circle rather like the Impis and the Masai in South Africa when under threat of attack. Here they erect their little tables and chairs in the centre and have communal holidays and they might as well be in Germany for all the contact they have with the locals. They are always polite and unobtrusive, but the Maniots do not welcome them; they spend no money, seldom frequent tavernas but look for bargains everywhere they go and, as in Crete, the last war is not forgotten. There are a few motor vans from Italy, but in the main they are from Germany and we have met them throughout the Peloponnese.

*

The *marmara,* marble man, is fixing a shelf for our small stove which at the moment sits so high up I can't see into the saucepans; he and his young helper drop one of the heavy slabs of marble and it splits in two. *Espase!* Broken! He announces in a voice heavy with a true Greek sense of tragedy. He is from Athens, this tiny, wizened man who wears a beret and big steel-rimmed glasses that keep slipping down his nose, a perpetual cigarette droops from his mouth. He is so slight one would think there was not enough strength in his thin frame to lift a heavy marble slab but he is agile, with small, deft, quick movements. He sticks the translucent marble shelves together with fast-drying glue, muttering to himself, watched a bit warily by his assistant; I suspect he might be somewhat tetchy and is certainly a perfectionist. Stephanos tells me the best marble comes from the centre of the Peloponnese in the Tripolis area and the cheaper quality is from local quarries south of here. We often see trucks carrying colossal chunks of marble, labouring up the steep roads, northwards; it is used everywhere in this part of the world. Finally, the shelf is mended, and my stove is relocated at a much lower level so at least I can now see what I am doing. I thank him and ask if the rest of the summer is going to be as hot as it is today, a sweltering forty degrees.

"*Auvrio,*" Tomorrow, he replies shaking his head like a terrier, droplets of sweat flying around. "*Pio zesti,*" tomorrow, it will be hotter! And off he goes on his tiny motorbike, putt-putting his way up the hill.

*

Summer siesta and I lie on the bed that feels too hot on my skin; everything is the same temperature, the air, the bed, my skin and hair, the water in the tap. I try to ignore the relentless heat drifting in through the windows, think of coolness, think of a deep, cold swim, but as I drift off, I am jolted back into consciousness by the interjection of the rhythmic sawing of a nearby single *tzitzik*, a cicada. Another joins in, and in a moment it seems as if all the *tzitzikia* in the Mani are part of a conspiracy to prevent siesta at all cost, mind you the decibels do wax and wane through the day. Outside the sheltering walls of our tower house everyone is asleep I suspect, but their chorus goes on incessantly and in my befuddled sleep-deprived state I reflect on how much I really do love this sound; it means Greek summer to me and as July creeps up, I wait to hear the first screech as they come into full voice during the first week of this month.

And now it is evening with the tower house filled with the glorious silken tones of Maria Callas. How that woman could sing. We are experiencing the second heatwave of the month with the temperatures again hovering above forty-three degrees. *The Athens News*, the English-speaking newspaper, reports that in polluted Athens the elderly and young are dropping like flies and that the heat will last another three days. Thank goodness the nights and evenings are a little cooler here than in Crete, in fact, and we are about to have one of Geoff's famed cocktails; the ingredients are red wine and vermouth—laced with tonic, slices of lemon, mint and plenty of ice. This long drink will be accompanied by *mezethes*—the Greek version of hors d'oeuvres. Our favourite home-made dip is *tzatziki* which is cold sheep's yoghurt mixed with chopped cucumber, mint, garlic and lemon juice. Replace the cucumber with grated carrots and we have the most delicious *karotta salata* that we eat with chunks of fresh village bread or crisp bread and tomato quarters sprinkled with fresh basil from our pots.

The lower terrace is our favourite sundowner spot, looking across the olive groves with the lowering rays of the sun slanting through the bamboo to the mountain range. This evening, the heat is oppressive and has captured the fragrance of the flowers and ferns which surround us; the atmosphere is so tropical I feel I could be back in my home in Dar es Salaam. Indeed, there is a similarity in our lifestyle in Greece to the early days in Tanganyika. But to the present. Callas is making me weak at the knees and I feel as if

I could cry, music can be uplifting but also damaging at times, yet I have nothing at all to cry about—perhaps my hidden tears are for her tragic life. I am reminded about my plans for my next life; I would like to either be a vocalist—preferably a second alto or a tenor—or a conductor. Dream on Valerie! Right now, her voice is fading away and a tear has fallen on my computer; I think the voice takes precedence. I can hear the ice clinking in the glasses as Geoff brings our cool drinks which is also music to my ears.

The Frankish figs that threaten to invade our tower house are in flower; olives and dark leafed carobs nudge the terrace and beyond the trees a delicate church spire and a lofty tower with a red design around the turrets, peers out from a forest of flowering Tree of Heaven. This feathery-leafed tree hails from northern China, is considered a menace as it suckers and grows with voracious energy in courtyards and empty spaces throughout the scattered buildings. And in the rest of Greece. All I can say is that it is a most attractive menace; the crowns of the trees are bright with yellow blossom that contrast gently with the pink blossoms of the Japanese Silk Tree which also flourishes in this part of the Mani. The walls of a crumbling tower sag above the greenery and pierce the skyline where the lofty bare peaks have captured a few clouds, unusual in high summer. The locals have another name for the Sangias—the *Kakovounia*—Evil or Bad Mountains. The Deep Mani was once a dark and forbidding region that is still reflected in the landscape, but for me, there is a beauty in the uncluttered shapes of the abandoned towers against the sky.

Around eight thirty p.m. during the month of July, the peaks turn from their drab daytime appearance to an astonishing shade of violet to amethyst to deep purple as the last rays of the setting sun give way to velvet night as it gradually descends. The *tzitzikia* continue to saw incessantly as the bats swing out of the spatulate fingers of the Frankish figs. How fast they fly, darting here and there so silently. It surprises me to find they live so close to the ground. Do cats eat bats? There are many half-feral cats forever foraging in the thicket of prickly figs. We are visited by a nervous jet-black female with swinging teats, a scruffy black tom with a white chest and a rather handsome ginger cat that leaps across the terrace, looks at us for a moment and disappears. One night we left scraps out for her but visiting friends swore they saw rats running across the prickly pears beside us, so we decided it was imprudent. Feed cats yes, but rats no!

Stephanos has remained true to his word and we are constantly surprised at the excellent quality of everything he has supplied; from the beautiful linen, outsize white towels and wonderful crisp sheets and pillow cases, soft new pillows and a perfect mattress—so rare in Greece where both pillows and mattresses normally resemble compacted concrete—to the swivel bedside lamps chosen by us in Sparta, and our modern desk lamps.

*

CHAPTER THREE

PROFITIS ELIAS AND BEAUTIFUL SAD MYSTRAS

Driving north, the coast road careers headlong down the tortuous escarpment into the bays where we swim at Limeni and Oitylo then drags itself up the northern side of the bay and continues its journey above the sea along a high plateau. It winds between walled fields of olives, spikey brown thistles and shimmering, golden grasses. Byzantine churches sit amongst the olives, weeds and grasses hiding their feet, their domed cupolas red and glowing in the sun. Langada is one of the prettiest villages, alive with summer flowers where elegant stone houses with balconies are festooned with startling pillar-box red and pink geraniums and creepers tumble down the stone walls—we smell fresh bread. Our nostrils lead us to the *fournos*, bakery, where we beg for *tyropitas*, those diagonal crispy cheese pies, but they are not ready. Later maybe says the old woman, she is not friendly. I have noticed in the Mani that most bakers seem to be either old or very old women—except for Milya in Areopolis, and they are reserved, uncommunicative, but it is a harsh life—always up before dawn to meet the villagers' demands for warm loaves long before daylight. Their distaste, or is it suspicion for foreigners is obvious—and I don't blame them.

We stand at the door of a most intricately decorated Byzantine church on a curve in the road through the tiny village and a gentle priest, good looking under his tall black hat, indicates we can enter despite our shorts, and shows us fragments of restored frescoes of intensely rich colours. He tells us sadly that it will take another ten years and *polla lefta*, a lot of money, to complete the restoration and rolls his melancholy brown eyes and rubs thumb and fingers together in the Greek way that indicates large sums of money. We leave our contribution in a shallow box and wish him well as we say our farewells, but our offering will not make any difference I am sorry to say. And then another dear little Byzantine church almost hidden by a stand of silver olives, sadly neglected, weeds grow from the old tiles but it looks so cute I want to take it home and put it on the mantelpiece. This area is rich in Byzantium—so many primitive chapels and enchanting churches, some sitting amongst the olives, others halfway up the hillsides their belfries delicate above the trees. There are several on the main road. The door of a miniature chapel in the hamlet of Nomitsa is open and as we enter, the smell of age and candle grease fills my nostrils. Every inch of the small interior including the dome is covered in ancient frescoes; the colours faded but in many places the drawings still amazingly clear. There are gallant knights on horseback, the shiny scales of a dragon and St George, the dragon killer himself, hollow-eyed saints all apparently in the last stages of tuberculosis, although the clearest is of a curious female figure carrying a lute and what looks like a violin bow.

Further along the road that runs along a plateau high above the sea, the tenth-century church of Agios Nikolaos with its three cupolas stands alone on a hill above a vista of sea and sky. Colossal stones were used to build this old church which faces onto an enclosed courtyard and I want to find someone with a key to the locked door as I understand there are fine frescoes inside. Even the gate into the courtyard is locked, as always in the Mani, yet one could easily get over the wall so there is no need for the gate. A pine forest full of buzzing *tzitzikia*, cicadas, at the side of the church offers a perfect spot for a future picnic we agree.

On we go to Stoupa which, albeit touristy and crowded with new buildings, is a pretty spot with masses of petunias and geraniums leaping out of pots, pink and white oleander in full bloom, shady mulberries, cypress and eucalyptus. Masses of trees. Busy tavernas shaded with leafy trellises overlook the long curving bay, umbrellas line the sand, fishing boats rock in the shallow, clear water. The Taygetus mountains, misty with humidity, rise to the east fringing the sky. The beach road winds round beneath splendid eucalypts in full leaf and flower; these trees do not appear to suffer the same disease and insect pests as they do in Australia and always appear to look finer and fuller in Greece. It is baking hot so we park in their shade and swim round a group of rocky islands in tepid water cooled by brisk underwater currents, then lie on silky sand on fallen eucalyptus leaves. It smells like Australia and makes me momentarily homesick. Far too many people around for our taste and unusually, we hear the muted tones of the British middle classes rather than the Birmingham and Manchester vowels I am so used to hearing in Crete when it is tourist time.

Fancying something sweet we go into an ice cream parlour and order cappuccino with lashings of real cream and I introduce Geoff to *galaktoboureko*, a traditional Greek dessert, a sort of custard-semolina pie in sweet syrup held together with layers of phyllo pastry, that incidentally and appropriately, comes from the Greek word *phyllon* which means 'leaf'. It is so delicious I have difficulty in resisting the impulse to order another of these huge slices of golden, crispy bliss bombs and making a pig of myself.

Driving further north the road clings to the steep sides of the mountain through greener, softer country than we are used to in the Deep Mani until we come to Kardamyli where my mentor, Patrick Leigh Fermor, lives. It was his book *The Mani: Travels in the Southern Peloponnese* written in 1958 that first attracted me to the Peloponnese. I first read it during the seventies when I was obsessed with coming to settle in Greece—although at the time it was not the Deep Mani but the island of Crete I simply had to see—but I do recall that even then, I was sure that one day I would find myself in a Maniot watchtower writing a book. Well, I am now—will anyone read it? No one can surpass the magic of Leigh Fermor's descriptions so I will not even try. He writes page after page about Kardamyli and captures this still enchanting village with his gift of words that leave me speechless, however the advent of tourism, that he was erroneously certain would never strike in that remote part, has certainly altered the main street and some of the ocean frontage. How he must hate the changes.

He writes of the houses looking like small castles built of golden stone and refers to Kardamyli as a castellated hamlet on the ocean's edge; his words instantly resonate in my mind as a painting of a place I want to know. He goes on to say he was very much tempted to settle in the small hotel in the village for months with books and writing-paper and says reflectively "the thought has often recurred". I am unsure as to when he and Joan settled in Kardamyli and built their house, but that is where they still live, he is now eighty-two years of age. The inclination to visit him is strong but I respect his privacy and resist the urge, but I did write to him when I first came to Crete and I have found his two postcards which I thought I had lost, to prove it.

The following is from my journal, scribbled on the rickety table:

"Kardamyli, and we are sitting at Lena's Tavern recommended by Hans and Iakovos for lunch. We found it easily as it is well advertised along the few streets and we are sitting at a table beneath hanging green grapes on a terrace with blue railings and flowering pots. Coppery gladioli sway in the breeze which smells of seaweed and below, against grey sea-worn rocks, pink oleanders in full bloom, their sweet perfume mingling with the inviting aromas from Lena's kitchen. Lena is a gaunt, very pale elderly Greek woman who was once Patrick Leigh Fermor's housekeeper; she looks unwell and is so over-worked I feel guilty increasing her workload. But we are hungry! Jutting rocky coves and inlets to the south and across a stretch of shimmering water, an island where we can see three ruined towers partially hidden by trees. We idly wonder if we should try to swim there to explore but Geoff, the ever-practical Virgo in my life, says we would need to carry our climbing shoes on our heads as the island rises sheer out of the sea and we would have to scale the cliffs once we got there. Waves pound on the rocks and curl and boil in dark caves and we agree we might manage to swim the distance but landing there would prove somewhat difficult. Geoff fixes me with his blue eyes and the decision is made without words; we will not attempt to swim to the island but will just have lunch and lie on a beach which is surely more suited to people of our age. But what after all

is our age? Are we not young and full of life and vigour? Indeed, we are. Age is only ever in the mind.

Lunch consists of a cool crisp Greek salad, fresh with slabs of white feta sprinkled with oregano and drenched with the glaucous green of virgin olive oil, warm brown bread that crunches noisily between the teeth and a glass of retsina, golden and glowing. Around us the pounding of waves as they fill rock pools and the chorus of tzitzikia like dry castanets rhythmically change tempo at a given signal; I wonder who signals this change of tempo? A chieftain or a conductor in the cicada tribe? Greek voices, bright, surround us, tables covered with debris from devoured lobsters and shellfish while laughing children play tag, chestnut hair burnished by the sun. Two grey and white cats look into my eyes anxiously but soon leave when they discover the fish aromas come from another table. The unrelenting sun pours through the vines and we are heady with heat, food, and cool white wine."

We drive slowly away in a stupor and find a long, pale pebbly beach where we snooze and later swim in a crystal sea. Families gather beneath umbrellas and an Italian couple nearby play with their children, she with nothing on but a G-string and bare and sun-blackened breasts. How ugly the human skin is when burned to a crisp. I have noticed that Greek women do not go bare-breasted at least in this part of the Deep Mani; the other women who do appear semi-nude are the Scandinavians, blonde long-legged and gorgeous and the equally gorgeous dark-eyed Italians who have an enviably carefree attitude to nudity and care not one jot for anyone else's opinion, nor, it would seem for the condition of their skins.

Evening and as we meander through the hamlet of Nitsis on the way home we come across little old ladies in black with walking sticks emerging from every nook and cranny, some in pointed straw hats over black scarves, most of them lopsided, limping. Arthritis? It is the hour for the traditional Greek *volta*, walk, stroll, also used to mean more precisely, evening promenade—even if it is along the busy main road in a hardly happening village. We arrive home at dusk, tired but in good spirits after another exhilarating day with my brain full of images and words waiting to be recorded onto paper. It is so good to be back in our tower; come to think of it, Geoff and I are living in an ivory tower in a sense, preferring to be alone and definitely shunning company. For the moment we are relishing the peace and quiet although I always look forward to hearing from my family and ring them now and then from Yiannis's outdoor telephone, carefully avoiding Azore, the growling black beast of a dog.

*

'The mystery of the white stones' I called this initially puzzling episode. One afternoon, following a long siesta, I wandered out onto the lower terrace feeling as if I had been hit by a sledgehammer for the sleep of siesta is another type of sleep and one wakes up with extreme reluctance and a very slim hold on reality. The silent, blinding heat, the incessant and rhythmic sawing of the *tzitzikia* plus the certainty that everyone in the village is still asleep behind their thick stone walls and closed shutters also has a curiously deadening effect on the brain cells and it takes longer than usual to come to life! Sometimes I think Geoff never entirely wakes following his siesta since he shows a strong resemblance to a zombie for the rest of the day, or at least until the evening cools—if it does. Mind you a swim invariably does the trick and after we plunge off the rocks at Limeni into cool clear water, we both recover.

Later, as I sat on the plastic chair trying to recover, my eyes focused as they invariably do on the gaunt slopes of Agios Elias, the looming mountain above Areopolis, and I noticed what looked like a white path zigzagging up to the miniature white chapel sitting in glorious isolation on the top. We had often wondered how one could get up to it, there being no visible path or means of access up the steep slopes, but of course, there had to be.

"Funny," I thought. "I haven't noticed that path before."

So I called Geoff who staggered out, bleary-eyed. He had not noticed the white markings earlier so we wondered if a little too much village wine was getting to us and that perhaps we should stop having a glass of wine at lunchtime. We finally came to the crazy conclusion that maybe someone had overnight, painted the stones along a path leading to the church. To show the way? It seemed a most unlikely answer to the puzzle, but also the only one. We asked Hans and Iakovos about it and they told us that the following day, the twentieth of July, was the name day *Panayia, of Profitis Elias,* and that indeed they were newly-painted stones marking the upward path to the summit. These days it was mostly the young who undertake the climb the night before; they built fires, feasted and indulged in fun, not much of it in the name of religion, although some of the older more ardent believers still made their way to the chapel to pray. The path is allegedly very steep and quite dangerous.

Sea fogs, thick and white, are a feature of the summer and occasionally during the afternoons I become aware of a change in atmosphere and watch a slow invasion of the land as the fog rolls mysteriously and silently up through the olive groves softening their contours and obliterating the mountain, then it settles for the remainder of the day and our evening view of the range is lost. The change in the landscape is spectacular and, but for the humid heat, it might be winter, so cool and grey is the scene from our tower. With the sea fog comes humidity that lays the dust; the air smells different, unlike the dry mood of summer, the table on the terrace has little drops of moisture on it and the geranium leaves are speckled with damp. During the afternoon of the 'day of the white rocks', a dramatic and heavy fog rolled in and totally obliterated the mountains around us, it remained until the next morning when the sun gradually dispersed the moisture. I felt sorry for the revellers on top of the peak, the temperature had dropped considerably and it would have been cold up there in the night sky. Next evening, we watched pinpoints of lights coming down the mountainside as the faithful and others made their way back and I thought how enjoyable it would be to go up and experience this feast day, but there is no way I could get up there short of a helicopter. Stephanos has just asked Geoff to walk up with him in the autumn and take photos one day. Good luck to them I say, I will wait in the village at the foot of the mountain with a small bottle of raki and medical supplies!

*

Sometimes we swim in the early mornings. I drag Geoff out of bed and we drive to the Bay of Limeni, scramble down the rocks and dive into the still sleeping water, the sun has not got around the mountain to wake up the day. Then home for breakfast, still glowing from our swim. For me there is nothing as sublime as an early morning swim in a silent, cold sea with no one around but my man. Far beneath me the seabed lies clear and detailed; patches of pale smooth rock, bright fish darting between gardens of waving seaweed, purple, sharp green, startling orange and further into the channel the deep blue-black of the depth that always makes me want to swim down to discover what lies beyond. I revel in the safety of the seas around Greece, in the ability to swim out as far as I like without fear, in contrast to swimming in Australia where the spectre of lurking sharks is always foremost in my mind, not to mention the occasional killer box jellyfish and other varieties. So different from the Indian Ocean that laps the shores of East Africa in Kenya and Tanganyika where there are sharks and jellyfish but no one, to my knowledge, had ever been attacked by sharks in all the years I lived and swam there. Mind you, when I was young, I was seriously stung by an invasion of hundreds upon hundreds of blue Portuguese man-of-war jellyfish floating on the water's surface. I had not seen their bloated blue 'floats' on the beach as I raced into the waves and was rescued by a heroic man who dived off the raft to take me to the shore on his back after I had swum as fast as I could, through the sea of poisonous tentacles to the raft. We were both hospitalised for a few hours, injected and rubbed with heaven knows what following the harrowing experience but we survived. Obviously!

I always thought they were jellyfish; they are not. Years later I discovered they are highly venomous predators that superficially resemble jellyfish but are actually siphonophores; the scientific name being *Physalia physalis*—their feeding tentacles sting and paralyse small fish, crustaceans and other invertebrates. these tentacles can be up to fifty metres, one hundred and sixty feet long and their multiple stings have been known to kill a human being.

The sea below the rocks at Limeni is full of ice-cold springs that instantly chill the limbs, even in high summer, and the water turns to the consistency of gin. The masks fog up making snorkelling difficult. We swim every evening, late, after the burning sun begins to sink, the summer holidaymakers are heading home and we have the rocks to ourselves as the sea becomes quiet as it cools and settles in for the night. It is a peaceful time and prepares us for the hot evening, the meal and the still, humid nights. If we miss our evening dip, we both feel somewhat wearier, even though we exert a good deal of energy when we swim it still leaves us feeling refreshed and less affected by the high and soaring summer temperatures.

*

Sparta, our main metropolis, is a little over an hour away. We haven't been there yet and as I roll the word around my tongue, I get a thrill—Sparta! It reeks of mythology and history and of that ancient race who believed that physical strength was the ultimate achievement and left their young out on the slopes of the Taygetus mountains to gauge if they were strong enough to survive; the ones that did were truly Spartan and the adjective remains in common usage today. I wonder what ancient ruins are to be seen, having read the following:

After Sparta's victory in 404 B.C. against Athens in the second Peloponnesian war, Sparta reached the height of its power. During this period the inhabitants evidently preferred to defend Sparta with men rather than mortar; no remains of city walls have been found.

My recalcitrant and silent laptop has given up the ghost and has to be fixed. I am bereft. I hate writing in longhand. I have been typing since I was fourteen when on holiday from boarding school, my mother suggested I learn to type since I was going to be a writer—or a ballet dancer—but where could one find a ballet school in Tanganyika? I did learn to tap dance at a young age and appeared on stage in Dar es Salaam where I did high kicks over a fancy walking stick. I wore a top hat and tails and it was fun—but my dream at that age, was to become a ballet dancer. My mother had an ancient and very noisy Remington portable that clattered away noisily as I sat at her desk and learned my way, on six fingers ignoring all her pleas to type more efficiently. I am still inefficient but can type at great speed and now I have a laptop with a spellcheck so my 'typos' are corrected. But I could always spell. As soon as my laptop packed up, apart from phoning my friend in London who has dealt with its vagaries in the past, I asked Stephanos what to do about it. He said he knew a man in Sparta who could help or at least get it quickly to someone in Athens, but for the ten days while the car was misbehaving, we didn't dare go to Sparta and I wrote in longhand and did not touch the keyboard. Finally, we are off to Sparta before the summer crowds arrive and I can't wait. Fancy going to an historically famous place called Sparta to get one's computer mended!

'New Sparta', founded in 1834 by decree of King Otto, stands on the site of the ancient city; it is a well-designed provincial town surrounded by ancient sites which intrigued me, but these could wait I decided. First get my laptop fixed since I could not bear the thought of writing longhand for one more day. We found the video games shop where my contact was employed, he was a young man, bright with very good English and he said yes, he could help and where was the laptop? As I opened the boot of the car to get it out, I had one of my psychic nudges—"I bet it's working"—and when we opened up the wretched thing—it was! The young man grinned with a slightly patronising air and went back to his desk. Home we came and I've been writing furiously ever since but with a new and curious set of problems, for now and then, it refuses to save or let me switch off and I lose everything which is an awful waste of time and effort. Then sometimes it suddenly switches off on its own accord and again I lose what I haven't saved. This occurs on certain days—Thursdays and Saturdays to be precise or am I bonkers? It refuses to read 'drive A' so I work in the hard drive and try to save everything; mind you the spectre of losing everything is beginning to take its toll. I suspect the tension is making me old before my time and is certainly no help with the creative juices which usually flow with great ease. I'm quick-tempered too. Poor Geoff.

"It seems to me," I said to Hans and Iakovos when we next saw them and I recounted the tale, "that this laptop needs the occasional *ekdromi*, outing or change, as we all do!"

This, they thought, was extremely amusing but I am sure it relegated me into the same category as being one of those eccentric Englishwomen who visit their guest house for spring and autumn walks "to take the air"! Anyway, it stopped working yesterday and no amount of persuasion made any difference; it sat silent and blank and overheated. I decided it needed a change, so I carried it around a bit then sat it on our terrace in the evening and invited it to supper. It was one of our good meals. We do occasionally have some really tasty ones such as grilled brown and crispy chicken, delicious roasted pumpkin and potatoes sprinkled with lemon juice and plenty of garlic, *horta*, the generic term for all green vegetables, such as wild spinach and dandelions, village wine— red of course—followed by cool half-moons of melon with sheep's yoghurt and golden coils of local honey. I ask you, could a gourmet computer fail to be moved by such a repast, sitting on our terrace with the moon rising above the bamboo screens and the scent of basil in the pots on the wall? And when I brought it in and switched it on, it worked again! What does one make of that I ask myself? I don't know! If it were not so frustrating it would be funny.

*

This morning we drove to beautiful, sad Mystras, the ruined fortress established in 1249 by the Frankish ruler Guillaume II de

Villehardouin, and the last stronghold of Byzantium in the southern Peloponnese. Its history is as bloody and as complicated as most of the other Frankish establishments all of which were systematically conquered by the Byzantines, Turks, Venetians and again the Turks from whom Mystras was finally liberated. This place and its history have long appealed to something deep within me; first of all, it overlooks the plain and city of Sparta that also draws me and I have a need to stand at the very top of the steep fortified hill and actually be there in order to seek the past. The ruins, reputedly the most impressive in Greece, lie along the northern slopes of the foothills of the towering Taygetus range, six kilometres north-west of Sparta. I could see the fortifications from afar, standing on the crest of a steep hill on the edge of a deep and dark ravine into which it is said the ancient Spartans threw their defective children. We parked at the highest level and headed for the top, despite the heat. I puffed and panted up the winding path with aching back, urging Geoff to go ahead while I rested in the shade; eventually I reached the impressive walls and sat beneath a stunted apricot tree, the wind in my hair until Geoff found me. I was pleased I had made the effort. The fortress was fast crumbling and many of the walls were only waist-high although those supporting the massive main gate were intact and had colossal arched windows. All was silent, few tourists. I noticed weeds sprouting from the cracks and felt a palpable presence of the past, of history and an awareness of ancient pride enveloping me. I have a strong sense of belonging in Mystras and Sparta—past lives?

Through the ancient crenellations, those fighting platforms and good vantage points from which soldiers could launch their arrows, I could see below, far, far below, the white town of Sparta shimmering in the heat on the Spartan plain, the landscape appliqued with tidy olive groves, green and brown—and beyond—ranks of fading mountains so pale they merged with the bleached-out sky. We spent a long time at the site talking of the past. I would like to have lived in that time on that splendid hillside with its backdrop of the soaring mountains. Further down the steep hill, the vast Palace of the Mystras Despots—once inhabited by the last

Emperor of Byzantium, Constantine XI Palaeologos crowned in 1448, stands proud although almost totally hidden by scaffolding over which workmen hang precariously. Why is it that almost everywhere I go, the place I most want to see is being restored? I want to explore the interior of the palace but I will settle for the Cathedral of Demetrios, the monastery and the archaeological museum which is housed in the cathedral, but not before I have had time to absorb my surroundings. The site is beautiful, steeply terraced and tree-filled. Cypresses dark and tall stand above the red-tiled cupolas of the many churches, cloisters shaded by pillared arches, gardens bright with summer flowers, tapering belfries and mellifluous birdsong. I sit in the shade as Geoff explores with his camera and reflect yet again how fortunate I am to be sharing these experiences.

We walked on to a many-domed church where, in a side chapel, Geoff discovered the fading fresco of the Birth of the Virgin, a beautifully expressive depiction which I found quite moving despite my heretic background. The church was crowded and as we started on the downhill journey back to the car, I noticed there were many more people around. For me the presence of others totally destroys the atmosphere in an ancient site so I was once again glad we had come early.

*

Geoff has had a bit of a run-in with the postal staff. It consists of a young chap Georgios, who speaks English but prefers not to, and a sour-faced middle-aged woman with pale hair and a tight mouth who barely returns my bright greeting. They have been allowing us to sift through and collect our poste restante mail for six weeks without showing them any identification after our first meeting, then, due to the presence of an older man, possibly an Inspector from Head Office—wow!—insisted on Geoff showing his passport having first allowed him to get the letters in his hand then refused to let him take them out of the post office. Back to the tower house he came in a sweat, very cross, he is not yet used to the vagaries of the Greeks but I found it amusing, I went in with him next time and Georgios, after glancing apprehensively at the woman behind the glass window—the official was still lurking in the background—asked for my passport.

I said, "But you know who I am! I am Valerie, this is Geoff. We live here and we have been getting mail without passports for six weeks." All in Greek which makes me think it must be improving.

Another exchange of looks and I thought for a moment he was going to relent, but no, he had to see our passports. Back we went to the tower house that should take less than five minutes but if one meets a car going in the other direction it can take up to half an hour because one of the vehicles is forced to back up the narrow winding streets until sufficient passing space is found. All quite quaint but often very frustrating. On this trip we met two cars and had to negotiate backwards and finally returned to the post office where Georgios checked my passport but couldn't find my name and sheepishly asked me to show him where it was. Then he opened Geoff's on the wrong page initially, then handed us our mail but for a letter from my old friend Brenda which was addressed to Valerie Helps, the name I use when writing. I was about to go into a long explanation about being a famous author and using two names but he accepted my statement that I was also Valerie Helps and off we went. Letters in hand.

Yesterday I went in with the passports in my bag although I was determined not to show them again. Georgios, who has beautiful eyes, looked at me, looked at Geoff and handed us the packet of letters without a smile or a word. The official, still lurking in the background coughed and turned away. I was quite disappointed as I had practised saying;

"Today I am Valerie Muir and also Valerie Helps and this is Geoffrey Bull. Yesterday I had the same names and the day before and tomorrow I will have the same names, and so will Geoffrey!" But I did not have to.

*

We have thirteen paintings, two of which are mine, ready for sale so we drive to Gytheio, en route we finally spot the remains of the Frankish castle Passava or Passavas from the French, *passe avant*, which translates as "'go farther down'" or "'move forward'" on the summit of the narrow gorge between Gytheio and Areopolis. This is the only pass through the Taygetus mountains and has always been the favourite spot for battles; we will climb to the top soon, it's not too high but is deeply forested and doesn't look what I call an easy trek. I always enjoy our trips to the town that generally commence with a hot and flaky *spanakopita*, cheese and spinach pie and a cup of Ελληνικό καφέ, *Eliyniko kafe*. Greek coffee comes in different levels of sweetness: σκέτο, *sketo*, no sugar,—μέτριο, *metreo*, medium sweet and γλυκό, *gluko*, sickly sweet, thick with sugar and if you must have it with milk—με γάλα, *me gala*, and of course, there's καφέ φραπές, *kafe frapé* which is iced coffee with a partly French name and is made with instant coffee, often Nescafé, and is not that exciting. We relax under striped awnings at the port as brightly painted caiques rock at our feet, absorbing the lively holiday atmosphere of mostly Greeks enjoying the summer break although I also hear Italian, French, a little English and lots of German spoken. The large square is tree-shaded, the esplanade long and lined with chairs and tables under multicoloured sun umbrellas, the shops are typical tourist shops interspersed with boutiques and at the far end near the old town, is Hasanakos's shop with his upper-level art gallery; there is a distinct possibility that we might sell some of our paintings there. We find Georgios and after a cursory glance at Geoff's folder he says he will take the lot! Did we hear right? The lot? How much do we want for them? My mind goes blank and Geoff does his calculations off the top of his head. Georgios looks slightly amused and offers him a few thousand drachmas less and we say "done" and walk outside—my brain swirling with astonishment. Selling our paintings wholesale? Well, I'll be damned! As we congratulate ourselves Petros his son, crosses the road and says his father wants some more local scenes of Gytheio please. So a commission for Geoff. We are even more pleased.

We find a long sandy bay slightly north of the port with a tatty nightclub on the edge of the sand. The beach is deserted and a perfect spot for our picnic and a swim. We notice what look like bamboo cages at various intervals along the sand and when I read the notice it asks people not to touch as there were turtle eggs beneath. I was so tickled to be swimming on a beach where there were turtles' eggs and I knew from Stephanos that they hatch towards the end of August. He told us that there is a Turtle Watch group from Athens in charge and that they work from a kiosk in the town; I intend to seek them out immediately and must see them hatching so I can write about them. It is important.

*

Today we tasted the first *frangosyka*, Frankish fig or prickly pear of this summer, my Polunin book on the Balkans calls them Barbary figs. What's in a name—the spines are still murderously prickly whatever these plants are called—and unsurprisingly, it is a member of the cactus family. The prickly pear, Frankish fig or *frangosyka* in Greek, is an exotic plant originally from South America, introduced to Greece in the early thirteenth century by invaders from Western Europe. The Greeks named them the 'Frankish people' or the 'Franks'—today's French—and *frangosyka* translates to '"figs of the Franks"'. It is believed they planted the ferociously prickly fig around their fortifications for extra protection from their enemies; the widely-spreading branches with their needle-sharp spines are as fierce as any guard dog.

Yiannis, one of the sons-in-law, was peeling one and offered me a plateful, he told me how to peel them and avoid the penetrating and almost invisible barbs by holding the fig in a fork, cutting each end, slicing the thick skin from each end and peeling it off. I brought them back to Geoff who ate them cautiously and commented on how many pips they had; he has a thing about pips and skins and removes them whenever possible. I think the figs taste like a good pink pawpaw; he thinks it is more like an Australian melon, not a Greek one as they are sweeter. Mind you he has never tasted a ripe, sun-warmed pawpaw straight off a tree sharpened with lime, and equates pawpaw with a bitter flavour, which they have when picked unripe. I had forgotten to ask Yiannis how to pick them so when I found him watering in the garden, I asked him. He dropped the hose with obvious delight and raced up to the house to bring back a long stick with a metal hook with which he proceeded to stab into the glowing figs and twist and they came off easily. One side of our tower house is surrounded by these figs, their spatulate fingers covered with fruit, but it is impossible to get to them as there is a fence around the property and our terrace is high off the ground. Yiannis returned with a ladder that is now propped up on the outer wall of our terrace so Geoff can climb down amongst the plants and pick them to his heart's content, and to mine.

I heard my name being called from Yiannis's house where his three daughters, sons-in-law and families are staying for the month, and I raced across to the telephone. It was Amanda. So good to hear her happy voice full of excitement and news of the music degree she is pursuing for the second time at the ripe old age of thirty-two—having neglected her studies of piano and flute when she was much younger. I am elated; she is after all a born musician. How I enjoy hearing from my family.

*

Finally, the last of the additions to the tower house have been completed. Christos the happy Pole came in with his baseball cap and vest and a cheery "*Kiria Valerie*" and glued three marble shelves at each end of our workspace. So now I can sort out my bits and pieces of manuscripts, paintings and drawings and be able to get to them more easily. The speakers of our new CD player sit on the top and Mahler booms out filling the room with his magic.

The weather has changed as it always does, I am reliably told, in the middle of August; thundery clouds roll in and the bleached-out summer sky has interesting shapes and shades of grey. I hear thunder. It is the fifteenth of August today, the Panayia, the Feast of the Assumption of the Virgin Mary. Most Greek churches dedicated to the Virgin Mary are called Παναγία, pronounced *Panagia*. Mary is considered the holiest of all human beings and, therefore, of higher status than the saints so the standard western Christian term of St Mary is rarely used in the Orthodox East. The town is full to overflowing with families here for the long weekend and the one-way system up into the main square is permanently blocked, so we have taken to using the side road that meanders through fields and towers and stone walls, through narrow laneways past my favourite little church with two towers, one graceful and tapering and the other domed, then we park at the side of the square. There are queues for the public telephones which at least means they are working for a change.

As Yiannis's family is here Azore for once, is shut away in his large compound and is going crazy wanting to join in. I feel for him, he is so playful, so fiercely playful that whenever he has taken my wrists into his huge jaws, he has drawn blood. And on Geoff too as he is totally untrained and leaps up like a wolf and wants to take you with him to play, hence the ragged wrists! The church bells clang at various intervals and we can just hear the spaniel howling away in tune, he is beginning to sound quite hoarse. God knows how he will sound by the end of Sunday with all the religious activities. The Panayia is, apart from Easter, the most important religious event in the Greek Orthodox church and the Maniot women are dressed smartly and spend a good deal of time at prayer. Their children are like dolls. I watch a little girl in a sailor suit dress dancing up the lane, brown curls bobbing, new shoes and socks; I want to rush out and hug her to death. And her little brother just tottering in tiny shorts and a smart shirt reminds me of my grandson Thomas, except for the hair. Thomas's is flaxen just like his mother's when she was a baby. Philippa is to have her second child in October and although I did not want to know its sex, it is obvious she will have another boy as she tells me she is so huge. His name will be Jack Hamish. I want to call him Hamish not Jack—not that that makes any difference. It makes me realise I must try to spend more time with Thomas who was two in May and my granddaughter, Alexandra who is now just walking. I miss them and how I wish I could be split into many parts and be with all my loved ones at the same time, missing nothing of the babies' adventures and development, yet also being here with Geoff, exploring, writing, painting and relaxing following the past few years when we were apart. The wise say we can't have everything but I wonder why we can't!

Awakened before dawn by the sound of children's voices, excited and loud. The bells toll in one of the two tiny churches just outside our gate and I hear singing from the terrace, I see a small procession of people walking up the lane carrying lanterns on their way to the church in the cobbled square. It is only a short, steep walk and for a moment I feel like joining them, but instead return to the welcoming arms of my love.

*

More rain heralded by deafening claps of thunder with brilliant flashes of lightning and an impressive downpour to wash away the summer dust. It has rained on and off all day hiding our mountain that sits sulking behind a bank of mighty clouds. We swim in the late evening in a calm smooth sea, the rocks feel cool. Wondrous rain—a gift from the skies.

Evening and we have just returned from a happy day's *ekdromi,* that ended with a refreshing swim at Limeni, diving through the clear water and swimming lazily out to our special rock past boats rocking at their moorings. Hardly anyone about at all. The grey skies have put them off, and of course, it is after the fifteenth of September when most families return to the cities to resume their daily toil while we stay on to swim in glorious isolation. It rained yesterday and cooled everything down and this morning the clouds were low and the sun nowhere to be found; an ideal day for exploring.

After breakfast a few days later, we drove to Pyrgos Dirou where the Wednesday market is held and purchased our fresh produce including a chunk of the most delicious feta from the cheese stall. The traders arrive in a variety of vehicles—including small traders' motorised bikes that haul containers on wheels to visit the peninsula's towns and hamlets throughout the week—and we are getting to know the cheery and chatty stall owners, as I did in Crete. Marketing entails a long and happy interchange covering an array of subjects, mostly with a political angle while trying to concentrate on the required list of items needed—it is so nice feeling that we belong here, even if for a short time perhaps. We continued southwards in light rain taking photographs and promising to return on a brighter day to sketch. I relish the overcast days after so much heat and brightness; the typical reaction of a colonial I believe. Geoff on the other hand responds like a typical Englishman—he loathes cloudy or wet weather, or anything remotely resembling the climate of the land he chose to abandon. The frowning sky was low above the mountains creating a splendid contrast with the pale towers in the foreground and Geoff thought he had taken some good shots for my stories.

On to Gerolimenas, remarking as we drove down into the enclosed harbour with the spectacular cliffs of Cava Grosso at the northern end, how much we liked the little fishing port when we stayed there for six days on our arrival in the Mani. We found our friends the Grumpy Brothers in the taverna and greeted the one whom we thought was Yiannis who was so friendly once he recognised us. Then a few minutes later we saw the second brother and realised we hadn't been speaking to him at all but to Theo, so alike are they.

"I am two and a half years older," said Yiannis when I asked if they were twins. And of course, they are grumpy no more. They told us the season had not been very good at all and was already winding down; they didn't mind in the least. We sat under the awning by the waterfront and enjoyed delectable freshly baked moussaka and green beans in rich aromatic tomato sludge while watching a spear fisherman in search of octopus. He speared one and, as he brought it back to shore, it latched onto an inflatable dinghy and he had the greatest difficulty unravelling its clinging tentacles. Poor thing, I cannot bear to see octopuses suffer because

I am sure they have highly-developed feelings—I turn away and try not to show what *I* feel in sympathy with these curious and fascinating creatures. Then followed the mandatory thrashing on the rocks one hundred times to tenderise it and remove the froth. I hate the procedure every time I see it, but I eat octopus nonetheless. In fact, I love it when grilled over open coals and it goes black and crisp. Yum! I have conflicting emotions, but they do not prevent me from indulging in my insensitive tastes so recently developed since arriving in Greece.

Λοιπόν, and now, it is evening and we are back in our tower house at our long white marble desk. Geoff is preparing for the next foray to Gytheio when he will take more scenes of the town and harbour to Georgios and I am painting several of my pen and ink sketches with watercolour and am quite pleased with the result.

"Bold," says Geoff. He likes them. But they are not for sale! One day some of my paintings and drawings will illustrate my journals. Wait and see I say!

Stephanos has just popped in. "I am running," he says characteristically and makes a to and fro-ing motion like a train with his arms to indicate he is in a hurry. This most congenial man is always in a rush but often sits and chats and has a drink and smokes endless cigarettes; his eyes are so tired yet great energy surrounds him and his brain is alive. He brings an attractive heavy cotton cover for our couch in flecked grey with strips of the Greek key design in varying sizes—it looks so smart. He accepts the rent which obviously doesn't really interest him and has agreed to help with our purchase of a car in September; he says that is the time when the Maniots have money in their pockets and they exchange their old cars for a new one. I wish we were getting a new one but anything will seem new after my dear old Blue Girl!

*

August is the month for fig jam; the fruit is from the spreading fig tree, *not* the prickly one but a member of the *'ficus carica'* mulberry family originally from Asia Minor. The prolific tree growing in the lower level of the garden is literally covered with green figs that burst open when your teeth cut through their taut skins. The smell of bubbling hot figs, cinnamon and sugar fills the solid walls of our tower and combines, not very well, with the slightly scorched smell of the red capsicum I am grilling for lunch. These *piperies* in Greek, have just arrived in the markets and we couldn't resist a couple; they are more expensive than the green ones which is ridiculous because they are the same type from the same plant but picked at a different stage of maturity! The green is picked unripe, the yellow is in between and the red with more sweetness is fully ripened, believe it or not. Initially I marinade ours in olive oil, garlic with thyme and oregano from the mountainsides and fresh mint from the terrace. The Greeks split them open, remove the seeds and lay them on an oiled tray and scorch them slightly beneath the grill, then after peeling off the outer skin they are layered in pure olive oil, liberally dosed with various herbs and offer them with anchovies and fresh crusty bread.

Back to writing with a vengeance. My motto has always been *"nulla dies sine linea"*—never a day without a line—and I am penning many lines daily. The latest is called *Men who live in Towers,* a piece about Hans and Iakovos. Geoff has taken slides with which we are quite satisfied although most of the interiors are too dark. He needs to come in closer for more detailed shots rather than the long views he prefers, however, each batch that comes back from Fuji is better than the last. I find it quite difficult keeping up with this journal as so much happens each day, life is so rich, full of texture and by the evening I don't always feel like writing, even if my brain is bursting with words. Our first story on the Deep Mani has been accepted by a glossy magazine in Australia—it is so rewarding being able to share our adventures.

The rain and cooler conditions have coaxed the birds down from the mountains. I heard the tiniest squeaking call the other morning from two finches with yellow breasts in the mastic tree outside our window, and today a swoop of house martins with split tails swerved into view darting and diving at insects. It is a delight to see and hear them once again; in Crete they don't return from the cooler mountains until late September and the summers are virtually without birdsong.

Early morning rain and thunder. Lightning. Dramatic skies and the summit of the mountain range obscured by wet clouds. The world is being washed clean by the downpour, even the Frankish figs look a darker, cleaner green without the accumulated dust, and the olives more silver as the leaves move with the light breeze. I can see the headlands to the north and south more clearly than ever before and there appear to be more promontories jutting out into the ocean than I have observed previously. The air, always fresh and unpolluted, smells different today; is there a hint of autumn thinness in my nostrils? No electricity! It goes off each time it rains. Hum! What of the winter I ask myself? But this is not my philosophy, live for this day for who knows where we might be in the winter? In the meantime, we are enjoying the cooler temperatures and our feet no longer seek the relief of the cold marble floors, in fact we are keeping our sandals on. This morning I am sitting in my chair with a bedspread over my legs, a harbinger of things to come and I'm not sure I like the idea. Although I am weary of the intense heat and humidity, the cold I do not welcome.

More fig jam on the boil, we will have it coming out of our ears but I will give away pots to our friends. The peach jam I made several weeks ago is quite delicious and the first batch of bitter marmalade made with νεραντζιά, *Nerantzia*, Seville oranges, is finished so we have made a second lot which will disappear rapidly. This orange is used only for marmalade and is known as *marmeláda*, or jam; the word comes from the Spanish *naranjas* while the common, sweet orange is known as *portokali* which is close to *portogallo*, a southern Italian term. It allegedly dates from the time when oranges were believed to have come from Portugal; in fact, the orange fruit originated in China, was brought to Europe by traders and eventually evolved into the English word 'orange' we now use to describe both the fruit and the colour.

*

Geoff has been unwell for five days now; it started with a heavy cold, blocked breathing passages then a bad throat which simply will not go away. On the second evening of his discomfort, I drove to the chemist in the pelting rain, had to reverse back down the steep hill of the one-way system three times for oncoming cars, then three times in the ensuing bit of narrow road for more cars that refused to reverse. All in all, it took me ten minutes to negotiate a journey which would normally take three at the very most. I wanted an antibiotic for what I diagnosed as possibly severe sinusitis, having looked up the words in my dictionary. In Greece, chemists are qualified to dispense antibiotics which they do with abandon which is a bit of a worry, but very useful for bypassing doctors when one is not really needed. The chemist had difficulty understanding what I was asking for when a rather suave young Greek came in and they greeted one another affectionately and launched into a lengthy chat about this and that, completely ignoring me. I waited at least three minutes by which time I was so annoyed I interrupted in my best Greek and said coolly:

"Excuse me but I am here to get some medicine for my sick husband and I am not waiting another minute."

The visitor stood back on his heels for a moment—surprised I believe, to hear me speaking Greek, then said in English:

"What is wrong with your husband? I am a physician." A physician in Greece is not what the western world knows as a physician, he is usually a GP with a grand title. I described the problem and he said he thought he should see a specialist in Sparta at which I shook my head and said I thought that all he needed was an antibiotic. Following some lengthy questioning about Geoff's condition he ordered a specific antibiotic and a throat spray for which the chemist charged twelve thousand drachmas, the currency at the time. Of course, I only had five thousand drachmas in my purse so had to renegotiate the journey home, still in the pouring rain which had turned the steep lanes into racing torrents. This time it was the cars coming *up* the hill that had to reverse while I waited, windscreen wipers barely coping with the deluge, the rolls of thunder echoing off the wet stone walls that line the constricted lanes and tight corners. I took the long way back to the chemist on my return, past the wet cows and their calves in the fields and droopy goats sheltering beneath olives, but it did not help. On the most confined strip of road, I met a gypsy truck followed by three cars and I had once again to reverse to a wider section, exceedingly difficult since I could not see through my rear-view mirror at all and barely through the back window. It took the best part of an hour before I finally sloshed out of the car with the antibiotic for my man; the main problem now, is his raw throat, he can barely talk and must feel dreadful, but he is a stoic and says he feels better. I hope he does.

*

A week has gone by; he is recovering. It is evening and we have returned from a rewarding couple of hours of photography around our vicinity; we discovered a group of dilapidated buildings in Kariopouli, a tiny settlement off one of the roads which leads away from here towards the sea. In between the ruins a vast tower mansion is being restored behind high walls. It has lovely curved stone walls, nooks and garden seats, a well, a barbecue area, high terraces, and a fireplace in the lower room which uses the original vaulted ceiling. The rectangular room at the top is huge with a bathroom and spa at one end. Incongruous in this silent, deserted village to find something so modern and seemingly foreign to the Deep Mani. Were the owners Greek-Americans perhaps, building for their future retirement? On investigating the narrow paths between their high walls, we discovered a quaint little church engulfed by the prickly arms of hundreds of prickly pears, their misshapen trunks swamped with ripening figs. There must have been twenty figs on each splayed-out leaf looking like deformed feet with too many pink toes. The sun was at an oblique evening angle and just caught the blonde grasses and the tips of a cinnamon-coloured plant with dried bobbles up its many stalks that grew in profusion beneath a lichen-covered olive with pitted branches, leaning over boulders. A photographer's dream. I must do some research on the Internet and learn to identify more of the wildflowers and shrubs.

Having exhausted all photographic possibilities, we wound through olives and rocky fields across the lower end of our village to the Panagitsa, the Little Virgin Mary, the only white church we have seen in the Deep Mani, all the others being of natural biscuit-coloured stone with Byzantine curlicues and decorations, red-tiled, towering belfries, some with seven tiers of bells. This tiny, unadorned Aegean-style church reminds me so much of Crete; it stands alone at the edge of the plateau on a promontory overlooking terraces of neglected olives, winding grey walls and, far below, the wild and restless sea. This evening the *meltemi* is blowing with serious intent and the olives are tossing their silver and grey heads above the swaying grasses and when we stood against the wall of the church on the edge of the cliff, the wind threatened to take us with it. Where would we end up, I wondered? What an odyssey that would be to write about. A spiritual quest at the invitation of the sweeping dry *meltemi*, also known by its old name, the Etesian northern wind, that blows from mid-May to mid-September, disrupting everything in its path: ferries, hydrofoils, small aircraft. In mythology the wind was controlled by Boreas, the god of the North Winds who occasionally caused problems even in winter. These gods were powerful indeed.

*

Stephanos has given us a television set. It was not on our list of requirements but here it is, sitting on a cleverly designed swinging arm at the side of our long desk. But viewing is another matter. We had occasionally muttered how nice it would be to see a movie, so we thought; or rather Geoff did, since I have seen Greek television on Francesca's black-and-white set with the jumpy pictures while living in Crete and know about the timing of films. At the very least, having a television set would allow us to enjoy the odd programmes and perhaps a film. Ho hum! The cold, bare facts are that the rare films mostly start around eleven thirty at night and always with a half-hour break at midnight for the news and weather. This, more often than not is extended to almost an hour then followed by numerous and dreadful ads by which time we have lost the plot and are almost too tired to go up the marble stairs to bed. We have seen a few films halfway through and one or two all the way through, finally stumbling upstairs at about three in the morning and wondering as we do, why we bothered! I must say though that foreign films with the Greek subtitles are excellent for my reading but as yet too fast for Geoff to pick up. It will come, if we can keep awake long enough.

*

We were in Gytheio enjoying a *café frappe*, iced coffee, on the waterfront when the President of Greece came through. I have never seen such a palaver or so many police in the Mani before, so I guessed it must be some political figure paying a visit to the sleepy port. Traffic police complete with pistols on their hips had closed off the one exit out of the town and were directing traffic in the opposite direction. Or trying to with little success. It was very windy and the detour sign kept blowing over, so there were two policemen standing a couple of feet apart doing exactly the same thing; leaping about like crazed puppets, arms flailing, gesticulating and blowing their whistles, getting more and more agitated and redder and redder in the face as it was also very warm. Then a fat Greek in grubby vest and shorts strolled past carrying what looked like a couple of rifles in fabric covers. No one looked at him or even noticed him yet he could so easily have been an assassin; when I mentioned this to the waiter he laughed and told us that the *Πρόεδρος,* the president was a harmless man and no one would want to shoot him! The chivvying of the traffic and the piercing whistles went on for a good half hour while he was having coffee in a nearby restaurant. Then the great man, who actually is very small and insignificant looking, walked past us accompanied by anxious bodyguards and the ubiquitous priest, robes flying in all directions and disappeared into a hotel nearby. All went suddenly quiet as if the world had come to an end. Cars and scooters began to flow normally and the exploding police collected in little groups, lit up cigarettes as they exchanged stories at top decibels awaiting his next move. They are so excitable these Greeks; I delight in being amongst them, joining in their little dramas or simply watching them.

CHAPTER FOUR

ON BUYING A CAR IN SPARTA

Finally, we are buying a car to replace my beloved, unreliable Blue Girl who really is on her last legs, but we have had such a problem trying to finalise the purchase. Initially, Geoff's money took forever to come through and it got nearer to the time for Brenda, who is eighty-one years of age, to arrive for a fortnight's holiday. I was not prepared to drive her even one mile in my old rust-bucket in case it broke down. When the money finally arrived, we phoned to confirm that the car we had chosen was ready; but Kyriakos, the very pleasant Nissan manager said it had been sold as we had taken so long to confirm the purchase. All this negotiation was occurring in Sparta and this was two days before our arranged rendezvous with Brenda in the city of Nauplion pronounced 'Nafplion', so off we went once again to Sparta and chose another car. It so happened we found a much better vehicle; a cream Hyundai four-door, power steering with a lovely shape, five years old with only forty-one thousand kilometres on the clock. Well! We thought everything was fine and dandy, but in Greece nothing happens simply; there are always complications and delays. But always. Kyriakos insisted that we supplied a paper from the tax department to prove we did not owe any tax before he could put the car in our name. And where could we get this piece of paper? Only from the place of residence!

Back we came to Areopolis—sixty kilometres and too late to find any government offices open, they close at one every afternoon—for siesta? But they do not open again after siesta we were told! Next morning, bright and early, we tried to find the *Eforeia,* Tax office and were finally led there by a very bright young man who seemed to be a clerk in the town hall, but also swept the streets. He waited around and made sure we found the clerk then left. We explained the situation to the young girl clerk, but no, she could not issue a declaration until she had a piece of paper to say we resided here and for how long. It would not be any problem she said, just go to the square and find a lawyer who would sign a declaration. To the square we went, the only office was shut. We began to think the entire transaction was jinxed beyond redemption, so I asked the man in the post office what time the lawyer might be there to open the office. One thirty he said but we knew the other office closed at one p.m. Then our street-cleaner-cum-clerk suddenly appeared, not surprising as Areopolis is a tiny, tiny place and found a phone number for the lawyer's home. I spoke to her; all this is happening in Greek mind you and my brain was about to explode. She couldn't really understand what I wanted but reiterated that she was on a holiday until one thirty in the afternoon; I phoned the tax office clerk in Sparta and asked if she would hang on until we got the paper and she said no, she closed at one p.m.—so I asked the lawyer to phone the tax clerk here to find out what we needed, then I rang her back. She said she would come in within thirty minutes but then rattled off something that I could not understand. We waited around for much longer naturally, and when she arrived, she told us that she had never issued a paper like this and could not do so, but she gave us three phone numbers of lawyers in Gytheio, which is on the way to Sparta, who would issue the paper. But of course, we would have to come back here to give it to the tax woman so she could issue the guarantee to prove that we owed no tax. Hell's teeth what a tangled web we have found ourselves in – not that we are practising to deceive, anything but!

By this time, I was in such a state of nervous exhaustion with speaking, listening and translating Greek to Geoff that he opted to phone the lawyers who luckily, spoke English though two of them had no idea what he was talking about and the third was out; we thought to blazes with this and drove to Sparta without the important piece of paper. When we told Kyriakos about it he said not to worry, his clerk could do it in five minutes and we could pick it up after we had been to Nauplion! It took them nearly two hours of mucking around plus a visit to the police station for more papers and stamps that happened so efficiently and quickly we were quite worried they had forgotten something of major importance. Finally, we got the car and drove off at three when the Nissan office was about to close. Geoff was wearing sandals and had driven only a few hundred yards when his toe got caught under the pedal and he realised that my advice given earlier, that he needed to change into his shoes, was valid. He stopped the car, changed his shoes but could not get the darned thing to start. Not a peep. And we knew the showroom was closing so he galloped back and luckily caught one of the young men who returned with him. It transpired these Hyundai cars cannot be started up without pressing down the clutch extremely hard till it clicks, this releases the gas or something, and they had forgotten to tell us about this most essential detail.

We left my Blue Girl to be sold in Sparta with a lump in my throat as we purred away in the super cream Hyundai with power steering—yay every girl should have one! We can now explore without the gnawing anxiety about breaking down that accompanied every trip in the old girl, but I do miss seeing her and I am now a woman without substance, as I told Geoff. But he loves me anyway he declares.

It was a fast trip to Nauplion from Sparta, just under two hours on a highway built for speed over the mountains and when we got to the waterfront, I phoned Iain of *'Beyond 2000'* fame and Trish his wife—journalist friends on a visit from Australia—to discover they too were about to arrive in Nauplion, from Corinth up the road in the opposite direction and could we meet them in the Venetian Square? I said I hoped so but discovered it was not marked on the town map which seemed to be quite believable, so we crawled down a narrow street filled with lively pavement tavernas and shops flanked by tall Venetian buildings, not knowing where to go but exploring the substantial city when a car in front stopped, blocking the road totally and a shaven-headed person got out. We both sighed and my comment to Geoff was:

"Those bullet-headed men, is he a British skinhead—they're everywhere?"

The person turned round—and it was Trish, Iain's eccentric wife who shaves her head. Was it not a most extraordinary coincidence that we should have chosen the same second to drive up that same road? Her sister, who lives in Canada and was visiting Greece, also shaves her head and they looked a little bizarre, these two lively, middle-aged women a-dangle with heavy bright jewellery and wearing curious eye-catching outfits. They are both potentially attractive, but I thought they looked masculine and slightly challenging whereas I felt incredibly feminine with my much longer hair! It was good fun meeting up with them again and we would like to have had longer, but Trish and Iain are returning to Australia then off again to places far away and back to Greece they say, so we will meet again. I do hope so—they were also in Nauplion to meet Brenda, our mutual friend.

This most elegant city in the eastern Peloponnese was the first capital of the modern Greek state; it is considered to be 'the most beautiful and romantic city in all of Greece'. We spent the night in the Hotel Epidaurus, once a Venetian mansion near the main square; after dark Nauplion is even more elegant with its tall streetlamps, soaring plane trees beginning to lose their leaves and the vast piazza with its shiny tiles that looks a bit like a skating rink. A small child, perhaps four years old and sucking a dummy, was riding a miniature, mechanical tractor round the outside tables of the two very smart Italian restaurants as we had our evening drinks in the cooling air; round and round he went, seemingly quite alone and unattended. Then he disappeared and returned with an even younger child with bouncing curls sitting on the back. This time there was a man in charge.

Later we wandered round the smart boutiques and shops, most of the displays marred by overcrowding as Greek windows invariably are. Why do they not know that a few well- chosen items will entice the customer inside to search for more, and that crowding is unnecessary? The shops stay open until all hours, often until two in the morning and open again mid-morning; a savvy plan in the evenings to catch customers when they are well-fed and watered and it is cooler.

Before we set off with Brenda we had planned to go up to the castle and take photographs, but the sky was frowning at us the next morning and Brenda, who had arrived at our hotel in the evening, was somewhat weary following her flight from Sydney—plus the taxi ride from Athens. She is after all in her eighties. We left Nauplion and hurtled southwards, we two girls nattering at full force catching up with the intervening months' activities. We drove through Sparta and I spied the Blue Girl sitting outside the Nissan second-hand car yard. She looked so small and unloved; sort of deserted and after all the good miles she has given me over the past years I felt I should be farming her out to someone who would care for her in her declining years, which let's face it, began some long time ago. We purred silently past in our cream vehicle and I felt like a traitor.

Back in our tower house and my dear friend is now ensconced in Yiannis's apartment above his three-storey house across the garden. The arrangement is working out so well and I am enjoying her bright company and talking books and writers, good and bad with her; we are a contented trio but she is only here for a short time which is such a pity. We will drive her to Athens to catch the plane then go to Crete to collect my remaining boxes of clothes, books and cassettes for the winter which we will spend here in our tower house.

*

We have just had an impressive earthquake and how the earth did move! We were in the sitting room with Brenda when it suddenly sounded as if an underground train was burrowing its way up through the floor beneath us and everything began to shake violently from side to side. The huge iron gate outside started to rattle and swing on its hinges and we all realised it was an earthquake and grabbed Brenda and hauled her outside by which time it had stopped. The epicentre was in the sea south of us which was, they say, just as well or else there could have been some major damage. As it is, the bell tower in the church has been slightly dislodged they tell us, and when we went to a dear little hamlet down the road the other evening, we found substantial stone walls had collapsed into the pathway almost blocking the way. Hans and Iakovos told us that the earthquake we felt was registered officially by the Greek authorities as a mere 5.9 on the Richter scale whereas the American seismological office, also in Athens, registered it as being 6.3. The boys said, with their usual cynicism, that after the scale reaches six the government has to pay damages, so no earthquake is ever permitted to go above 5.9! Later when we took Brenda to Mystras, we were unable to go up to the castle as the episode had displaced some of the larger walls. Earthquakes are common in many regions of Greece and have been responsible for most of the damage to ancient places—the tall columns being particularly vulnerable. The last major one in these parts was in 1927, the northern region of the Peloponnese often has them but apparently, they are quite rare in these southernmost parts.

*

We are steeped in manufacturing greeting cards assisted by Brenda who gamely tears up thousands of little bits of paper of all types to make recycled paper. It all seems a bit daft to me but the resultant textured sheets are most attractive and have been converted into Christmas paper. However, she has only made a couple of dozen sheets and between us we need more than a hundred—so we bought sheets of stiff cardboard in several shades of green, scarlet and blue and Geoff carved a Mani tower, a Byzantine church, cypresses, cactus and a caique, traditional Greek fishing boat, from potatoes and we are into the printing business with a vengeance. We might even register ourselves as *'de Villehardouin incorporated'!* It is interesting to see how things evolve, the style which pleased us so hugely initially is no longer good enough as we go from strength to strength. We now have speckled cards; Geoff uses paint on a toothbrush and faint towers have been the result which we have titled either *'Mani towers in the mist'* or *'in the snow'* depending on the effects achieved. We are also into making calendars of entire villages in a variety of colours all of which look fabulous; a pale sickle moon lies sideways in a dark green-blue night sky and ghostly white moonlight shines on the appropriate part of the Maniot skyscrapers that range from pink to purple to ochre to bottle green. There is always a white church or chapel, of course, guarded by cypresses. We are mightily pleased with ourselves and have worked for long hours, always to music on our cassettes—from Beethoven, Bruckner, Mahler and Mozart plus a few operas; fortunately, Brenda also loves classical music. When I told Amanda that we were making our own paper for cards she responded jocularly:

"Oh no! You aren't going all folksy are you, have you stopped shaving your legs Ma?"

This has got me slightly worried; I mean does one automatically become the clichéd alternative lifestyle freak if one makes paper? In the past I have always drawn or painted my own cards whenever possible but maybe the combination of recycling, designing and printing from a carved potato is a bit over the top? Anyway, it's been great fun doing them and I am not wearing dungarees and braces yet, nor a floppy hat and if I needed to I would shave my legs, but I am a blonde and don't need to! It is rewarding to have a partner with the same interests and Brenda's input has been invaluable; Geoff and I have both remarked on the fact that this is the first time in our lives we have ever shared creative activities like these, although when my children were young, we always made our own family Christmas cards. It was such fun.

The nightmare of driving in Athens had to be faced when we took Brenda to catch the plane back to Sydney. There is a new highway that dissects the entire Peloponnese and it is magnificent, but it cuts out the old Corinthian bridge over the Corinth Canal where we had planned to find an Athens road map at a comfort stop but there was nowhere to stop so I drove into Athens 'blind', so to speak, and 'map-less'. Iakovos had suggested we should go to the airport via the port of Piraeus and avoid the centre of the city, but unfortunately, we got there mid-afternoon, which is when all the workers and builders knock off so the road was packed with motorcyclists, trucks, lorries, taxis, all hooting and driving like lunatics. The *nephos*, pollution, was so thick we could hardly breathe and of course we had a deadline; Brenda had to be at the airport by four o'clock. We had left in what we thought was plenty of time to get there, got lost several times and somehow or other we arrived at a quarter past four after a hair-raising hour which involved stopping at least five times to ask a friendly driver in a passing car at the lights, how to find the airport. The Greeks are always incredibly helpful and we had plenty of good advice, one chap actually followed us then passed us and shouted directions when we most needed them.

After we had said our tearful goodbyes, we spent the night in a hotel then headed towards Epidaurus via Ancient Corinth on a bracing day and sat on cold stones against the columns of the Temple of Apollo, the fortified castle of Acrocorinth looming massively to the west, the crenellations like cardboard cut-outs against a sombre grey sky.

"Do we want to go up there?" asked Geoff.

"Certainly not," I replied emphatically. He was not feeling his usual energetic self nor was I. A large group of elderly Americans approached, both men and women wearing the same squeaky-new clothes, gleaming white Reeboks, jeans, peak caps, the women mostly trim of figure but with lined, anxious faces; the price of retaining a slim silhouette when middle-aged is urging them to spread a little? Their hair was uniformly stiff with gel, permed, dyed, and the smell of deodorant tainted the air; their body language appeared to me to be unusually aggressive with the men lagging behind somewhat hesitantly. We moved away to the Pereian Spring and the Roman baths and an overweight, camera-laden American man with a red face said loudly to no one in particular and certainly not to us as he looked down into one of the underground springs, "A nice spa-art for fishing what?" We moved on quickly out of earshot.

We left Corinth and as I was driving to Epidaurus, we experienced two major earthquakes but did not quite realise what was happening; suddenly the road appeared to be extremely bumpy and the wheel jerked between my hands and I wondered what was going on as the surface was smooth. Geoff also noticed something strange but neither of us thought to mention it until we discovered they were big ones, 6.9 on the Richter scale which even the Greek authorities recorded faithfully for a change! It damaged some houses but nothing more.

*

I hear from Francesca in Sydney; I still call her 'Chanky' her childhood nickname remains in my brain. She is having a busy time with little Alexandra's teething and related problems, she is now fifteen months and into everything which is exhausting, fortunately she has a coterie of good friends and her sisters and brother nearby. She misses life in Crete and if I had the means I would fly her back there tomorrow to help her live there at least for a few carefree years, with her little girl. I realise with astonishment that it is a year minus two days since we three flew to Australia from Crete; I to return—but mother and baby to remain in Australia.

Also in Australia, speaking to my good friend Anne on the phone, with whom I had worked closely for many years, is dying from a rare form of leukaemia that was only discovered recently when she was over-tired and bruising a lot. Indomitable, strong, self-sufficient Anne, reduced to a hairless skeleton with awful tubes coming out of her middle into which they put the chemotherapy and all sorts of other chemicals. She was going to have to make a decision this week whether or not to stop the therapy and I believe she will refuse further intrusive treatment. All this confirms my unshakeable belief that it is imperative to do what one wants to do if one can, because one never knows what is around the corner. Anne always envied me my courage which was more like desperation on my part when I left my position in the

Sydney Opera House and headed for Crete. She wanted eventually to quit her job as concert manager in another orchestral establishment to run a nursery garden with a friend, but now it is too late sadly. She felt the need to hang on to her high-stress career of many years in music management to wait for a pension. And where has it got you my dear friend? Into a premature grave. Personally, I could not have cared less about a pension—*carpe diem*—seize the day. One simply *has* to. And never fear Richard Bach insists that:

One should not be distressed at goodbyes, they are necessary before one can meet again, and that meeting is assured for those who are friends.

I really do believe this to be true—Anne and I will be friends forever. I really loved my stint in the Opera House but was exhausted and suffering from unrelenting pain from my spine. I had a warning that the same thing could happen to me if I did not radically change my stressful working hours; so, at the age of fifty-five I fled to Crete to a totally different life-style accompanied for a while, by members of my family. I missed being involved with music and my musician friends; I missed the majesty of the grand operas and the graceful, gentle ballets; missed the fast-moving nights of drama and the highs and lows of my work, but also knew that I needed to heed the warnings and move on. It was the right decision.

*

November and we are in Skoutari, sitting on the beach against a wall made of multicoloured sea stones in varying shades of rose to lavender to strawberries and cream to royal purple, still to be found along this sandy beach. Oleanders in seed lean over the sand, their dried pods hanging down; caiques piled up with yellow fishing nets; a single taverna tightly closed with the detritus of summer littering the surrounds; crates of empty bottles, red plastic chairs, broken tables. Behind me, right on the beach stands a squat and weathered Byzantine church of rough grey plaster with many apses facing the sea. Faded and pitted fresco remnants of a saint can be seen in a false window, some of the colours remain; faded Reckitt's blue, saffron and terracotta washed away by the elements. It is the Byzantine church of Aghia Varvara, Saint Barbara that dates back to the tenth century and I have tried to draw it but the curves and many domes defy description, the exterior walls wander at random and seem to make no sense. Outside, a rusted metal framework holds a brass bell and what looks like a weathervane on top of the dome. We push open a metal door to reveal more frescoes on the many walls, including the ubiquitous St George on his white steed and the dragon and newly-framed, gaudy picture of the sad-eyed Saint Barbara depicting a woman of tragic implications holding an ear of wheat in a large and discoloured oil painting. There are the usual accoutrements to be found in all these churches and chapels; a tray of sand, candles and matches, a bottle or two of liquid, usually alcohol, plastic flowers and a dried- up bouquet to show that someone takes care of the saint whose tiny church is only visited on her saint's day, whenever that may be. The music is the ever-constant swoosh and swish of the waves on the fine, sandy beach; not a soul in sight, we are alone in this world of worship, sand and sky, the wide bay flanked by low green hills behind which tree-dotted mountains thrust upwards out of the sea. Looming towers top the lower hills to the north and the roofs of miniature hamlets peep above the demarcation of stone-walled fields, no longer tilled or productive, though the broad valley grows citrus, grapes and some vegetables. It is hot and humid here and obviously enjoys a microclimate of its own just twenty minutes away from cold and windy Areopolis. On the low headland between the two bays a sign in Greek:

"Yes, to health and life. No to death and drugs."

Indeed.

Later, after due research I discover the unimaginable details of the tragedy that befell this poor nun Saint Barbara, if indeed she ever existed. Doubts on her authenticity have been unearthed by the Catholic Church and I wish that I had not found out how she died.

*

CHAPTER FIVE

RUINS AND A SECRET GROTTO

Continuing our castle quest, we drove north along the coast road in search of the remains of Beaufort Castle established by Guillaume II de Villehardouin in 1252. Iakovos told us the site was between the main road and the sea at Agios Nikolaos, but we were waylaid by the ancient settlement of Pano Oitylo, Upper Oitylo, pronounced *'Eetilo'* once the most important settlement in the Mani. It stands in a magnificent position on the edge of the gorge above the Bay of Oitylo where we swim. As we wandered through the mostly ruined buildings, an elderly man insisted on showing us *mia poly orea thea*, a very beautiful view, and pointed to a picturesque monastery perched on the slopes of the deep ravine that we had often seen while swimming; it looked Italian surrounded by the dark shapes of cypresses. He told us it was fifteen hundred years old and had been taken over by the occupying armies during the war and that the locals had suffered in their hands. Greek monasteries are not only religious centres but seats of wisdom where those who refuse to be subjected to brutality, gather and plan strategy.

We had coffee in a shady *kafenion* beside a row of Seville orange trees with their white-painted trunks. The abundant fruit of these fragrant trees that line the sidewalks, squares and parks and flourish almost everywhere throughout Greece, is seriously bitter thus never eaten in its natural state. Maturing and ripening in winter the golden orbs glow against the dark glossy leaves and one has to control the impulse to pick one—which is not permitted—peel it hastily and put a segment into one's mouth expecting an explosion of sweet citrus flavour only to end up with a shock, puckered-up lips and a mouth with a million wrinkles that resembles the ravages of old age following years in the sun. The attentions of a beguiling bat-eared kitten with huge eyes kept us entertained as she purred and pleaded for a crumb of our delectable *loukoumades,* fritters; these honey-flavoured bliss bombs are a decadent delight and one of the oldest desserts recorded in history. My oh my! Have I gone to heaven? The kitten asked the same question as she gathered honey on her whiskers. I noticed there was still some blue in her amber eyes and I wanted to take her home but Geoff demurred; anyway, we had no permanent home! Tall, double sunflowers of gigantic proportions leaned over a garden wall and interestingly, and unlike anywhere else in the Mani, the vocalist was a popular American folk singer.

We drove through the upper village of Agios Nikolaos, the patron saint of sailors amongst others; many of his miracles are related to the sea. The village stands high above the ocean but we found no roads leading towards the sea, nor any sign of a likely looking hill where there might once have been a castle. On we went, and as usual, became distracted from our goal and stopped to see the enchanting Byzantine church of Agios Nikolaos with its three-domed cupolas; it stands just off the main route on a plateau overlooking a sweep of coastal plain. We sat on a stone wall with the world beneath us and picnicked on crusty bread, feta cheese embellished with roasted red capsicum soaked in herbs, garlic and olive oil, cucumber in chunks and basil-sprinkled tomatoes in quarters—never sliced, they have less flavour—finishing off with translucent green grapes still cool from the fridge. Later, beneath a stand of secret pines, we rested on a bed of fallen needles; soaring above us birds of prey checked the ground for movement, otherwise nothing stirred. Even the *tzitzikia* were resting oddly enough, since siesta in Greece is not always observed by all; if I were asked to define the word 'tranquillity', I would reply a 'Greek siesta'.

Rousing ourselves with reluctance we left the pine forest to continue our search for Beaufort Castle. The main road northward descends in a tortuously winding escarpment to Agios Nikolaos and then leads on to the fishing hamlet of Trahida that sits peacefully at the end of the coast road. We had been here before and Geoff recalled seeing a flat-topped hillock near the sea—maybe the castle had once stood there? We would go and find out. The ocean road clings precariously to the mountain edge and falls steeply away through massive outcrops of layers of pale grey and white rocks to the sea. It was hot and the sea most inviting; crystalline inlets with every speck of sand and weed clearly visible enfolded by pale overhanging cliffs beckoned us. But first the castle. We found the hillock and we walked up through the scrub to investigate, but the ruins were of a crumbling tower house and surrounding walls with no sign of ancient stones or of a castle to be seen. Disappointing. Would we continue with our search? It was mid-afternoon, the inhabitants of Trahida were fast asleep but for a weary woman who sold me two lemonades and agreed it was *poly zesti* and was I German? The perennial question. Must be my fair hair.

Later, coming home from our evening *volta* with the sun a bright red ball behind us and the soaring mass of mountains alongside our little town turning violet then purple, the castle and old stone towers glowing copper and gold in the last rays of the dying sun. The rapidly changing colours are spectacular but only for a very few minutes when a metamorphosis takes place, and the outlines soften and fade as smoky-grey clouds gradually obliterate the peaks. This is quite the most dramatic and exciting place I've ever lived in and the oldest and least spoiled. At night, when we come back from a meal in one of the tavernas, we wander down the narrow, cobbled lanes enclosed by high walls and I find it hard to believe we really are in the twentieth century. Tonight, the moon is high and becoming brighter by the minute, the air is cool and clear and tomorrow we will spend the day writing, painting, studying Greek, reading, swimming at our special place and then taking our evening *volta*. Or at least a few of those enjoyable occupations.

Castles could wait, we decided some days later. The glistening sea begged to be savoured so we drove back to a gorge we had noticed earlier then clambered down a rough and rocky path over outcrops of grey and white boulders to a secluded and magical grotto. The sandy seabed some three metres down was as clear as if seen through glass. Tiny fish fed on weed as bright as malachite between the starry black shapes of hundreds of sea urchins that littered the ocean floor; shadowy caves held secrets in their dark recesses and on three sides, precipitous cliffs hung over the translucent water. Within seconds we had thrown off our clothes, climbed down the vertical rocks so hot they burnt the soles of our feet and dived into the depths followed by shafts of bright bubbles; the water cold and silky on our hot skins. Fish darted in all directions hiding behind weed and rocky ledges, the clarity of the water was such that there was no need for face masks. As we emerged, smooth as seals from our deep dives we found ourselves in a glimmering green and gold world, the refracted light of the sun together with the aquamarine of the sea and the pearly grey of the overhanging cliffs cast a kaleidoscope of colours onto the surface. I looked at Geoff in silent awe, my heart almost bursting with the utter beauty of our surroundings and as I write I realise there are no words to describe the intensity of my emotions as we swam side by side in the enchanted grotto. Heading out beyond the cove in very deep water we discovered another inlet and an underwater ledge covered with soft weed and just beyond the ledge a deep rock pool with a layer of sand at the base, the water tepid and inviting. The sea washed in and over the ledge cooling the tepid water as we floated together in our ocean rock pools; later we lay on a sun-warmed rock feeling the afternoon heat on our skins and I felt the world was ours and would be forever more.

*

It is autumn and on the way down the hill to Limeni for a swim today I noticed between the dried-up thistle heads and the candelabra arms of the yellow mullein, the tall leafless spikes of sea squill rising phoenix-like from the earth, prompted no doubt by the last rains. Soon the metre-long flexible stems will be smothered in delicate white flowers and the bare hillsides will take on an air of spring. The hanging of the sea squill bulb from a doorway was regarded as an attribute for fertility in ancient Egypt and Greece, so if they grow near you watch out for possible pregnancies! All I can say is it would take more than a sea squill bulb to make me pregnant, but my youngest daughter Philippa is expecting her second child and she is going through a difficult time with extreme discomfort with yet another big baby, due in two weeks, and I am a little anxious.

I have been reading about the ethereal sea squill, *urginea maritima;* this charming single-stemmed plant with flowers resembling hyacinths, produces clusters of two to three hundred ivory 'stars' with a green band on the inner side—and at the apex of the elongated spike there is a crown of purple hairs that seem to cast a mauve wash that resembles a faint shadow over the pristine petals. The buds on these slender spikes begin to open at the base and each day a group of some thirty blooms appear above the previous day's, which then wilt. The stems grow from over-sized bulbs that in winter—not spring—have tall fleshy blue-green leaves that die off before the spring to be replaced by the showy blooms. A curious phenomenon.

There is a red variety but I have not come across it in Greece and in this region, I have only seen them growing near the sea, none inland so far. I read that in the Middle Ages the toxin in squills was used medicinally both as a poison and as a cardiac stimulant, which seems to be a contradiction to me. The tall spikes sway gracefully in the breeze and when the breeze develops into a gusty ocean wind, the sea squills dance.

*

Yesterday we drove to Gytheio to the 'bazaar' then discovered to our chagrin, that it did not really start until the evening, but it is on for a week so we will go back to wander around the stalls that border multiple streets and sell everything. I will be searching for birthday gifts for our two daughters, Amanda and Karen, as well as anything else that catches our interest. I love Greek markets; I enjoy the sounds and smells, the groups of gossiping women often in black with lined faces but alive and well with smiles displaying either a few remaining teeth or often none at all in pink gums. The hint of something tempting as it sizzles away on the spit issuing aromas that force us to stop or savour as we stand absorbing the ambiance, the all-enveloping feeling of being surrounded by friendly people. The town was sparkling with a brisk wind the day we visited the market; a slim-lined cruise ship was moored beyond the pier and the port was busy with tourists, some smart and some distinctly tatty-looking. I could not hear what language they were speaking and I wondered how our young friend Petros was faring in the shop with his father. They need tourists but dislike most of them so we went in to find Georgios looking black as thunder, his barely concealed rage aimed at a small blonde child who was sucking a dripping water-ice as she handled his books and magazines. He asked her politely to go out and she ignored him and moved deeper into the shop; he asked her again more strongly and appealed to her English father who was leafing through a nude magazine.

"G'arn outside," the man said. Then "G'arn," again, and went on reading. The little girl turned her back on him and shrugged, sucking away noisily and once more ignored the father's half-hearted command. Georgios, now apoplectic with real anger, grabbed a mop and followed the child around mopping up behind her, gently nudging her towards the open door. Her father saw what was happening and slowly ambled out of the shop followed by the defiant and recalcitrant child. No wonder they dislike some of the tourists. Geoff had no paintings for sale as he has been somewhat *hors de combat* since he had flu and is still on antibiotics for the throat infection and hasn't felt like painting, and last week I finally succumbed to the virus and I am still blowing, stuttering and coughing like an old tramp steamer; we were neither of us feeling up to scratch.

We spent a fruitless hour looking for sunglasses; they are all streamlined and narrow, not a shape suited to my bone structure and we were unable to find sandals for me but did acquire a pair for Geoff. In the past, I often found bargains in Crete and I still have a pair of beautiful Spanish two-toned leather boots that had most likely fallen off the back of a truck, they were being sold at half price the gypsy told me. Hum! Nothing remotely resembling a suitable birthday present presented itself so we thought we might go for a swim. Did we have the energy? No, we did not, so we decided on the next best alternative and had a leisurely lunch at a fish taverna beneath octopus drying in the sun. Once again, I agonised at the fate of these poor creatures and questioned my own integrity but shrugged it off. I still enjoy the new seafoods I am experiencing in this part of the world. It was a late birthday lunch for Geoff as he had been too unwell to celebrate on the day, and what a delicious repast it was. Making up for lost time, we ordered far too much and as the afternoon dreamed on, we managed to pass the time in the best possible way, as the Greeks do better than any other nationality, in my opinion. Time means nothing, it is the moment that matters.

Like most meals in Greece, it began with crisp *horiatiki salata*, Greek salad, followed by small portions of *ktapordhi salata*, octopus salad, which is basically octopus vinaigrette, tender and white and seasoned with oregano and other herbs with a small salad. This was followed by a colossal mountain of crisp *marithes*, a delicate and indescribably delicious type of whitebait, deeply fried and crunchy without a trace of oil and washed down with a regional and refreshing white wine. What bliss! I did some research when we got back to our tower and learned that the Peloponnese had been known for its wines since Homer's time, three thousand years ago, although some historians date the production of wine in this region back seven thousand years. Homer referred to the region as *'Ampeloessa'*, meaning 'Full of vines'. Today the Peloponnese is known for wines of diversity and complexity due to the many areas of microclimates and we have, now and then, been occupied in researching these claims and can confirm almost all of them!

The weather is cooler now and the evenings are perfect for

walking. Our little town sits on a rise leading onto a plateau a kilometre or so from the cliffs and far below a series of narrow ledges to the sea. The road past our tower house leads immediately to a patchwork of endless stony fields bordered by stone walls, old and oblong in shape with what might be the remains of old threshing circles. A few buildings between the olives and carobs and several restored tower houses, stern behind their closed wrought-iron gates, stand above the ruins and tiny churches enclosed by glistening olives. The walled lanes meander between smallholdings and fields that the farmers use for their stock, and this evening we came across two glossy cows and a newly-born calf, cocoa and white in colour, with a perfect white blaze down his brown nose. We called him and he came towards us, ears flicking then pranced away, playfully kicked up his fluffy back legs then jumped sideways, tossing his head. It was the most enchanting thing, watching this young creature play with us; his mother looked up briefly then continued feeding as a grumpy old shepherd milked her into a bright red can. Further on we came across two superb, sleek black horses grazing quietly in a field; horses are plentiful in this part of the world, unlike Crete where mostly donkeys and mules are to be seen. More, little farmlets along the road lined with shacks and shanties roofed with slabs of grey slate, tethered, bored watchdogs sitting in their wooden boxes barely notice us, plots of neat rows of vegetables, chickens, ducks, the occasional turkey and four more handsome cows and another calf, this time pale cream in colour. I believe they are Charolais, a French breed, and in a separate field is a big bull with a square muzzle, a superb creature Ahead in another field we discover a sow and seven piglets snuffling and snorting into the dirt beneath large stones that they were shifting with their snouts. We couldn't see what they were eating but there was something under the rocks, maybe grubs Geoff thought. "More likely roots," was my opinion. When we leaned over the wall, they all looked up at us with their little piggy eyes, they really are a bit ugly at first glance; curiosity satisfied they flicked their huge ears and went on snuffling and digging. They were absolutely filthy and stank to high heaven, but were nonetheless kind of cute. Nearby in a pen, eight snow-white goats fed from a trough and a friendly farmer with bright blue eyes greeted us with a smile. What troubles me is the cruel way they hobble their animals; the goats had each hind leg hobbled tightly to each front leg and they could neither jump nor run nor exercise at all. It is the ultimate cruelty for goats are such lively, frisky animals and they need to jump and play around; but they are healthy as their coats show, so maybe they don't mind—but I definitely do.

*

Occasionally I call in at the guest house, Tzimova, to have coffee with Poppy and her mother. I receive such a royal welcome it is quite embarrassing, but I do enjoy going there, they are so lively. Thea speaks only Greek at a million miles an hour and Poppy tends to lapse into Greek in the presence of her mother, forgetting that for me to comprehend, the language must be spoken at a reasonable pace. The other evening, Poppy came to see our tower house bearing a cardboard carton tied with shiny ribbons full of fattening and delicious chocolate goodies as Greeks often do when visiting—and before she left she said she had a secret to tell me. She seemed quite strange and showed the whites of her eyes as she rolled her head around, then she announced that she was pregnant.

"But please you must not to tell to anyone, especially my mother Mrs Valerie and Meester Geoff." She has always insisted on putting a handle to our names so we promised not to tell anyone, especially her mother, as she continued, rubbing her plump stomach.

"I have two babies, a boy and a girl."

Well, I didn't quite know what to say as she had been in Athens for a month seeing a psychiatrist for her nerves and I thought maybe, just maybe, she had found a man though it was unlikely. I gulped and said:

"How do you know, Poppy?"

She said she had symptoms, hunger, felt dizzy, etc and that she was one month pregnant; on hearing that I knew there was definitely something weird going on.

"Are you going to be married?" asked Geoff, his Virgo need to keep things tidy coming to the fore.

Ignoring the question, she replied, "He is the father," looking upwards to the heavens. I took a quick look at her. She was deadly serious and when I asked:

"What did your doctor say?" She snorted dismissively.

"He says it is nonsense it is all in my mind." But I'm afraid this is true, it is so profoundly sad, all she wants out of life is a man and babies and it is doubtful she will ever have either. I have heard subsequently that there is a history of mental instability in the family and that the guest house, which is two hundred years old, was once the family mansion belonging to Poppy's aunt, whom her father Georgios, had committed to an asylum. He then moved into her home and converted it into a guest house and has made a lot of money, which the villagers say is not his.

*

Last night we saw a wonderful programme on Maria Callas; it was the anniversary of her death. What a consummate actress—she simply *was* the role she was singing, oblivious to all else. It was a televised concert held in the Paris Opera House in 1958 in black and white of a 'concert performance' which is not a full-blown opera but consists of substantial extracts with choir on stage together with soloists. Tito Gobi was the baritone performing with her. Callas walked onto the empty stage looking so thin and fragile, the camera work was excellent with wonderful close-ups of her flashing eyes and strong features. She was totally enclosed within herself as she sang and acted every word with such brilliance it brought tears to my eyes and I noticed Geoff sniffing surreptitiously. Seldom have I witnessed such acting nor heard such a commanding performance. The commentator said that she had brought new life to opera and that it was now split into two parts, BC and AC, Before Callas and After Callas, when opera singers were called upon to act as well as to sing.

*

The town is once again back to its sleepy old state. The visiting Maniot families with their children have returned to their various homes and schools, leaving a small population of now familiar faces all of whom are revelling in the peace and quiet. September conditions are perfect, growing cooler by the day and the beaches are wonderfully deserted. On our way back to Gytheio we swam at Mavrovouni which is the longest beach I have seen anywhere in Greece and there were eight people on it. The water was as soft as silk. There are lots of sandy bays and beaches round this peninsula as well as interesting rocky coves with deep pools, we have so many choices; life is one long adventure.

On our evening stroll yesterday, we followed a different road bordered by grey stone walls and under the olives and around the boulders, we spied pools of pink and white flowers. On looking closer we discovered they were miniature wild cyclamens brought on by the rains, so pretty, peeping through the dry grasses. It is almost like a second spring, the dry twigs of oregano that grow profusely from the stone walls are producing little rounded leaves and the tall spikes of the white sea squill are in flower—and a carpet of bright green grass covers the brown earth. How wonderfully rewarding it is, living in the country and being close to nature once more, quite like Ellinika in Crete where the passage of the seasons and the night skies were part of my world. They are again now—and I am content.

I have just been to see Kyriakos, the young dentist here, a kind and gentle-eyed Maniot who said that I did not need to have my broken back tooth capped, but suggested I let it stay as it was after he smoothed off the jagged bits which my tongue had been probing for weeks. That decision of his, which he agreed ruefully was good for me but not for him, saved me thirty-five thousand drachma and a long session. He cleared plaque off and dug away into the gums most painfully and I was grateful I had not had major work performed by him; perhaps he is inexperienced as only once have we seen anyone in his smart and very modern surgery. In fact, he spends his time across the road chatting with a cousin until someone calls him to make an appointment. It is such a congenial laid-back way of life here, so much more relaxed than in east Crete where tourism has geared the locals into a frenzy during the seven-month season, and they lose their sense of humour and joy, not surprisingly. Geoff mentioned to Kyriakos that he had bumped into Poppy who was having problems with her teeth. He said, "It is not her teeth that are Poppy's problems!"

When I asked why she had gone a bit funny he said it was a tragedy and that when he was growing up, she was the slimmest and most beautiful girl in Areopolis—until she was jilted—and following a period in Athens at university she had become unbalanced. The secret starts to unfold. I shall ask her cautiously what happened when next we speak, but I will not ask her if she is still pregnant poor girl. As we left, Kyriakos invited us to his house which is where we swim off the rocks at Limeni and said we should eat the figs on the tree that grows over the wall into the road. A nice young man and possibly a new Maniot friend to add to our few acquaintances; a welcome thought.

*

We have been to Sparta where another computer shop is going to order my printer cartridge and we visited the only two remnants of ancient Sparta. Earthquakes, combined with the Spartans' indifference to creating anything of beauty or aesthetic value, has left nothing to posterity but the adjective. The town for once was bearable; it normally suffers from a blinding sizzling heat off the plain but today was cloudy with threatening skies, that made a pleasant change.

The heavens have opened up. Wonderful, soaking rain, the sort of day I always welcome as it means I do not have to go out, or feel I have to go out and can write or sketch or read to my heart's content. Geoff, like all the Englishmen I have known, feels the need to get outside and misses the sun, he keeps looking to see if the sky will clear while I hope it will remain just so, but not for too long—I would miss our daily swim too much. It is also quite cool and I am wearing slacks and a T-shirt with sleeves instead of my usual almost non-existent clothing, which consists of a sleeveless top, or tank-top I believe they used to be called, and what the Swahilis call a *kikoi*, the Hawaiians call a *sarong* and the Australians call simply a wrap-around. I have two most attractive lengths of fabric and feel quite glamorous when I wear them with my gold sandals. All I need is a hibiscus in my hair but there are few in this region, although there is a magnificent shrub on the road to Oitylo whose scarlet flowers shout at us as we drive by.

*

Hans and Iakovos are coming to supper. I'm making cauliflower cheese with potatoes and onions in the large oven tray beneath the grill, and when I pour the cheese sauce over all the vegetables it bubbles and goes a wonderful brown. I cut the enormous cauliflower into four and the huge portions barely fit in our small Greek bowls, we will eat on the terrace although I noticed yesterday evening that the air was chillier than usual. Later, it was almost too cool by the time we felt like eating Geoff's dessert of fresh fruit soaked in brandy with sheep's yogurt so we moved indoors. As always, we had a lively evening; Iakovos is a mine of information and he tells us so much about this place and the Mani in general and Hans's humorous interjections have us falling about with laughter. He is a droll man. I always enjoy their company. They are still terrified of Azore who comes bounding up to the sliding gate as soon as he hears a strange voice and then behaves as if we are being attacked and is prepared to defend us and the property to the death. Geoff has to call him off and distract him while I shepherd the boys out into the night with fond farewells until the next time; I am sorry for the dog; he spends his day in a yard at the back of Yiannis's house and is only let loose at night when the gate clangs shut. He is quite friendly towards us unless he is chained outside Yiannis's house and is on guard then, if we come near, he goes berserk and is extremely threatening.

In the evenings he gambols and plays like a clumsy puppy with huge paws and is most endearing; he keeps racing back to his 'bed' a soft patch of weeds beneath an olive tree. When I approach him, he crouches down and watches me with his yellow eyes as I say, *"Azore, those mou to balla,* give me the ball". He leaps up instantly, rushes out of sight and returns with the ball that he drops in his bed. I repeat the sentence and to my astonishment he picks up the ball and leaves it at my feet. The moment I bend down to pick it up he whisks it away and charges back to his safe place, tail wagging, loving the game. I do too.

*

It is the twenty-sixth of September and I am a grandmother again; Philippa has given birth to Jack Hamish by planned Caesarean section, after a few months of anxiety, partly brought on by the unforgettable trauma of her first son's difficult birth two years earlier. I almost flew back to be with her but felt deep down, that she should handle this crisis without me; after all she has a husband but tends to lean on me if I am around. I felt dreadful with the stress of it all but she rang me this morning on Yiannis's phone and said cheerily:

"So, what was all the fuss about?" Sounding bright and positive and just like my youngest daughter again.

*

The Greeks use the word *tramontane* for the ferocious north wind that yesterday and the day before, turned the town into a film set with newspaper and chairs being blown around like props made of balsa wood that swirled around my legs as I telephoned Philippa to see how she felt the day after the operation. Meanwhile two tiny, thin kittens miaowed at me from the woodpile beside the telephone box, dust and wind blowing into their wide-apart eyes which were full of alarm. I wanted to collect them up and bring them home. But I resisted. The *tramontane* hurled my pot plants off the terrace and removed the autumn splendour from many of the deciduous trees; I was reminded strongly of the winds that battered and buffeted Crete so often. *Tramontane* is a classical name for a northern wind, the exact form of the name and precise direction varies from country to country; the word derives from the Italian *tramontana,* that developed from the Latin *trānsmontānus*, beyond the mountains or across the mountains, referring to the Alps in northern Italy. Another old word which I heard when I was talking with our fisherman friend at Mesapo, was *fourtouna*, which means storm. He said that the small harbour was no good in the winter because of the *fourtouna* although Mesapo, together with Gerolimenas and Limeni, have been for aeons regarded as being the safest harbours on this western coastline. Finally, the *tramontane* has died down and the air is calm and peaceful without a breath of movement. The days are perfect, pure autumn with those quiet mornings where not a ripple disturbs the water's surface—not that we can see it from here, we cannot—but when we go for our swim generally around midday, the bay lies still and so clear one can see thirty feet down to the seabed which is starred with thousands of sea urchins; then a cool breeze springs up so we don't lie on our rock for as long as we used to. The weather pattern is remarkably similar to that affecting Crete but the Peloponnese, being further north, is slightly cooler.

*

Today is the first of October, my daughter Amanda's, birthday and also Karen's, Geoff's daughter; although they are a year apart; how curious it is that they share the same day. I find I come closest to my children on their birthdays; the link is somehow reforged annually and my memory is brilliantly clear. I recall every detail of their births and the emotions and sensations I went through each time. I wrote to Amanda today, telling her about the circumstances surrounding her birth:

My father died from the Asian flu epidemic that swept through far north Queensland; he became rapidly unwell and died within two days on the ninth of July 1964 and you were born on the first of October of the same year. Less than a week after he died, my mother had a massive coronary thrombosis which seriously damaged her heart and she was as near death as anyone could be. She had no wish to go on living without my father and, in a way, I didn't want her to survive either; theirs had been the perfect marriage and they loved each other deeply. But of course, the doctors worked to pull her through. They were very concerned about me as I was seven months pregnant with you Amanda, when he died and I had a difficult time trying to cope with everything. I was experiencing Braxton Hicks contractions and was ordered to rest, but every day I drove twenty miles to and from the hospital in Mareeba to see my mother. Most of the trip I was heaving with early contractions and not knowing whether she would still be alive when I arrived there, she was so dangerously ill. But she pulled through and was in hospital for three months and we made history in a way; after you were delivered by emergency Caesarean there were three generations of our family in the same hospital at the same time. I was so happy with my new and beautiful little girl, but it was also a nightmare time made worse by the knowledge that my mother had lost the will to live and I was intent on being positive and cheerful towards her, while grieving for the loss of my beloved father. But life goes on and you, darling Amanda, were born and you made all the difference to me and to us all.

After I had sent this to Amanda, I was looking through some old papers of my mother's and found this poem by Algernon Swinburne. It was copied in her beautiful handwriting and I remembered she had told me it was their best-loved poem of all time. So here it is for my mother and father, and thank you Mr Swinburne, for these achingly touching words.

AH! TAKE THE SEASON

Ah, take the season and have done
Love well the hour and let it go;
Two souls may sleep and wake up one;
Or dream they wake and find it so,
    And then—you know.
We stand on either side of the sea
Stretch hands, blow kisses, laugh and lean
I toward you, you toward me;
But what hears either save the keen
    Grey sea between.

*

CHAPTER SIX

TIGANI PENINSULA AND CRETE REVISITED

Now finally, so many months after we first looked at the Tigani peninsula and the rock where Guillaume de Villehardouin II built his magnificent castle, the Grand Maina in 1248, we have decided to go on our long-planned expedition. And why had we waited so long? First of all, we needed a reliable car and almost more importantly, the weather was now cooler. It was obvious that the trek from the mainland down the steep hillside and along the pan handle to the rock itself was going to be a long and difficult walk at the best of times, but in the heat, it was out of the question. Once again, we could not find the road that led to Tigani; there were no signposts on the main road and our memory was not serving us well as with the last time we wasted a good twenty minutes or so trying to find the path which led down to the Tigani peninsula. The tower on the cliff that was a beacon on our previous trip, kept disappearing behind undulating slopes of olives so we drove round and round and backtracked several times until we finally spotted it and parked the car with relief. After packing our picnic and cameras in our rucksacks we set off downhill with our bulging packs after closing the blue gates as the sign requested, so bizarre in that remote part of the world. Close the gates to where? The road deteriorated rapidly into a rocky track that careered down the steep hillside between round bushes of grey-green euphorbia, also called Greek spiny spurge and dried thistles however, following the recent rains, lush green grass covered the stony ground and we discovered miniature crocuses in flower, lilac and mauve, growing on shorter stems than those in the more protected fields around our town. Nature adjusts to the climate so effectively; another white star-like flower lay close to the ground between the grey boulders, cyclamen too, just a few.

We stopped to take photographs and to absorb the impressive landscape. the rock with its 'handle' stretched out below us with the bluest of seas on either side—to the north-east across six kilometres of water the open yellow cliffs of Mesapo harbour framed by a scattering of white buildings—and to the south great headlands rose perpendicular to the crashing seas. I wondered how Guillaume de Villehardouin II, the fourth Frankish prince of the Morea, first discovered this inhospitable place. Did his ships seek shelter from a storm in the harbour—and did he see the elevated plateau jutting out of the sea with its long, natural causeway joining it to the mainland, hence its name *tigani*, frying-pan? It was the obvious place for a fortified castle and eight hundred years ago the flinty rock-strewn approach would have made access from the mainland an impossibility. No horses could have traversed those sharp rocks, no wagon wheels could have survived that hostile terrain; access by sea must have been the only way until a track was cleared between the mercilessly sharp rocks of the handle and the plateau where he built his impressive fortress. Historians believe this was known as *Megali Maina*, the peninsula was formerly called the Maina, and the inhabitants were formerly known as Μανιάτες, Maniots.

As we neared the summit, the great bastion of ancient stones on the south-east corner of the plateau and sadly, one of the few remnants of the mighty castle, loomed larger and larger but it was not until I stood beneath the wall that I appreciated fully the magnificence and the size of this medieval citadel. It was quite inspiring standing there with the wind in my ears—and was it martial music and the bright call of trumpets I could hear? Or was it my imagination? We clambered higher and the precipitous path curved abruptly and fell away alarmingly on both sides to a sheer drop of a hundred metres or so down a jagged cliff-face to the churning, crashing sea below. Turning away from the vertiginous drop a shallow, stepped ramp had been cut into the rock—for the cavalry? It led to the plateau and there before us were the remains of the fortress of the Maina. Majestic in its day and so sadly neglected today.

At the edge of a cobbled street stood a slender marble column carved with a fine cross of St George, or the Knights Templar, and what resembled a walled, extensive graveyard with open tombs of different sizes and lengths with slate slabs lying beside them; were these tombs—if indeed they were tombs—once covered by these slabs? Or were they shallow catchment areas for rainwater, leading to deep cisterns? I almost stepped back into an oblong underground cistern still holding water, it had just rained. Patrick Leigh Fermor writes that the Maniot women he met were collecting salt when he explored Tigani, they told him that the shallow diggings which we thought were graves were cisterns leading into deep wells, and that there was one for each day of the year. There were certainly a lot of them, but not three hundred and sixty-five. All around me, collapsed walls, sizeable blocks of carved marble, fallen pillars with square bases. A superbly carved horse's head on a pillar. Evidence of a culture long gone.

We sat in the sun on a marble slab against an old wall protected from the wind which was too cool for comfort, the scent of bruised thyme filling the air with aromatic perfume. I wondered if the little fishing ports on the mainland south of Tigani could smell it too. Wandering around on the soft young grass, I followed the broad ramparts of the castle that must have covered some four to five acres, looking for signs of the past. But grass and weeds obliterated much of the fallen masonry and hid the contours of ancient walls and structures; I felt somewhat melancholy that the centuries had taken such a toll on what was once a proud fortress. Looking back towards the mainland the long handle of jagged rocks stretched out and we could see that the rough trail we had followed was marked by stone cairns; this was the only possible approach hopefully to avoid ending up with a twisted ankle or worse. Ancient salt pans lay along the approach where the women once gathered salt during the summer months; it must have been unbearable on that diabolical stretch of land. Even today, with the autumn sun partially masked by a film of light cumulus, I could feel the heat beating down. From crevices in the rocks, delicate sea lavender with purple papery flowers grew on long, slender stems and shy cyclamen peeped out from the shadows. I gather there was a spring of brackish water there but I saw no signs of this. I could hear the waves crashing against the northern shores of the peninsula but noticed that on the southern side it was calm and still. We swam in a cold sea after clambering down tiers of jagged rocks in the little bay we saw on our way down; it was out of the thrashing hot wind mercifully, and we found a narrow ledge and briefly dried ourselves before facing the long haul back to the car.

I do so love coming home after a day out. On the car radio we discovered Radio Moscow was broadcasting English songs of the sixties and seventies. Patches of wild Michaelmas daisies lined the road, and now and then a glimpse of crocuses and cyclamen as we sped along, our muscles tired, and the tight skin of sunburn on our faces. It had been an absorbing day of discovery, living in the past.

*

"In November the ferries to Crete leave Gytheio on Fridays and Sundays at four p.m." Geoff announced on his return from a visit to the port and next week is the last boat to Crete for the winter. I raised an eyebrow as I had heard this before. We had been given incorrect information last year in Crete when we tried to discover whether or not the ferries were running. So, we went to Gytheio to buy our tickets and the disinterested woman in the travel agency told us that the Friday boat was now not leaving until two o'clock on Saturday morning. I had the temerity to ask why and she sighed, gazed at her immaculate nails and said in a monotone,

"The boat must to call to Kythera to deliver petroleum because the government it has decided this."

I came to the grateful conclusion that the government in all its wisdom had determined that it was unsafe for a ferry full of gasoline tanks to also carry passengers. We dismissed the early morning departure as being too awful to consider.

"Bearing in mind our advanced years," Geoff said with a grin and, after obtaining her assurance that the last boat to Crete this year was on Sunday and that it was undeniably sailing at four in the afternoon, we went home. We realised that we would now have to return to the Peloponnese via Piraeus on the overnight ferry from Crete since the shorter journey from Kissamos to Gytheio would no longer be in service. Sunday came and we were at the ticket office; this time it was a grey-haired and very polite man who served us and when I asked him if this was the last boat to Crete, he gave me a kind of pitying smile and said,

"No I am sure not! This is not the last boat."

When I pursued the matter, he said politely that the Head Office—and he said it in capitals—would certainly have the correct schedule and it was in Chania we would be spending what remained of the night following our arrival at ten o'clock in Kissamos, the port in north-western Crete.

Our journey to Crete was enjoyable as always. We went aboard at Gytheio at four and I waited at reception while Geoff negotiated the car deep into the bowels of the huge ship between lorries and trucks. It is not so bad boarding the ferry, but disembarking is a nightmare as the driver must get into his car some time before the boat docks and wait in suffocating fumes emitted by all the surrounding vehicles until he can move. Mind you, I have always been amazed at the dexterity and speed with which Greek ferries dock and disgorge both passengers and vehicles. A great deal of shouting and gesticulation goes on especially on some of the smaller ferries where the vehicles have to back across the ramp into the boat. Hair-raising to say the least, with half a dozen or more Greek officials giving conflicting directions assisted always, by various members of the public who must impose their views often in conflict with those of the people in charge. A lot of *scase*, shut-up, and *feyg*, get lost, and stronger words to that effect, is heard, mostly good-natured but not always. Greeks are hot-tempered but it is of short duration. Before departing there is an announcement on the loudspeaker; first in Greek, then English, German and Italian. A disembodied, very English, male voice says in the best BBC manner:

"Visitors are requested to disembark—the ship is about to sail.

Thank you." The carefully modulated Englishness of it all is so incongruous on a Greek ferry boat. Ten minutes later the same voice reminds us that

"Visitors are requested to disembark immediately. The ship is now sailing."

We settled ourselves into comfortable reclining aircraft seats and spent the seven-hour journey to western Crete reading, dozing and doing crossword puzzles refreshed by several cool drinks. After calling in briefly at the island of Kythera we heard this formal message over the airway:

"May I have your attention please? Passengers who wish to dine may come to the dining room now. Good appetite!"

Followed by the usual *'achtung, achtung'* and the message in German which always reminds me of films about concentration camps. The public areas on these large ferries are quite grand; heavily carpeted with leather arm-chairs and couches, comfortable upright chairs and tables and muted lighting. The main problem is the frequency of television sets—often one in each corner of the lounge and each on different stations. And of course, one could state truthfully that nearly all Greeks smoke, so the air is thick with tobacco fumes which normally I have never objected to, though have never been a smoker myself, but after the clean air of the Mani I find I react severely to cigarette smoke in a confined space; my eyes itch and I sneeze and am generally miserable. The dining salon is smartly appointed with starched white linen, good cutlery and glassware and a waiter to each table and the service both in the lounge and dining room is excellent, the food quite palatable both in the cheaper, self-service area and in the main saloon. While on board we asked two different officers if they knew the schedule for the next week and neither of them did. Did anyone know, we wondered, or does it just happen at random as things often do in Greece?

We arrived in Kissamos near midnight, drove to Chania and next day, after a good half-night's sleep in a converted Venetian mansion, we found the Head Office for the ferry line. In we went with no expectations whatsoever of getting any useful information.

A plump, blonde Greek female with an unnerving wayward eye asked if she could help us.

"Yes," we answered brightly. "Could you tell us if the ferry boats are going to Gytheio next week?"

She looked vaguely at us as though we'd suggested the ferries were going to the moon and replied, "To Gytheio?"

"Yes, to the Peloponnese from Kissamos?" encouragingly and with a smile. She thought for a moment and asked another woman about the boat schedule who looked equally as vague and shrugged her shoulder.

"You must to come to see me tomorrow."

"Will you have the information by then?" I asked knowing full well the futility of my question.

She hesitated then said cautiously, "Yes, must to be."

"We will not be here tomorrow. Can we telephone you?" She looked relieved and agreed that this was a good idea and it was patently obvious that she thought it an equally good idea that we would no longer be in the vicinity to ask her awkward questions about ferries. I asked for her name and phone number which she gave me with reluctance and I saw her show the whites of her eyes to her colleague as we walked out into the street. I did not phone her, there was no point, so we never did find out whether or not there was another boat direct to Gytheio from Kissamos.

*

I am sitting at the marble table on the terrace of my old top-storey apartment in Agios Nikolaos in eastern Crete. When I first lived there I called it 'the penthouse,' its views are stunning. A Schumann piano piece is calming me but my mind is in a whirl of mixed feelings and I am a bit low. I am missing Francesca and the baby almost more than I can bear and long to see her happily hanging out her washing on the miniscule rear balcony of her eagle's nest apartment across the house-tops, and to hear her cheery greeting before going our separate ways. I have felt choked up and sometimes close to tears since we arrived, and Geoff is unable to comprehend neither my mood nor my apparent despondency. I suppose it is because the last time I lived in Agios Nikolaos I was totally involved with my daughter's pregnancy, the birth of little Alexandra and then the first six months of her babyhood. Every waking hour was spent trying to shore up my daughter's spirits and planning for the birth of her first baby. It was an emotional period of our lives and, when we departed on the plane for Australia with Alexandra, I was sure they would be unlikely to return to Crete at least for a while, and I also felt that I would probably not live in this part of Crete again. I was ready to move on with Geoff, so here I was temporarily back in my old penthouse in Crete that Pat and Graham, old friends currently on a short visit in Britain, had taken over when I left for the Peloponnese with Geoff; all rather complicated but it had worked out well. Today so many emotions and memories keep flooding into my mind, some joyous and others reflective and somewhat wistful. We think "if only" or "were things different" but life continues along the path we have chosen I believe—and we need to make the best of it. And we do if we are able.

Beyond the dome of the church and past the untidy rooftops, the bay is tranquil, the sun casting a baby-blue sheen on the water. A long line of white clouds, lie along the Tripte mountain range in a ghostly wraith, a shining ghost, white with dove-grey shadows. Birdsong from the trees in the street behind my apartment. The tiled terrace is washed and wet from the rain which has poured steadily for a couple of days, and my pot plants, unseen for five months are thriving. The salmon-coloured geranium, whose particular shade I was unable to capture from my child's paintbox, is now bursting out of the painted petrol tin and the white geraniums are in full flower—but my Cretan eyrie and terrace is no longer the private and peaceful place it used to be. A huge building partially completed, now blocks out the view of the entire south-east is an abomination; a concrete structure rising higher than any other, its walls actually touch those of my apartment, the tiny bathroom window is blocked up by the rising wall and there is now no exterior vent at all in the bathroom. My friends Pat and

Graham will be leaving soon; they liked the penthouse partly because the wide terrace was so private and the view stunning.

Crete makes me melancholy now. The magnificent coastline is even more littered with half-finished concrete structures; empty hotels and rent rooms, tacky tavernas and hundreds of billboards line the main coast road. In between the towns, as one climbs into the hills and over the peninsulas, one can still see what the Great Island was once like. I feel very strongly that Crete has lost her identity to the foreigner and the face of the island is changing, indeed has changed since 1989 when I first arrived with members of my family; unlike the Mani, that takes pride in its past and clings determinedly to its roots and makes no concession whatever to tourism. It has consequently, retained its identity. But it was good seeing my friends though several had left the island; there is quite an exodus of expatriates returning to their various countries of origin since the general decline of tourism from the UK that began three years ago. This year was apparently a little better although the tourists were, in the main, from the old communist bloc, Russia, East Germany and Poland. They were mostly nicely mannered, hesitant and they came with very little money so the island did not benefit from the greater numbers.

I discovered that a custom that I initially so enjoyed has been discarded; after living there for a few years, whenever I went to an old haunt I was greeted like a long-lost friend and presented with a tiny glass of raki and a plate of delectable μεζέδες, mezethes, while I decided what else to order. Following prolonged small helpings of a variety of delicious dishes and feeling totally satiated they would offer me a platter of fresh fruit! This charming tradition died out four or five years ago when Cretans in their affluence, began to take tourists for granted, forgot their customary hospitality and demanded higher prices, offering little in return. Eventually the tourists went elsewhere, many to Turkey which must have infuriated their arch enemy—the Greeks!

When we finally said *αντιο, goodbye,* to Crete and returned to the Peloponnese we caught the overnight ferry from Heraklion to Piraeus, the port for Athens which we do know has ferries that function every night, summer and winter unless of course there is a gale force wind in which case nothing sails or flies for that matter, and Crete is isolated and remains so until the winds subside. From Piraeus we took the ferry to Gytheio, our port in the Deep Mani, then drove back home to Areopolis. The seas were calm and kind on our ferry trips and we returned with our remaining winter clothes, more cassettes and books from storage and a small supply of raki, Cretan firewater which we prefer to the local brand. It is so good to be home back in our cosy tower house, or castle as Geoff likes to call it.

*

One evening following a visit to Sparta, where the Taygetus mountains radiant with thick falls of snow looked so splendid against the bluest of skies, we brought with us the new laptop which is a Digital from the USA. It has Windows 95 and we have Internet and email and fax facilities. It has an inbuilt mouse which one works by moving one's finger across a pad at the base of the computer itself, quite amazing but I am used to working with an external mouse. The problem is we cannot get either the fax or the Internet to work, Geoff is almost as hopeless as I am with these sorts of things and we have no manual. Tasos, the Greek in Sparta, has told us he has sent a manual by bus but it hasn't arrived so we are powerless; I am convinced he is lying. I am getting really fed up however, Geoff's son Robert, who works with computers in London, is coming for Christmas and we will have to wait for him. I am not using it at the moment as I have so many letters to write I prefer my tried-and-true laptop, even if it does keep switching itself off with gay abandon.

There are still a few 'shooters' around; old and young macho men in their pseudo army fatigues bought from the nearest supermarket where they hang by the door. They continue to arrive in their jeeps, guns in the back and head for Porto Quaglio also called *Porto Delle Cailles*, Port of Quails, since this is where migratory birds, mainly quails and turtle doves find rest during their southward travels. This southernmost port of the Deep Mani, once a pirate base, has been in use since the fourth century and today is a charming little settlement with dreaming yachts in the calm bay; but to me the atmosphere filled with the cries of dying birds can still be heard, although the netting of the flocks has long been banned. Georgios, the greengrocer, tells me there are restrictions about this frenzy of shooting that starts in September and continues for several months, it is now the end of November but no one takes any notice of the law and thousands upon thousands of birds are shot annually. We sometimes hear scattered shooting quite nearby and duck down low for a moment or two!

*

It is December and Hans and Iakovos have given us an outsized paper bag half full of chanterelles—those golden toffee-coloured fluted mushrooms that grow near the base of mainly oak and pine trees. We have eaten them for breakfast cooked in butter, olive oil and rosemary on toast, with chicken and almonds for supper and Geoff combined them with eggs and bacon one late lunch when it was cold and we were too hungry for mere salad and cheese. Chanterelles certainly live up to their reputation as being the most desirable mushrooms in the world; I gather that in America there are blue chanterelles—these I might not fancy, food is not usually blue. Naturally enough, the boys refuse to tell us where they find them and when we ask, they look slightly shifty then reply airily:

"Oh, somewhere up in Parnon and Taygetus." These are the two colossal mountain ranges that stretch halfway across the Peloponnese. Hum! It takes but a minute for us to decide to seek the elusive chanterelles somewhere on Parnon and Taygetus! Quite mad we agree, nevertheless, armed with coats, gloves, scarves, several Mahler and Verdi tapes and high hopes we set off on a sparkling wintry morning to visit the Mount Parnon heights.

I last passed through this region with Amanda and Tom on our way to the Deep Mani. Each time I step into the Hyundai, either to drive or as a passenger, I get this wonderful sensation of pleasure and a complete absence of anxiety which I realise must have accompanied every journey in the Blue Girl during the five years I owned her. Geoff has given me security in so many ways and I never take it for granted having lived without it for so long.

So—we are having a musical *ekdromi* today and our ears are filled with the sombre chords of Mahler's *Ninth Symphony* as we wind our way smoothly across the plains north of Gytheio and through citrus groves with enormous crops of golden oranges glowing between the dark leaves; some of the branches are so heavy with fruit they are touching the ground. Then we come across a curious sight—several broad paddocks lining the road are covered with carpets of ripe oranges spread across the ground being eaten by sheep and goats and, in a bare space between the two farmhouses on a small hill, sitting on a chair, I see a woman reading. My imagination was immediately fired. It is seldom one sees a Greek sitting outside with a book, and certainly never a shepherd or a shepherdess.

I wanted to stop and ask her what book she was looking at but came to the conclusion she must have been a foreigner to sit outside on a rather cold though sunny day with a book. Probably English but I will never know however, I could write a short story about her. We collected a few oranges from the ground and they were the sweetest I have ever tasted; no wonder the sheep and goats devour them.

The road to Geraki and its castle on its heights beckoned but we drove straight ahead up the winding road into conifer country which I always find exciting, perhaps because I have never lived in a high, cold country where conifers thrive. Mahler boomed from the speakers in keeping with the grandeur and starkness of the terrain as we kept an eye out for mushrooms but saw none in the green fields of new grass beneath the olives—and none beneath the stands of pines and spruce that covered the mountainsides as we climbed higher. Patches of purple *erica*, heather, struggled in the wind, which was now accompanied by driving rain, but no mushrooms. There was a barrier across the road at the entrance to the mountain village of Cosmas so we parked the car and stepped out into an icy blast of wind. Putting on everything we could find, we hurried through fine stinging rain into the square with its church and into the nearest taverna for a coffee. Inside, the usual *somba*, wood stove sat in the centre pumping out heat within and smoke outside through a pipe stuck through a hole in the wall. News on the television, that several Greeks were watching, showed the devastation caused by the bushfires in Australia then moved onto a programme in English on London today and the new Covent Garden complex, more restaurants and fashion, it sounded like a country on the move. We sat in the warmth, eating chunks of bread and goat's cheese with our coffee while watching the rain drench five magnificent plane trees, heavy with conker-like fruit and a covering of emerald green lichen on their broad trunks.

As we stepped out and walked around the side of the church, we came across a bizarre sight on this biting wintry day; outside a small deserted restaurant stood half a dozen red plastic covered tables and chairs standing with their feet in a stretch of water, as if waiting for customers. There was no one around—but for two chained dogs with expectant lifted ears and wagging, wet tails observing us as we admired the semicircle of tall old houses that faced the square. This little mountain hamlet had a lovely feel to it, despite the weather, and we agreed that we would spend a few nights here some time. It was too cold to explore further so we headed for the car and the dogs turned away with a dejected droop to their ears and tails. Craving more music, we exchanged Mahler for Verdi's *La Traviata* and the soaring aria *Sempre libera* replaced the wintry silence as we farewelled this sleepy place. Before departing, Geoff dug up a tiny spruce for Christmas and cut some branches for decoration, and we picked some holly, which Hans later told us was not holly! But it will do.

> *Christmas is coming, the geese are getting fat,*
> *Please put a penny in the old man's hat;*
> *If you haven't got a penny a ha'penny will do,*
> *If you haven't got a ha'penny, God bless you!*
> *(published in 1882)*

As usual when quoting anything at all, the copyright search has to be addressed, and on looking up the publication date of the above I also discovered this somewhat surprising edict from the great Queen Elizabeth I who, in 1588, ordered her subjects to eat goose for their Christmas dinner in a celebration of England's victory over the Armada, which suggests that it was not the most common meat served. I imagine goose might have been quite expensive in those days.

I have borrowed a recipe book from Iakovos so I can make my first Christmas pudding ever—but am not quite hopeless because in the past, in East Africa and in Australia, I had always made the Christmas cake several months before Christmas and on Christmas Eve the mince pies but had always *bought* the pudding. This year I decided no cake but would attempt to make a Christmas pudding and lashings of brandy sauce, but it was not as simple as it sounded. It took some weeks before I finally found crystallised fruit, peel and ginger following a search both here and in Gytheio. Last of all we looked in Sparta in a spacious, western-style supermarket on the outskirts of the town. I was about to give up altogether and noticed on the delicatessen counter huge bowls of fruit floating in syrup. green stuff that looked like angelica, pink things which were not cherries but red strawberry grapes, small pale bobbles that turned out to be white sultana grapes and chunky orange rolls that I discovered was bitter orange peel preserve made from *Nerantzi*, those glowing Seville orange trees that grow in public squares throughout Greece. They are for decoration only, and they ripen like all citrus fruit in winter so provide a bright splash of colour amongst their dark leaves. This selection of preserved fruit in syrup is called *glyka tou koutaliou*, spoon sweet, and is a traditional Greek offering to visitors served with a glass of iced water, although sadly this custom is fast disappearing in favour of sticky cakes and mock sponge and cream slices bought from ubiquitous *zaharoplasteia*, patisseries which can be found in every Greek town and village. Even Areopolis boasts two on opposite sides of the only street so we bought a handful of each of the sticky crystallised fruits and came home triumphant, ready for battle.

The recipe was for three plum puddings. I had planned to give one to Iakovos and Hans and, since Robert would be with us, I decided to make the full amount. Not a good idea I discovered! The problem was where to put them once mixed, and how to cook them as we are not well equipped with bowls, basins or saucepans. Having completed the mixing which was wrist-breaking and required Geoff's strong and willing hands, I greased two glass ovenware bowls and a yoghurt clay pot, then placed the two smaller puddings in water in the oven tray, and the larger bowl in a saucepan on top of the stove, tying the tops with kitchen cloths as instructed. I was unable to boil two puddings at once on the hot plates and have the oven on because this stove, like many Greek portable stoves, does not permit one to have both the oven and two hot plates on at the same time. One hot plate, yes, but two, no. It blows the fuses! For some reason the water in the flat oven tray was reluctant to boil and after an hour, as the pudding in the saucepan boiled away merrily, those in the oven were definitely not cooking. It was obvious I was going to have to boil them in relays in the large saucepan on top of the stove, but this was going to take over six hours and it was already late afternoon. I thought I would try putting the grill on, this always made the entire oven very hot and would possibly get the water to boil. A few minutes later the strong smell of singeing fabric told me that this was not such a good idea and I removed the two bowls from the oven and red-hot grill just before the two burned cloths on top of the two puddings went up in flames. Geoff somehow prepared the evening meal around the puddings and, when I finally turned them out, they looked and smelled good and now I am dribbling brandy on to them daily and am sure they will be delicious.

*

This afternoon we went down the lane to photograph the baby donkey and her mother who is always tethered when not being ridden. I could see the foal was a female and I have named her 'Flossie' after one of my oldest and dearest friends in Sydney. The foal is a most beguiling little creature and we instantly became acquainted as she nuzzled and nibbled at my fingers with her soft mouth, watching me through the longest eyelashes I have ever seen, in an oval of pale creamy fur around her dark eyes. Both mother and daughter have coats of pale tan with a dark chocolate stripe down their backs and muzzles and Flossie's coat is thick, soft as velvet, with legs and hooves which seem to be too delicate to support her body. I think she looks a bit like a raccoon or some such animal from Disneyland. Her mother was tethered with the usual wooden saddle across her back, but the owner was nowhere to be seen; he is very fat and flops over on each side of the saddle when he rides and he is immensely fond of the foal that follows them everywhere, trotting daintily on her tiny, shiny black hooves. When we tried to leave, she followed alongside us like a big dog and was visibly perplexed when we clapped our hands and said, *exo*, shoo!

Calves, lambs and kids have recently appeared in the paddocks down the lane; a white goat with yellow eyes has triplets, two white and the other is the most delicious mixture of soft *café au lait* and chocolate. Their winter coats are thick and woolly and they have really solid furry legs like stuffed toys; they are curious and so friendly. I do revel in this rural scene that surrounds us, our walks are always so interesting, pretty too with the fields now full of white crocuses whereas a month or so ago the mauve ones were out in their thousands. Geoff has taken some super photos of them.

We have ordered and received a selection of mineral salts recommended by Brenda for various ailments including one for nervous tension, excitement, stress etc and when Geoff was trying out the new computer, I was feeding them to him by the handful. We both got so ratty I began to take them myself but it didn't help. He has been unwell again with another cold, throat infection and a chronic cough which he never seems to throw off. He eventually agreed reluctantly, to take antibiotics after a month of coughing and congestion. I have run out of ideas as to what causes this condition to keep returning so frequently and I just wish I could find a Chinese herbalist; he would fix Geoff's problem pronto.

*

Areopolis, City of Ares – the ancient Greek God of War

Summer in Limeni Bay

White church near Areopolis

Taverna festooned with drying octopus – Gytheio

Church of Aghia Varvara – Saint Barbara

Deserted tower house – Kotronas

Tapering tower – a familiar sight

Summer sunset

Porto Quaglio – Port of Quails

Vatheia – village of towers and ghosts

Byzantine church above Oitylo bay

Mesapo harbour – Odysseus's fleet destroyed

Taverna on the beach Aghia Varvara

Nestling in the olive grove

View from Nysi

CHAPTER SEVEN

A WINTER WORLD AND CHRISTMAS

Winter has brought a change of colour and texture to the landscape, the leaves are no longer on the deciduous trees and the autumn tints have faded but it has, of course, its own particular stark beauty which I almost prefer. The weather is most changeable and one never knows what to wear, for instance it is almost four o'clock, we are sitting on the terrace and have just finished a late lunch of chunky golden pumpkin soup with equally chunky slabs of a grainy brown loaf from Milya's bakery finishing up with goats' cheese with our home-made chutney. Now sitting back replete and soaking up the atmosphere with the sun on our faces a cloud creeps across and goodbye warm sun; it is immediately too cool, so we move inside which is equally chilly since no sun comes through these tiny tower windows. I have changed into heavy slacks, a jumper over a warm top and slippers and socks. The air conditioner is now on so all is not lost, but the plunge in temperature as soon as the sun is lost is staggering, it must only be about eight degrees outside and even more frigid indoors.

A few days later, it is evening and we have lit our first fire of the winter. Yiannis has a pile of olive logs beneath a tarpaulin and Geoff had no trouble lighting the wood, in fact the fireplace was so effective he had to block off the flue hole on the terrace to prevent the wood being consumed too efficiently. No smoke to be seen. We put two huge logs on and lay on the couch sipping Cointreau and watching television after supper, Jean-Claude Van Damme and a silly blonde defying all odds as the logs turned to glowing embers. Snug as two bugs in a rug we were, the problem being we didn't feel like going up to our cold bedroom and kept delaying the move until it was far too late.

I have just read Louis de Bernière's *Captain Corelli's Mandolin*. My archaeologist friend Don, sent it to me and it's one of the best novels I've ever read, set in Cephalonia during the Italian occupation. I have never heard of him yet he has written four books and they have all won prizes; he writes rather in the style of Gabriel García Márquez—thickly worded with miraculous word pictures. The difference is that he is English, even if his surname sounds French!

It is the thirteenth of December and my eldest daughter Francesca's birthday. I traced her in Sydney, by ringing Philippa who was on her way with the two little boys to a barbecue at a friend's house to celebrate the birthday. All the family was there and I should so like to have been as well. Alexandra is now seventeen months, a baby no more, growing so fast and a bright little thing from all accounts.

As I sat at my desk a robin arrived on the terrace, his breast was bright red and his legs very thin as he hopped about quite impudently, he appeared to be quite tame but when I made a move to give him a titbit he flew off. I have heard his curious staccato call each morning since then but have not seen him again; there are precious few birds around now and the cats are on the prowl most nights.

Two days of torrential rain and I can smell snow in the air. Geoff has gone out into the wild wind to Sparta to once again see if he can get the wretched problem with the computer fixed. I am too cross with Tasos and never want to see the man again. We have had a difficult time leading to many tiffs over our new acquisition that held so much promise, with its access to research on the Internet, fax, email; all these modern things to keep us in touch when we want to be with the outside world, yet we can access none of them because the modem is not connected properly to the computer, or so we suspect. We asked for a manual which we had presumed would be supplied in the box with the laptop and have walked up to the bus station at least half a dozen times to collect the parcel; rung the patient woman who works there so often that she just says *opxi, δεν έφτασε,* no, it hasn't arrived as soon as she hears my voice. Tasos has solemnly sworn that he has put the book on the bus four times and insists,

"You will have it in your hand tomorrow for sure".

His excuse last time we confronted him with the non-arrival of the manual was that it has gone to Neapolis instead of Areopolis! I am wondering what excuse he will give Geoff today. The man is shameless; he lies without blinking an eyelid. So here I am alone in the tower house with the heater on and Liszt showing his true colours, outside it is true *Wuthering Heights'* weather with a fierce gale raging around in gusts that threaten to uproot the olives that are showing their silver leaves as they are tossed about unmercifully. Just as well most of the crops in the surrounding fields have been harvested or there would be nothing left of them. The mouth-watering smell of another soup bubbling on the stove is dragging me fast away from the keyboard—I simply must taste it! In the cast-iron pot are bones from a leg of lamb Yiannis the butcher hacked to bits for us with onions, leeks, potatoes, carrots and celery tops flavoured with herbs from the garden. Our tower house is reeling with the aromas; it is going to be good.

Later, and I have been writing all day with no interruption. Not that Geoff seriously interrupts, he does not, but I am always aware of spending too much time at the keyboard so try to limit my hours. I have finally caught up with my journal and have noticed that the weather is even wilder than it was yesterday, with the mountains sulking behind a thick, thick pale cloud. I feel as if I am the only person in this world, a familiar feeling which I enjoy. I have always needed solitude but also find I am waiting for the return of my man who has just rung me; he is on his way home and says he has got the computer problem sorted out and is bringing a bottle of champagne to celebrate.

Evening, and I think he spoke too soon about the computer and the celebration! Geoff is sitting beside me looking a bit grim and not managing to access the programs he found this morning in Sparta; so maybe we will not open the champagne? Oh yes, we will! Later we did and temporarily forgot about the computer.

Λοιπόν, lipon, so now a red-letter day. We have finally

managed to receive a fax; Hans sent the word TEST on a page and it arrived, but we do not seem to be able to send him one, although I did manage to the other day. We have won some and lost some. It is evening and Geoff is still sitting like Geppetto over his wooden carvings, gazing into the screen through his granny glasses and frankly getting nowhere. Later, and Greek roasted chestnuts from the market taste like sweet potatoes I think, and we have just roasted and tasted *our* first home-prepared chestnuts and they are delicious, hot and steamy and soft and sweet and straight out of the embers of our fire. Yum.

*

Evening on Christmas Day—and what a happy day it has been; the cooking was interesting, but I should begin at the beginning. We found a turkey much to our surprise, one of four birds complete with head and feet hanging up in Yiannis's shop where the dogs steal in beneath his gigantic wooden chopping table and help themselves to discarded chunks of fat and gristle which he throws onto the floor, while outside, multicoloured felines sit on their hunkers beneath any car parked close by watching the goings on, and now and then come in cautiously and take a piece. But they are not hungry; fat as butter are the cats of little Areopolis, there are after all, three butchers and a new fish shop plus all the leavings from the tavernas. So—on Christmas Eve we bought the turkey home, a decent-sized bird *sans* head and feet which Yiannis the butcher felt we really ought to buy as well, for some reason. Geoff and I had prepared stuffing and brandy sauce—as usual without any electrical gadgets—which meant hours of beating the butter and sugar until it was smooth and creamy, then adding the brandy with multiple sips for us both to help us on our way.

Robert should have arrived yesterday, but he unfortunately took the ill advice of a taxi driver who said, "Take a train to Sparta and then bus," and he, not realising there was no train to Sparta but only to Tripolis, which is another hour away from here, was left at the railway station. After queuing for half an hour, he discovered the destination of the train and rang us sounding quite distraught. He said the traffic was appalling and it had taken him an hour to do a ten-minute journey to the station and it was too late to take a bus. I advised him to stay another night and be early at the bus station the next day—but he was not up early enough and finally arrived well after midday, having taken a taxi the full distance. A young man unimpressed by the Greek public transport system which, in the end he did not use at all.

Christmas morning, we put the bird in the oven which left no room for anything else at all, so initially I had to arrange the potatoes, onions and golden chunks of pumpkin in the large frying pan on the top of the stove to cook and when the bird was done, I took it out and covered it with foil while I fast roasted the vegetables. It all tasted pretty good but the vegetables were not crisp enough—we do like crispy roasted potatoes. I boiled the plum pudding for two hours and the rich slices tasting of oodles of brandy that we poured over the top and lit—then liberally topped with cold brandy sauce which began to melt down the sides—was scrumptious and one of the best I have ever tasted, although I say it with a lack of modesty, I do realise we even managed one of the mince pies Robert had brought with him. He arrived with goodies galore including curry powder and paste, chutneys and poppadums pre-ordered by Geoff and several boxes of chocolates, half a dozen CDs and a beautiful blue and purple graded scarf for me, soft and glamorous; something I have occasionally coveted on other women. He is a most generous and delightful young man.

*

Boxing Day to the glorious music of Verdi's *Requiem* on cassette sung by Marilyn Horne and Luciano Pavarotti with conductor Sir George Solti—who has recently died—what a loss. I dislike clichés and never ever use them if I can possibly help it, but this music does truly transport me; my soul soars and I am filled with an overwhelming fondness for everything and everyone, but most especially for Geoff who has spoiled me rotten this Christmas. He even asked Robert to bring some chocolate ginger, my favourite, favourite flavour of all time and unavailable in Greece. Geoff has given me so many gifts including a gorgeous amber pendant and, on Christmas Eve he solemnly removed the pillow slip from one of our pillows for my presents after I had told him our family were in the habit of putting gifts in pillow slips at the end of our beds; then he brought me coffee and we lay hugging tightly, agreeing that we were indeed the fortunate ones.

*

Next day and I am on my own. The menfolk have gone around the Mani peninsula and I intended to complete an article about Epidaurus but am unable to as I am compelled to listen again to *feel* the Verdi Requiem. *'Sanctus'* is now playing, and I remember so well singing it in Verona's Arena di Verona in the summer of 1992 with Pavarotti in glorious voice, Lorin Maazel conducting, a tiny figure, miles down from the tiers of three thousand choristers from thirty countries accompanied by the Moscow Philharmonic Orchestra. What an experience. Now *'Agnus Dei'* with the threads of melody joining the voices of the soloists still gives me goosebumps! I notice in this recording Pavarotti's voice was lighter than it is now. What made it extra special was meeting up again with Patricia from Sydney, an old friend from my North Queensland days. We had what could be called a 'fantastic time.'

*

New Year's Eve 1997 and it is morning and I have just seen our robin on the terrace bobbing about very cheekily on his skinny little legs, he has a beautifully rounded red breast and is very talkative; it is nice to have a resident robin around our tower house. We are listening to Puccini's *Tosca* on Philippa's most welcome CD—a Christmas present—and finally the damp and dreary weather of the past few days has cleared to reveal a bright sunny morning with clear skies of a pale duck-egg blue, a bit washed-out but blue nonetheless. Faint wispy clouds are being thrown around by a capricious high wind.

*

Geoff is laying the fire; we have just returned to our tower house after spending New Year's Eve in Gytheio. I am replete with good living and have had one of the most enjoyable New Year's Eve's in my life. Geoff concurs. Yesterday afternoon we left Areopolis with a change of clothes and a bottle of champagne and drove to our hotel on the waterfront that, we were assured, was the best hotel in town. It had heating in every room that would certainly be needed, although it felt comfortable in the sun. Our room was pleasant but small, enhanced by a narrow balcony overlooking the harbour and the jetty where the ferries tie up—and inland the Taygetus mountains gleaming in the evening sun. Quite splendid. Two chairs on the balcony invited us to have our drinks outside but the air was bitingly cold. After a long and desperately needed siesta we dined at a very quaint and tiny restaurant which has no name other than that of 'General Store'. It is in the older, less salubrious end of town away from the waterfront, owned by a Greek with a Canadian wife and is partly a restaurant and partly a store that sells home-made produce of all kinds, chutney, jam, preserves, marmalade, thick yellow local honey and wine, beautifully packaged. A small *somba*, wood stove, in the centre just managed to keep the chill off but I was glad of my jumper and enveloping black shawl even if it makes me feel like one of the chatty and ubiquitous Greek widows who can be found in every village in Greece. The owner is called Pierro, which is an old Greek name and means 'with flaming hair'—that he doesn't have—or 'rock'. Whatever his name depicts he is a most affable dumpy Greek with a big moustache that I normally consider to be Cretan. The only other person for the most part of the evening was a single white-haired man who turned out to be a Norwegian philosopher; he was imbibing great quantities of red wine and became seriously loquacious towards the end of the night. I thought of Herman and his lively mind and depth of conversation, nothing trivial ever came from him and this man also had a lot to say. He considered Greece to be the most interesting country in Europe, following its layers of civilisation and thought the Greeks themselves really did not know what their identity was; they had lost a sense of purpose. I agreed wholeheartedly and reiterated a point I often make about the Minoans; in my humble opinion they created perfection in both their jewellery, ceramics and their architecture and nothing has ever surpassed or even reached their artistry and exquisite workmanship. He said he was wandering the world, looking for somewhere to settle and that it would definitely be in Greece.

I liked him and would have enjoyed talking with him at length were it possible. *"Ships that pass in the night,"* as Henry Wadsworth Longfellow wrote in *Tales of a Wayside Inn*, a collection of his verses. We could not keep awake any longer so finally said καληνύχτα, good night to our philosopher friend and drifted off just before midnight; remembered to put the champagne bottle outside in the cold air and in the morning, after an excellent breakfast, left to explore Mavrovouni, a village two kilometres from Gytheio that has some ancient remains and a Mavromichalis castle. We found the ruins, as always on top of the rise, magnificent views all round and in the distance once again the snow-radiant peaks of the Taygetus. An old Greek bailed-up Geoff and chattered non-stop to him, these elderly men are always so friendly and interested in foreigners even if they speak no Greek and they invariably pick on Geoff, being a man who flounders shyly and is often relieved when I come to the rescue. But I love to listen to them nattering to him, on and on they go, gesticulating, telling him about the castles and towers we visit, or the Germans and he mentioned angrily that the castle had been wrecked by canon fire. Whose canon fire I wondered? Possibly that of the Egyptians when they sided with the Turks and tried to wrest the Mani from the Greeks in 1862.

Later—and we are on one of our favourite beaches sitting on a log in the sun that was so hot we considered diving into the enticing waves; it was deserted but for a fisherman and his friendly dog, so we resisted the impulse to shed our clothing—with reluctance. We didn't exactly have a picnic since we had not planned one, but had brought tangerines, nuts and sultanas that went down well, although I did have a strong hankering for a chunk of bread and feta cheese, and olives of course. The anemones were out, spring must be on its way with delicate colours; mauve and violet and some a deep shouting red in stark contrast with their black centres. As we picked them another old man, a shepherd, stopped and had a lengthy talk with Geoff. He chatted on and on and I could see Geoff squirming a bit from my spot on the top of a small hillside amongst the anemones; he was also pleased with himself as he managed to understand a few questions and answered them quite correctly he thought. The delicate anemone blooms are now rearranging themselves in a glass pot that once held honey.

On looking back over many years, I have in general, found New Year's Eve to be an anticlimax and often a bore but the best year's end party for many aeons was last year's—my first with Geoff in Sydney—when we went with all my family to Julian and Nathalie's timber house on an island close to the mainland to dance the night away. A major feast had been prepared by Nathalie with her usual French flair and her decoration of the long table on the 'front deck' resembled a photograph from a glossy gourmet magazine. She is an artiste in every way.

At our urging the musical members of my family played the most amazing quartet arrangements of Mozart and Beethoven pieces with only one of the four playing the correct instrument. Philippa, a violinist, led the strange assortment and she and her husband, Brendan, a trombonist, wrote the brilliant arrangements and he played the viola part. Amanda, a flautist, played the transposed part for second violin while Linda, a musician friend and a bassoonist, played the cello line! The performance was entertaining and hilarious when Brendan with his usual wit, bent several notes on the trombone at the most inappropriate times following which laughter and the sound of appreciation raised the roof. We all stayed the night, what was left of it, on various beds and couches and gradually found our way home the next day, taken to the mainland in Julian's little 'tinny,' motorboat. It is always fun watching my son take the helm, hair flying in the wind and a wide grin as he shouts greetings to passing boats. The island is a friendly place.

*

Early January and we are back home suffering from slight nervous exhaustion brought about by driving Robert to Athens airport, two days ago. We left Areopolis late morning, had lunch in Ancient Corinth and visited Helen, a friend with whom we were to stay on our return trip, then headed for Athens where we became seriously disorientated in peak-hour traffic. It did not help that various squares in the city were boarded up and the road signs obliterated—if indeed they were ever there. After what seemed like hours of nightmare city driving and being squeezed by trams and abused by irate Athenians who have to put up with this chaos every day, I was quite shaken. It was after dark when we finally reached the airport, less than an hour before Robert was due to depart so we said our goodbyes with reluctance and began driving west out of the city. Happily, it was relatively easy as the roads seemed to lead us by the nose to the outskirts and on to the highway to Corinth and to the villa where a warm welcome awaited us from Helen, her mother and young Leo her four-year-old live wire. We had not seen one another for several years and as the fire, good food and wine soaked into our jagged nerves we relaxed and then slept like the dead, until ten the next morning.

Coffee and breakfast revived us as we stood and tried to take in the stunning view from the villa that stood in an orange grove in full golden fruit; brilliant sun, high and hot, cast shadows on the hill of Acrocorinth that overlooks the ancient town, the castle crenellations jagged against the sky. To the north we could see the luminous summit of Mount Parnassos rising high above its snow-clad range across the Corinthian Gulf and to the west, the far hills of the Peloponnese frosted with snow—and southwards the deep blue waters of the Saronic Gulf. It was, like many places in this land, almost too beautiful to absorb. Almost too much to take in. Can there be a too perfect day where everything one looks at fits in with one's preconceived ideal of perfection? If so, this was one of those days and perfection of the day continued as we drove south through the centre of the Peloponnese, flanked on the west by the Taygetus mountain range radiant with winter snow against an azure sky. Around each corner some other scene presented itself and we kept stopping to take photographs, mind you once outside the car it was bitingly cold. The towns of the central Peloponnese are ugly and untidy like many Greek towns, but the villages are enchanting with their old stone houses and cottages, worn steps leading upwards through intriguing moss-filled laneways, many of them cobbled and always a church, invariably pretentious, too large and out of proportion with the surrounding buildings, a central square with spreading plane trees, lichen-green trunks, leafless and heavy with conkers. Many trees winter-bare others holding onto the last russet tones of autumn; shaggy chrysanthemums, roses still in bloom and the copper berries of cotoneasters.

At Sparta we called in to find Tasos, the ashtray had been emptied and there was no coffee cup on his desk so I guessed he had not been in that day so we drove to the foot of Mystras and lunched in a taverna in bright sun, then returned to see if he was in his office. And he was, and as evasive as ever and I lost my cool; I said I did not want the computer and demanded our money back or I intended to contact Digital to complain about his lack of service. When I challenged him about the manual and his many assurances that he had "put it on the bus for sure", he said the manual didn't have that sort of information in it anyway. He lied so boldly that it almost took my breath away and the confrontation almost ruined the day, my frustration simmered almost all the way back to Areopolis. But this calmed me; as we were driving along the plain towards Mystras I had the strangest sensation that I had been there before, long, long ago. Everything was familiar to me, could this have been during a previous life as a Spartan? Seeing the castle on the crest of the hill with the precipitous sides plunging down into the ravine, and the now ruined city standing proud and high along the hillside, I felt as if I knew this place and that I was coming home. I must explore this further.

*

CHAPTER EIGHT

HALCYON DAYS AND OLYMPIA AT LAST

Bumping along a very rough road mostly washed away by the rains we came across a profusion of wild irises, dew-soaked, glistening in the sun, delicate butterfly-thin with yellow centres with spotted stripes on alternate petals like exotic insects. They grew along the steep edges of the track and on the banks above. I noticed that the flowers were larger than the wild irises I have seen before but on shorter stems and the euphorbia was out in a flurry of vibrant yellow-green flowers shaped like tiny parasols in triumphant clusters. It was warm, in total contrast with the day before that held us in the grip of a heavy sea fog that obliterated the world around us until late afternoon when, according to mythology, Helios, the sun god, also called a Titan, finally peered through, decided it was not his sort of day and departed in his golden chariot pulled by four winged steeds named Aethon, Eos, Pyrois and Phlegon. Helios flew across the sky from east to west then sailed around the northerly stream of Ocean in a huge gold cup, a ship or a golden bed—depending on which myth you read!

As for us, we left the car and followed a deep ravine for a good kilometre down an unused road, bypassed a makeshift barrier across the road by climbing over a stone wall until we reached the crashing sea. It was a glorious day with cottonwool clouds frolicking around the top of the mountains whose smooth flanks were a pale grey. It is amazing how the colours of the mountainsides change depending on what time of day one looks at them in detail. I watched a mischievous cloud break away from the mountain and drift westwards across the land towards the sea where it vaporised within seconds. "Serves you right," I thought, leaving your safe base and striking out, but then that's what I did eight years ago and look at me now. Happy. Free of constraints and in love at the unlikely age of sixty-three! Break away I say to all and sundry. Never follow a pattern unless it fulfils you. Do as Richard Bach advises; let go of the bottom of the river and see where the current takes you. It takes courage but everyone has that if they delve deep enough, of that I am convinced.

A sturdy young bull with a fine head and thick coat of deep mahogany gazed unblinkingly at us as we passed; he was not really interested just observing the intruders I thought. I noticed that he was hobbled and was in magnificent condition unlike the solitary and somewhat emaciated cow further down. Nothing else stirred around us, we were alone with the mountains, the ravine that was lush with ferns and moss, while on either side, low hills swept away towards two gigantic headlands that enclosed the wide bay where we were hoping to find a private beach for the summer. But no, the land ended in a ferociously rocky ledge metres above sea level and there seemed to be no way to get down to the water.

St Anthony was a Franciscan monk, born in Padua in the thirteenth century, still known as the patron saint and finder of lost things, of the illiterate, the poor and the saint of small requests. I don't have a religious bent, but I do occasionally invite this catholic saint's assistance when I lose something and he generally assists me in finding whatever it is. Or is it just my psychic leanings working again? It might be! We were about to take a happy snap of the two of us with Geoff's camera which has a neat, portable tripod when we discovered the gadget was missing. I thought it might have dropped out at the top of the hill near the car but nonetheless had a word with Saint Anthony and knew without a doubt, that we would find it on our return trip. It was unbelievably hot as we trudged up the slope and I was wishing we had not walked so far from the car as we searched in the almost treeless terrain for a patch of shade to rest from the oppressive heat. Dripping with perspiration we finally found a rock shaded by a shrub and as we gulped water from the bottle guess what we saw at other the side of the path? The lost tripod! Interestingly, it was on the far side of the road on the verge and had we not crossed the track to find shade we could easily have missed it. Thank you, St Anthony!

Driving further south after our picnic, Geoff showed me where he had picked the jonquils he brought home recently, their heavy scent had almost knocked me out and was too cloying for our living room which now of course has all the windows closed. We found the field just off the road to Tigani and he picked another bunch that will replace the fading anemones we found the other day. The irises I have will go with the chamomile daisies in the bedroom, how I enjoy being able to bring fresh flowers home from the wild whenever I wish. Each time we go out we discover something spectacular, beautiful or interesting for Geoff to photograph. On our way home, we left the main road and followed the lower flanks of the mountain range through several tower villages and stopped outside the tower hamlet of Paleochora, old village, to photograph a superb old tower house built into the hillside. A half-moon hung in a sky so intense it was almost a summer blue, cloudless but for the gathering of fluffy white youngsters that hang around the peaks all the time.

A little further on, we pulled in beside a well-kept tower house to look at a ruin when a white-haired woman called out to us in Greek. I thought she asked me if I thought the house was an *ómorfo σπίτι*, a beautiful house? I replied *nai, polý ómorfo*, yes very beautiful and surprisingly, she disappeared into her beautiful house. I waited as Geoff took a photograph while her dog, a well-groomed hound of uncertain ancestry befriended me; he wagged his tail with a slightly embarrassed air then barked half-heartedly at me as if realising he was supposed to be a guard dog but did not really feel like one. We were about to leave when the woman reappeared holding a tray with two glasses of water and plates of *gluka*, sweet Greek pastries dripping with honey and nuts, sprinkled with icing sugar. The three of us ate them sitting on the steps in the sun while she chattered away at great speed, challenging my brain. She asked the usual questions: where were we from, how many children did we have and I resisted the impulse to admit we had eight between us, where did we live now, and did we like the Mani? She told me she had three children and five grandchildren all of whom lived in Athens, they came and went from time to time. Her husband had died a few years before and she lived alone and was obviously delighted to break the tedium of yet another long solitary day. Her name was Maria and her friendly dog that cowed when she chastised him for being so friendly, was called, bizarrely, 'Dick' named by the grandchildren I suspect. We shared the sun, the delicious goodies and her generosity which is renowned all over Greece; the word *philoxenia* is literally translated as a 'friend to a stranger'. Geoff took a photograph and we promised to return with a copy and to have a meal with her and her family in the future. This we must do.

*

It is Twelfth Night—in Greece the Epiphany feast day known as *Theophaneia* or *Fota.* The most important ritual is the 'blessing of the waters'" which is performed by the Greek Orthodox priest and celebrated on the sixth of January. It is the day when people traditionally celebrate the baptism of Jesus and the official end of the Christmas period. Moreover, in folk culture, the feast day is associated with the banishing of the Christmas goblins and ritual purification. A variety of celebrations take place across Greece on this day, and in Crete I watched a small group of young lads freeze in the name of the feast day, by diving into the icy waters in Agios Nikolaos in search of the Holy Cross that had been thrown in earlier. Eventually, blue and shivering, some lucky boy found it on the seabed and as he erupted gasping out of the water holding the cross like some blue and shiny dolphin, a roar from the onlookers and a tangle of willing hands pulled him and the others onto dry land to be instantly surrounded by fussing mothers and bespectacled black-clad *yia-yias* grandmothers, who rubbed the cold bodies down, tutting and remarking as they worked. There is always a blessing invoking good luck for the winner that lasts until the next year's icy immersion and I understand each region clings to traditions that date back thousands of years.

On arriving back home, we take down our Christmas cards and the trimmings off our tiny spruce which is still growing in its pot. Many of my cards have not arrived in Australia yet; friends say they are finding it difficult to keep up with me, some write via Philippa or to Francesca in Sydney, others to Agios Nikolaos in Crete, not the Agios Nikolaos in the Deep Mani—while others have most likely given up the unequal struggle and will wait to hear from me. Francesca has sent a most welcome Christmas parcel containing cosy bed socks stuffed with packets of Thai and Indian curries, powdered coconut milk and pappadums and two days ago, Karen's parcel arrived with… guess what? Curry powders, pastes and pappadums to add to the supply Robert brought us. Thus, our menus have taken on a new and hotter look due, no doubt, to our frequent complaints to our families that these products are not to be found in these remote parts and we now have curry coming out of our ears!

January's calmer days are here and as if to prove this, the first asphodels are out, masses of candelabras of pink flowers are thrusting upwards on long stems from sheaths of sword-shaped leaves; the evergreen wattle also called mimosa—a member of the acacia genus—is smothered with frothy yellow racemes on the tips of the branches that remind me of Mitisaba, my home in the highlands of Tanganyika where my father planted wide strips of wattle as a quick-growing windbreak and for firewood. Yiannis has a young tree in his garden that is covered in powder-puff blooms; it is quite rare in this part of the world. I also glimpsed my first scarlet poppy amongst the bright starry faces of hundreds of chamomile daisies lining the roads and footpaths. Nature has fooled everyone this year into thinking spring is already here, I am certain it is not because Stephanos says this warm weather is unusual and that we have already had our main rains. This morning we again woke to a day of bright sun, and in the living room last night's logs were still smouldering and the tower house was quite comfortable. Most mornings it is absolutely icy upstairs because I like to have a window slightly open, even in winter. We are revelling in the twenty 'Halcyon Days' of January at the moment;

the weather is calm and sunny with clear night skies brilliant with stars. The Greeks refer to these days as the *Alkyonides Meres.*

Today we have breakfast and lunch on the terrace and find we are avoiding the sun it is so hot—but once inside these thick, protective walls the temperature is too cool so we light the fire or switch on the heater. The term comes from a charming old Greek myth; Alcyone or Halcyone which means kingfisher in Greek, was the wife of Ceyx the legendary king of Trachis. He drowned and when she heard of his death, she hurled herself into the sea and they were both changed into kingfishers. Zeus, god of all gods and humans, keeps the Aegean waters calm during the twenty halcyon days of January so they can build their nests and hatch their eggs on rocks in the sea in safety. It is an enchanting fable and as refreshing to contemplate as are the calmer, balmier days and it seemed to me quite extraordinary, that in the middle of a northern winter, the weather more often than not becomes tranquil during most of the month of January. Could the gods indeed have had something to do with it? Possibly, but after some research I discovered that this phenomenon also has a meteorological explanation; this time of year, the barometric pressures between Northern and Southern Europe are equalized, resulting in milder temperatures thus protecting the nesting kingfishers that do not migrate in autumn but in early spring. Even in the depths of winter, mild weather and sunny days often shine through.

We are off to explore the north-west, to find the Castle of Chlemoutsi and to visit Olympia, the latter has been one of my goals ever since arriving in Greece. Driving towards Kalamata, the landscape after Kardamyli is transformed and the road leaves the coastal strip, steep pine-covered hills close in as it winds tortuously and tiringly through deep ravines and up yet another steep incline. Chamomile daisies and purple irises grow on the roadside and along the ridges and we have an occasional glimpse to the east, of the glistening peaks of the Taygetus mountain range. Now and then we see a tower house high on the crest of a hill between cypresses pointing to the blue sky; it is another golden day with lukewarm sun but cold when the car dives into the shade of yet another ravine.

Finally, the Bay of Kalamata spreads out before us, we are relieved to be able to avoid the city and head north through disappointingly arid countryside. We stop for a picnic in an olive grove bright with clover and Richard Strauss on cassette reflects our mood that however, changes later in the day when we become totally lost trying to find Killini, the tiny stopping-off place for the ferries to the islands of Zakinthos and Cephallonia. We figure that in winter, hotels and rent rooms in the smaller villages would be closed but that the ferry-boat port would have rooms. It took us well over an hour of wrong turnings on deserted roads that dematerialised into tracks and then nothing. We were both very tired and I was quite demoralised as we wound to and fro, completely lost in an ugly landscape. I have no idea why I felt so bad. Am I getting a bit old for adventure and prefer not to struggle any more? How ridiculous you are Valerie, pull yourself together!

Eventually we booked into an empty hotel and were asked summer prices for a rather dingy room, but after bargaining with the pleasant owner, he reduced the cost by two thousand drachma and honour was satisfied. We could have searched further but we were so tired that all we wanted was warmth, hot water and a bed that following a quick meal in a fast-food joint, we achieved. In the morning we left the desolate port and set off for Chlemoutsi castle, built by good old Frankish Geoffroi de Villehardouin I in the early1220s it is considered to be the finest fortification of the early Frankish rule to be seen in Greece. I read that Palaeolithic implements have been found on the site, so occupation took place ten thousand years ago or more. My solar plexus leapt with excitement when above the olives, the castle came into view, its crenellated outer walls dominating the cypress and pine-dark hillside that rise out of the flatlands. I was filled with a sense of grandeur as if all below stood in obeisance as I am sure people experienced all those centuries ago. It is not surprising that the fortress was deemed unassailable; the eight-metre-thick walls of the fortified keep that surrounds it, stand strong and sturdy withstanding time and the elements. Once inside the imposing main gate we came to a large hall with an amazing, vaulted roofline that continued round a long curve into a church and out of sight; the graceful ceiling was still intact but for one area where bricks had collapsed and I could see the sky. The rest was perfectly preserved, such is the strength of the curve. As I climbed up worn steps to the broad ramparts noisy black choughs wheeled and whirled around before settling on the other side of the walls. Down below the world spread around me. To the west the misty isles of Zakinthos and Cephalonia barely visible on the horizon, in front of me the untidy village of Kastro lay dominated by its church and in the south the coastal plains led into the distance. A group of workmen and weary-looking archaeologists sat in the pale sun within the castle walls eating, drinking and talking.

As I sat there hearing the birds, I could feel the past within these mighty walls, much of it filled with pain. A book by an unknown author tells me:

"Khlemoutsi, as it stands isolated by the edge of the sea and the plain, seems to sigh as it is swept by the winds. Legend says that the sighs and groans which are heard are the lamentations of a mother for her lost child. She had given it to her sister, who was shut up in the fortress and the mother was never permitted to see her child again".

An unspeakable act of cruelty, but I have been unable to find out whether there is any basis to this legend, although history does relate a Frankish tragedy. Marguerite de Villehardouin, the younger of Guiillaume de Villehardouin's two daughters, was deprived of her rights to the throne following the death of her father and sister. She approached the enemies of the Franks, the Catalans, for assistance and was imprisoned at Chlemoutsi until her death in 1315. Perhaps it is her voice that can be heard wailing in the wind?

We returned to the car as a party of boisterous school children in their mid-teens came roaring into view, their loud voices and laughter echoing off the old walls. Many of them greeted me in English, that surprised me; why didn't they speak to me in German? Most Greeks do. Then a solitary young boy greeted me in French, after all this is a Frankish castle. I replied in friendly fashion but to my surprise I found the group to be more cheeky than friendly, they giggled and jeered as they passed by; perhaps it was just their awkward age. Then one of the girls saw our Greek number plates and I heard her say in Greek, "Maybe she is from Athens," and their attitudes instantly changed and they hurried past politely. They spent at the most, ten minutes at the castle and there were no teachers with them, they were probably enjoying a welcome coffee in the *kafenion*, free for a brief moment from their exuberant charges who were now occupying every bench and seat in the village. Greek school children are generally polite, always well dressed and groomed, the boys tidy, short haired and the girls in jeans, glossy-haired with excited eyes and voices—not at the prospect of visiting a Frankish fortress but due, no doubt, to the presence of young boys with not an adult to be seen!

*

Olympia at last and I am sitting beside the ruins of the Temple of Zeus in the Sanctuary of Ancient Olympia. A robin is looking at me, head tilted on one side. He gives two staccato cheeps and flies to another branch. He is perched in a wild olive that grows exactly where my map marks as the site of the sacred olive tree from which leaves were picked for the crowns of victors of the Olympic Games. The tree was named 'Olive of Kallistephanos' meaning 'beautiful crown'. Following a sacrifice, a child of living parents climbed the tree and with a golden knife, cut branches to be plaited into crowns. There are conflicting myths about this tree; it was either brought by Heracles from the land beyond the North Wind or, following a prediction by the Delphic oracle, was found wrapped beside Zeus's Temple in a spider's web. A crown of the wild olive was the most idolised aspiration of Greek youth and the contests at Olympia took place for "spiritual improvement, the harmonious development of body and mind and for the worship of nobility and beauty". Perfection personified. Olympia was finally destroyed by the Romans. The mad Emperor Caligula wanted the twelve-metre-high ivory and gold statue of Zeus taken to Rome with the intention of replacing Zeus's head with his own. The temples were eventually shattered by earthquakes and completely covered by five metres of silt when the two rivers nearby flooded and changed course. For hundreds of years Olympia lay forgotten and was only excavated in the last century and today the sanctuary is full of graceful wild olives, laurels, cypresses, prunus and Judas trees that will in a few months, be covered in purple blossom. English daisies grow in the thick grass, wild irises too, purple with lemon yellow freckles and I hear fluting, echoing calls from a hidden bird quite similar to those of an Australian bellbird.

At last, the sun is out. Geoff is relieved since he prefers to take colour slides with sun and shadow and as the winter sun is low, the shadows on the ancient columns are already beautifully elongated on the grass. The fallen columns and bases of the Temple of Zeus are gigantic—oversized—and no one knows how they were erected but they were felled like dominoes by earthquakes and wisely, excavators have left them alone as they returned to the earth in sad remnants. I can easily imagine the terror the inhabitants must have felt as major earthquakes struck. Behind me Kronos Hill, covered with pines as black as raven's wings, looms above the ruins; at its feet the serene pillars of the Temple of Hera glow in the grey overcast day. It is cool but not freezing, for which I am profoundly grateful since exploring acres of an ancient temple in either extreme of temperature can be very uncomfortable. I have gone into a state of suspended animation which seizes me in these ancient, quiet places; I sit on the old stones and dream, letting my picture of the past drift into my subconscious. Apart from Geoff there is no one to be seen.

I have been reading a most informative booklet on Olympia. The rules governing the Olympic Games were strictly observed and when infringed, the punishment was severe; fines, disqualification and public floggings were inflicted depending on the severity of the offence. Slaves were forbidden to participate, the athletes had to be Greek freemen who had a record clean of crime or impiety, had not broken the rules of the games or the

Sacred Truce and had trained for ten months prior to the onset of the games. Non-Greeks were allowed to watch but not participate. The Sacred Truce declared the district of Olympia and the state of Elis to be inviolable; no army or even armed men were permitted into the sanctuary. Wars and hostilities throughout Greece ceased initially for the month when the Games were celebrated and then for three months. Later, the rules were extended and the Games became Panhellenic and later still they included Roman athletes. Women—but for the Priestess of the goddess Demeter Chamyne—were not permitted to watch the Games although Pausanias, who wrote succinctly on this subject, said the prohibition related only to married women. Interestingly, a women's festival featuring foot races honouring the goddess Hera was established many centuries earlier, the participants were virgins from Elis. The races were judged by a group of Eleian women who lived in a special temple in the Sanctuary. These games were not held at the same time as the Olympic Games but took place alternately every four years before or after the main Games. There are conflicting views on the presence and participation of women in the Olympic Games as females entered, and indeed won, some of the equestrian events. This is verified in the New Museum of Olympia where the statue base of Kynisca, sister of the King of Sparta, refers to her victory in the horse race. The female charioteers, however, won no prizes; these went to the owners of the chariots who, of course, were men!

The oldest Doric temple in Greece and Olympia's finest building is the Temple of Hera, built in the seventh century BC for both Hera and Zeus. She was both his sister and his wife and was reputedly so jealous of his infidelities that Zeus moved out and established his own, magnificent temple. Today the Olympic flame is still lit in the Temple of Hera then carried by athletes to the place of our modern Olympic Games, wherever they may be. I was overjoyed when I heard that Greece had won the 2004 Olympic Games venue but I do wonder how they will cope with the influx of visitors. It is a bit of a worry.

We spent the night in a rather grand hotel and had a good meal in a taverna. The village of Olympia nests comfortably in and down the curve of a hill and is quite tastefully geared for tourism. As we were going to bed Geoff said, "I think I've left my jacket in Kilini". We rang to find out and, yes, it was there and certainly too good to abandon, partly because it was a Christmas present from me and was rather like a smoking jacket with velvet bits, navy blue with a thick lining and he feels warm and looks somewhat affluent when he wears it! After an early breakfast the next day, off we raced back to Kilini, the hotel manager expected us, handed it over and we returned to Olympia to the New Museum. It took two hours out of our day, but it did not really matter.

The museum at Olympia is impressive with the statues well displayed and spaced apart with each item clearly described in several languages. I was enthralled by the magnificent, larger than life statues that originally occupied the pediments over the entrance of the Temple of Zeus and the depictions of Heracles's Twelve Labours. Some were only fragments but others were almost intact; hundreds of pieces had been carefully pieced together and beside them was a clever sketch of each frieze.

*

In search of the hidden monasteries of Lousios Gorge we left Olympia and went inland into the high country of Arcadia to find the three sequestered monasteries which lie along the banks of the gorge. I drove down almost inaccessible roads on endless hair-raising hairpin bends into the deep gorge of the Lousios River where I was confronted by a very narrow bridge with no sides that I was certain could not have accommodated anything wider than a normal car; it spanned a rushing, freezing stream and I was somewhat nervous about crossing it. How stupid! We stopped at the 'new' seventeenth century Philosophou monastery that unfortunately was being restored and was festooned with scaffolding; I wished that we could have spent the night there. On the side of the canyon, the earlier AD 1270 Philosophou monastery is built into a vertical cliff above the darkening gorge and looked so precarious I wondered how any human being could have built there, or indeed, could live in such a precipitous and exposed environment. Only monks, strengthened by their unassailable belief that denial is their lot, could still be living there. All we could do was look from afar. It was getting late, an eerie and cold mist was enveloping us, so we turned round and Geoff drove back, negotiating the scary bridge and corkscrew bends with aplomb. Then we had to negotiate our way up the escarpment to the main road that took hours on a different, disused and bad track where much of the surface had been washed away exposing sharp rocks and deep ridges where the recent rains had raced down; huge boulders had come away from the slopes and driving was in bottom gear most of the time. There were no sides to the very narrow track and the land fell away steeply for what seemed like miles down to the Lusios River which was by then, obliterated by mist. It was a hair-raising trip but luckily the car is a four-wheel drive and is superb on bad roads and he is a good driver which helps.

Evening in the mountains, five o'clock and we are in Stremnitsa, one of the most picturesque villages in Arcadia—surrounded by tall, three-storied austere houses with jutting wooden balconies, windows and shutters closed and attractive Byzantine tiles on the rooftops; extraordinary architecture so unexpected somehow and surrounded by soaring mountains with the skeletal shapes of bare winter trees. The buildings meander up the hill with the night mist stealing in and blotting them out between the tall, bare trees. It is so steep they are built amphitheatrically around the hillside; I find it quite strange, eerie in fact and now it is snowing big soft flakes. The only sign of life that I can see is a pair of scraggy chickens, maybe everybody's dead? Well, we are not, but there's not a soul about and I read somewhere that the population is one hundred and ninety. Where are they all? I feel numb with tiredness, so we've just taken our mineral salts for nerves following that drive up from the Gorge. How daft is that! Higher and higher we climb and Geoff is still taking photos—click, click—but right now I am in dire need of a hot bath to sooth my aching back. Finally, we find a few people wandering around and a couple of dogs so there is a bit more life than the two chickens, it is like a dead village nonetheless. The atmosphere is stern, unfriendly, but it could be due to the winter weather. Above us, the mountains are obliterated by low cloud and the buildings go on and on up, the road starts to descend towards another lower hillside covered with houses and a church and there is smoke coming from a chimney; someone else is alive after all. It is a hotel actually, and of course it is closed. No δωμάτια προς ενοικίαση, rent room signs around either. Geoff, intent on the architecture, tells me the houses have Georgian proportions and some are quite handsome with their wooden balconies and shutters but frankly, at the moment I don't care, let's just find one that's open whatever its appearance, but we fail totally so we plan to return in a few months' time, when the spring flowers are out and the worst of winter is over. Since we were virtually in the middle of the Peloponnese, we hurtled southwards to the city of Kalamata—where we promptly got lost! Fortunately, we knew of a taverna at the coastal town of Kardamyli—and it was open with a roaring fire and a warm welcome to boot, so we had a restorative meal and got home at about at around ten thirty, worn out! Our total driving time was roughly six hours, excluding the quick stop at Kardamyli and I thought the next day, that maybe I was getting a bit old for so many kilometres of driving, which we do share, but then we did not know when we set out, that it was going to be as long and wearisome, nor did we imagine we might get lost. Blame the conflicting maps or no maps at all of some areas!

*

We have just returned from a quick walk to the edge of the plateau where the wind off the restless sea was liver-chillingly cold and the low evening sun across the water, was blindingly bright:

"Like the kind of light one sees, when a vision is about to appear," I commented.

Geoff said, "Do you often see visions then?"

I replied, "Of course, doesn't everyone?"

The northern headland and bay were blotted out by steel-grey clouds full of moisture, thunder grumbled overhead and, on our way back we got caught in a heavy rain squall and then hail came hurtling down, dimpling the flooding road ahead of us. Before we got home the road became a torrent as the water poured down from the town that stands on a higher plateau than our tower house. We were totally drenched despite our raincoats and raced inside to change hurriedly with me complaining repeatedly that we should not have gone for a "stupid walk" when we suspected it was going to rain! Geoff, ever the pacifier, has made coffee and we've had two coconut macaroons so I am fine once again.

About our pig friends, when we set out, we take bits of bread and leftovers from the kitchen to the enclosures along the rough paths that lead to the cliff's edge. One of them is a young pink and black boar with huge ears that is getting to know us and is quite endearing; today we saw him a long way down the narrow field and called out to him. Squealing with anticipation he gave us a straight, old-fashioned look when he found that this time, we had nothing to offer and I am sure I heard him grunt as I shook the empty paper bag and perhaps he muttered:

"I knew it, you can't trust human beings,"—*sniff sniff grunt grunt,* eyes a-slit before he turned away in obvious disgust—*trot trot trot trot* on short stumpy legs, pink and black bottom swaying from side to side and his tail slightly uncurled. This boar has a highly developed sense of right and wrong and is not afraid to show it. I have named him Menelaus, King of Sparta, brother of Agamemnon, although since he is young, perhaps he should be called Prince of Sparta for the moment? As for the ugly, mature pink sow in another field down the road, she shall be called Helen of Troy, wife of Menelaus and Queen of Sparta. I do not mean to demean these marvellous characters from Homer's *Iliad* and the *Odyssey* but somehow the names seemed right and they became more appropriate, as did my fondness of them as I got to know them better, and my recognition of their intelligence and inner beauty soared; pigs are some of the smartest animals on the planet I do believe. This pig knows our voices and snorts and squeals at us when we lean over the stone wall, but she is unable to move far as she is tethered to various trees around which she creates a perfect circle of mud from her snout; the field looks as if it holds the remains of threshing circles but they are just pig circles. I hope one day she will be freed and be able to gallop or canter up to the wall and share the morsels we want to give to her.

*

It has been chilly the last two days and has rained unceasingly for the past four. I think the halcyon days of January might be over for a while and certainly the land needs some rain as it has been dry for at least three weeks. We went out to Xanthi's our favourite taverna the other night with Hans and Iakovos who are trying in vain to sell their beautiful guest house and other properties and move to the island of Ikaria, where Iakovos' parents live. The daunting task of selling three establishments is beginning to depress them. They have been here twelve years and I think they have become bored with life and the Mani, although Iakovos loves this place deeply. He was saying, and I agreed, that only a certain type of person can handle the Mani—others are afraid of it. I can understand how a city dweller who comes to the town for a holiday might not appreciate the medieval austerity of the buildings and towers, and not like the closed wooden doors, high walls and shuttered windows that retain the privacy of the Maniots—so unlike other more outgoing Greeks. Most of the streets and lanes are dark at night, and when we wind our way downhill after a meal in a cosy taverna I feel safe and content in the silent walled world that encloses me echoing with the hollow hooting of the owls, but I can appreciate these dark lanes and tall, dark towers could make some people nervous.

Xanthi's taverna is a typically no-frills place with a tiny courtyard where we sit in summer. Inside it is wonderfully cosy in the winter. The large room is heated by a wood stove on which Xanthi cooks, using heavy pottery casseroles and outsize saucepans, there is also a spit where she braises an entire lamb or a pig over red hot coals. Tonight, we were served chunks of tender lamb in a sauce with artichoke hearts and it was one of the tastiest meals I have had in a long time. The only other vegetable was cauliflower which perfectly complemented the lamb which was redolent with rosemary. Gosh Greeks can cook! A local red wine combined the flavours perfectly and, in typical Greek tradition, there were no desserts; these and coffee are traditionally not served at tavernas per se; one goes elsewhere to the local *zaharoplasteio* to gorge if one wishes, on delicacies such as one of our favourites, *bougatsa*. These utterly delicious cinnamon-and-fine-sugar sprinkled multi-folded custard-filled sheets of buttered phyllo pastry can be found throughout Greece and words to describe that heavenly flavour as one bites into a *bougatsa*, now fail me. These should be eaten warm in a *kafeneion* if possible; they are not the same when cold. Greek desserts are primarily made with honey, nuts, cream and fruit, these scrumptious treats will surely tempt even the reluctant weight-watching human being!

Another of our preferences is *melomakarona*, these delicacies are simply delectable! No—scratch that—they are divine! These small, round bliss-bombs are dipped in honey or syrup and covered with ground walnuts. Mainly served during the Christmas holidays in Greece, *melomakarona* are decadent and scrumptious and everyone should have at least one in their lifetime.

*

Now that Yiannis is in Athens with Azore, his black Alsatian, we don't have to face him bounding up to greet us, almost knocking us both over, taking our hands in his mouth and trying to drag us off playfully. He really is more like a sort of friendly wolf than a dog and I do miss him charging around with the large ball plus the tennis ball, chasing up and down thunderously and returning to his safe place beneath the olive tree.

Evening, and we are sitting by the log fire trying to ignore the gusts of air which are being forced down the chimney by Aeolus the god of winds. He has been busy today and our tower house is being bombarded by glacial winds which come in gusts which would knock any normal building clean over. But this wonderful stone tower house stands solid, impervious to the gales. No wonder the Spartans and later the Maniots their descendants, built like this, anything less substantial would have been blown away by the first winter hurricanes that are channelled through the gap in the mountains that acts like a wind tunnel. I can hear the wind hurtling round and I have been watching the torrential rain through the windows; it is coming down at an angle, carried hither and thither by the gale force *tramontane* which struck during the night. The mountains have disappeared, and I can smell snow, I am certain it is snowing up there as the rain is like sleet, and the temperature is below freezing. Winter is really here today. The olives are tossing and twisting and any minute now I expect to see them being carted off into the sky and thrown into the sea far down below our plateau.

Next day I wake to a still and wondrous world of snow-white mountains so close to us. I am excited and keep leaping from window to window and back onto the bed. From beneath the blankets Geoff says, "Yes, it's very beautiful—inside!" The hurricane had given way to a calm day with occasional bright bursts of sun that glistens on the white slopes. Heavens, I love snow! I love the cleanliness against the blue sky and am able to reach the very soul of the bare trees etched like a woodcut against the white and pink of the setting sun as it discovers new angles as it sinks, setting the sky alight.

We discover that the bedroom roof light, against which the rain had rattled tumultuously all night, had been leaking and my clothes were soaking wet so we called Michal, who spends a lot of his working time in Yiannis's shed behind the house up the slope. He has a fine sense of humour and was his usual cheery self. Now that Yiannis is in Athens he is the master in charge of ceremonies, and we call him for all our problems—mainly leaks—and we have had some! The tap in the kitchen has leaked into the cupboard and onto the floor for months, and one morning the pipes suddenly ruptured. Luckily Geoff knew where the main stopcock was and, amidst clouds of boiling steam and torrents of scalding water, raced to switch it off. Thank heavens he was here; it was early in the morning and I would not have known what to do. He made three attempts to fix it and finally pronounced the problem solved, then the downstairs lavatory leaked for a while, but stopped of its own accord much to our amusement. After Michal arrived, he made a comment about it being a cold morning and that he had decided to stay in bed or go back to bed after doing some small chores. When we asked if he often stayed in bed, he replied, *panda*, always, with a cheeky grin on his wide Polish features. I said *ti krima*, what a shame, and he said that it was not so much a shame as a tragedy having to get out of bed! Nevertheless, he hauled the ladder onto our upstairs terrace and we could hear him working in the freezing wind that comes straight off the snow-topped mountains beside us. He blocked the edges of the roof light with the ubiquitous yellow gluey stuff which comes out of a cylinder like an enlarged bicycle pump that can be found around the windows and doors of most Greek houses. But not this one, until today.

*

I am painting to the familiar sounds of Liszt's *Years of Pilgrimage* and have finally finished a watercolour of an impossibly tricky little church with help from Geoff. I intend to illustrate my journal which is going to see the light of day somewhere. I have loads of watercolours of Crete but few of here so far, somehow writing has taken precedence. There is so much to record but I don't want to not draw. Is that good grammar? No. But I know what I mean. We are doing well locally with my stories and Geoff's sketches and photos; the *Hellenic Times,* a weekly ex-patriate newspaper based in Athens publishes everything I send and both our sketches come out extraordinarily well, though Geoff is having a problem with the human figure never having drawn from real life before. I don't even try. I have sold five articles so far—but no money in my account as yet—hum. Not much luck overseas yet which is disappointing, still last year was the best ever with pieces published in the UK, Greece, Australia and New Zealand and the best payment, a thousand dollars for a thousand words with one glossy magazine that I could not have done without Brenda's help, so I shared the pickings with her. I have a rather black short story in my head but it is partly based on the experiences of a close friend, my stories often are and I would hate her ever to read it—although the ending will be different. I must write it since it is already in my head waiting for me to sit down and type.

 We are having some fun with the computer finally, having been assisted by J.D. in Sydney who has sent us pages of advice by email. It is a relief to be able to send and receive help within a few seconds, provided we get the time right since we are either ten or eleven hours behind Australia throughout the year, but the fax still poses a problem as it does not appear to receive unless we actually tell it to and that's not the point. I need it to work when we are out or away. J.D. says in a phone conversation that we should not bother with internal faxes, they are always a problem he assures us. I have been looking up de Villehardouin and Frankish castles to complete my journal and am blown away by the concept that I can now access a library anywhere in the world at virtually no cost on the computer.

*

CHAPTER NINE

CHASING CASTLES AND KING NESTOR'S PALACE

It is February already; what have I done since I last sat down to write my journal? Not much, and I have been cold all day, fooled by the presence of a clear blue sky and what seemed to be a warm sun I wore ordinary stockings under my ski-pants instead of the sensible heavy winter ones I normally wear. I wish I had not. Partly to warm up we went out for a stroll through fields that are already scattered with scarlet anemones, their bright blooms opening to the afternoon sun showing their black centres. The tendrils of a wild legume that smother the stone walls on either side of the road are now sporting delicate mauve and white flowers and, deep in the grass, I catch sight of a Reckitt's blue flower with a white centre. Most wildflowers, apart from the red anemones and poppies, are quite delicate in shape and colour; nothing vulgar or common about us they say. We have picked a few stems of exotic flowers with speckled leaves, the small velvety-brown blooms have pale ivory, purple-tipped stamens peeping out from the centre. I think they might be orchids but I am not sure, I must check. Orchids are common in this region.

When we go on along this path, we pass a concrete shed housing two nanny goats, the common name for female goats, the males are billy goats and the young are called kids. One of the females had produced endearing snowy-white triplets and had unusually heavy udders full of milk, the teats almost touch the ground, poor things. The females are hobbled and unable to move about easily, while the kids are free and today the triplets were feeling particularly frisky; I was delighted since some young animals are also hobbled in Greece much to my dismay. The enclosure gate was open and the kids were racing out into the field, around an old olive and up into the lower fork down again then back inside the fenced area, stopping for a moment, tilting their cute little heads then did it all again at great speed. Gambolling and leaping in the air, turning their bodies in mid-flight while tossing their heads that already sport tiny 'hornlets' then landing on stiff legs before taking off once more and colliding with their mother. She was becoming irritable at this lively display and each time the kids hurtled past her she butted them with her sharp horns. On our return we saw the little group on the far side of the field, the hobbled nannies walking in orderly fashion and the youngsters still leaping up and down the wall, chasing one another and avoiding the mother's rebuffs.

"Just like we used to!" Geoff commented and I agreed.

"Take the kids for a walk to wear them out!" It is interesting that he and I were doing much the same things with our separate families at much the same time, with different partners and in different countries.

*

I am disinclined to mention the computer but I will. Briefly. We were quietly celebrating our success with emails and the Internet when it suddenly slowed down, the mouse button would not click, the arrow became a line and collected icons and shifted them like ghosts across the screen. Once again off to Sparta, could not find Tasos so we took it to another computer shop run by two young brothers; they looked at it and came up with the startling information that some essential files had been deleted and they needed one of our floppy discs to reinstate them. On our return home, we sent the floppy to them on the Sparta bus and a few days later we went to pick up the computer. The two brothers had done all they could but were unable to open the laptop as it would break the guarantee and they could not fix it. Fortunately, this time Tasos was in, and his brain was functioning better than usual; he checked for viruses and agreed that it was *árrosto ypologistí*, a sick computer and that it should be returned to the company. So there we are. No new computer for the moment but thankfully my old faithful is still working even though the battery does not function.

Enough about computers, Geoff says they have taken over our lives and they have for a while but for no longer as I have no further expectations. Instead, I am trying to concentrate on my Greek studies but somehow find it difficult to do every day, something else crops up and before we know where we are two days have gone by with not a Greek book opened. The road to hell is paved with good intentions and from tomorrow morning I am going to do at least two hours of Greek and maybe I will coax Geoff to join me for half that time as I am trying to teach him. No! It can't be tomorrow because we are going out early if I can get my man out of bed to explore the remains of Passava Castle—no—I think we are going to King Nestor's Palace. Well one day we will recommence our serious language studies, maybe.

Speaking of Greek, Francesca has signed up for a Greek correspondence course in Sydney so she doesn't lose touch with her good working knowledge of the language. She has a natural aptitude for Greek and speaks it well. She tells me that Australia is experiencing a horrendously hot summer, the first in many years and that her small flat is quite airless and she and the baby are uncomfortable day and night. Amanda phones, also from Sydney and says she would rather be in London with its damp grey winter because she hates the heat and her fair skin is covered in insect bites which always go nasty. She is not a summer girl. Philippa and baby Jack Hamish are feeling the heat but with the pool in their garden they can cool off, she takes him into the water with her and young Thomas is rapidly learning to swim. I am relieved not to be visiting Sydney this summer although I do enjoy much that is associated with summer, swimming, feeling healthy and lithe, but not the intense heat and I believe I am beginning to prefer the opposite—the winter! Maybe because a northern winter is a relatively new experience to me and I delight in the changing seasons and the contrasts that are so vividly announced by nature's hand.

*

Today I am sixty-four. How can anyone be this old I ask myself? It amazes me when I stop to think about it, which on reflection is not a good thing to do—but I certainly don't feel my age except when Geoff refers to me as the "older woman!" but he will be the same age in August. Luckily my age whatever it has been, has never worried me at all; I regret the gradual appearance of more wrinkles and wish the sides of my cheeks were not floppy, but otherwise who cares? Not I. We celebrated in various ways as we are wont to do – and a fun day was enjoyed by the two of us.

*

Finally, we have conquered ancient Passava or Passavas, the remains of the Frankish castle built around 1222 by Jean de Nully and most likely built on the site of the earlier ancient acropolis. Apparently, the walls are still relatively intact, but all other traces have been lost except for a few that probably were mainly Turkish. We climbed a mountain the other day to find this castle which when we began, looked just like a big hill but some time ago I reached the conclusion that no hill in Greece is ever what it promises to be. It is always further, higher and rougher than at first sight and the problem was we initially couldn't find the track, there were no signs although we had been told there was a path of sorts. I had asked a man at a nearby petrol station if there was a road, *Oxi*. No, he replied and lifted his chin up slightly, both eyebrows went up into his hairline, the way the Greeks describe the negative and then said, *me ta pothia*, slapping his thigh delightedly. 'with the feet' I translated to Geoff as the man gesticulated towards a house on the other side of the road; we parked the car and found a well-cleared path wide enough for a car, that looped up and around olive trees and the curve of the hill. However, we decided to walk and set out with joyous step thinking the ascent would be a breeze, but within a few minutes the road petered out to nothing, no track or even a path so we struggled up the heavily wooded hillside that was already beginning to feel more like a mountain. The incline was almost perpendicular with colossal boulders, rocks and overgrown with trees and a tangle of impenetrable bushes, many of them horribly thorny and wet with dew. It took ages to get to the top and I moaned and groaned as I dragged myself up behind Geoff, breathlessly hanging onto his hand and sometimes his trouser belt. I am sure I even suffered slight altitude sickness at one stage but dismissed the thought as I puffed like an old grampus and had to sit down several times to catch my breath, my heart racing and nausea rising in my throat. I kept slipping on the dew-wet grass despite Geoff's support and I began to feel like a sack of potatoes being hauled up a hillside, my description not his. It was a steamy day and we poured with perspiration and stopped to rip off our winter clothes—then had to carry them.

It was a glorious moment and worthwhile as the far Taygetus range drenched in snow came into view against a clear azure sky and there, on the small plateau were the ruins of Passava Castle whose jagged parapets we had seen from the road since our arrival in May. There was not much else to see regrettably, only a long line of wall crowning the western side of the plateau and a magnificent bastion to the east; the inner walls had collapsed long ago, and the interior was so overgrown it was almost impossible to fight our way through the undergrowth. It must have been a magnificent place at the time of the Franks when the castle guarded the only passage through the mountain range between Areopolis and Gytheio. While Geoff explored, I sat on a tumbledown wall amongst brilliant red anemones, daisies and wild iris and beside me a wild plum with its roots in the walls of an old building, its delicate branches festooned with the lacy-pink flowers of spring.

I wondered if my back might suffer a bit as on the descent, I kept sliding down the muddy slope and landing on my bottom with a thump. Next day I had a few tired muscles and some bruising, but no serious back pain; what a relief! It is like being born again with a stronger body and I wonder what the reason might be. I believe our lifestyle has brought fulfilment and a lack of tension combined with swimming, walking on the beaches through summer and exploring the countryside year-round could be the reason.

The countryside around Passava is bright with flowers, in particular a tall plant with bracts of fragrant mauve flowers that look suspiciously like 'lunaria annua', otherwise known as 'honesty', 'money plant' or 'silver dollar plant' the last mentioned might be the American term. In winter the dried silvery seed pods are charmingly delicate and long lasting when there is not much else to put in a vase.

I am writing al fresco. The midday sun is inviting and Geoff has found an extension cord and my laptop is now on the terrace, we've finished a salad and fresh fruit lunch with a small glass of village wine and I am replete, relaxed. Recently we have enjoyed quite unseasonably balmy weather and I am surrounded by sunshine and birdsong and am already much too hot, but as usual, within the tower house it is seldom warm enough and I generally freeze while I work.

*

Last week we were away for a three-day *ekdromi* and explored the western peninsula of the Peloponnese that I have been dying to see for months. The coastline has the most heavenly beaches with fine white sand and fascinating castles in total disrepair steal into view without warning. There is a certain magic about this land. Many of the fortresses are mentioned by Pausanias and make such interesting reading. First, we visited the port and town of Corone, about an hour south-west of Kalamata, driving through a gentle landscape with undulating and orderly vineyards. The houses have curious roof shapes and the little port could be charming but is entirely geared to tourism; all the signs are in German and they have virtually taken over the area with many restored, newly painted houses and newly tiled roofs. It is not exactly what we expected and it is a shame, otherwise it is an attractive little port but we would not stay there except perhaps in winter when there are no tourists around. The impressive Venetian fortress built in the sixth and seventh centuries keeps guard above the town with its great bastion standing in the waters of the Gulf of Messenia. The much-photographed arched gateway leads to a tranquil and sprawling monastery that takes up the entire plateau on the hilltop and also looks down over the town. There was no one to be seen, the place appeared to be deserted, yards of blue and white bunting stretched between the monastery buildings implied that someone important was either coming or had been. We wandered around knee-deep in lush grass and wildflowers and along the edge of the crumbling walls that plunged straight into the sea.

We then went northwards up the west coast to Methone to explore the immense ruins of the fortress whose walls also jut out into the ocean; the two moats now filled with grass are spanned by a beautiful stone bridge with fourteen arches. We walked along the spit on ancient stones and springy grass that led to the Turkish built *Bourzi*, fortified island which is in perfect condition. Once again, we were alone, around us the sound of pigeons' wings fluttering inside the tower and the crashing of waves against the rocks below.

I have a book on the Peloponnese that I bought when I first visited this region briefly with Amanda and Tom Forge. Among many other graphics was a photograph of a stunning horseshoe-shaped sandy bay called Voidokilia, Ox-Belly Bay, that is encircled by two towering rocky headlands known as Cape Koryphasion, joined to the sea by a narrow channel. This bay is now considered to be Homer's 'Sandy Pylos,' the port from which King Nestor's fleet of ninety ships sailed to join the Greek armada to lay siege to Troy. This is the bay where earlier on, Telemachus, Ulysses' son, who was becoming increasingly annoyed with the suitors who were pursuing his mother Penelope in his father's absence, came to seek news of his father. He arrived to find King Nestor and his entourage sacrificing jet black bulls to the sea god Poseidon and he was invited to spend the night at Nestor's Palace.

For centuries a great deal of controversy surrounded this bay and the grassy plateau halfway up the headland; Pausanias placed the Palace there and local tradition asserted that there was a cave known as 'Nestor's Cave' and that this site was where the palace and ancient town had been. Three Homeric archaeologists dug and searched for clues. Schliemann excavated in the cave and found pottery both too old to be from the time of the Trojan War and too modern, so abandoned his search in favour of Troy, Dorpfeld did much the same and finally, an American archaeologist, Carl Blengen, placed the palace firmly and indisputably ten miles inland on a low hill known as *Epano Englianos*, the Hill of the Englishman. I wonder why that particular hill was so named? I must try to find out because tribute is given to the American for finally establishing the exact site of King Nestor's Palace; most of the artifacts discovered dating from thirteen hundred BC. Being surrounded by so much ancient history gives me a real buzz; it makes every outing a thrilling adventure.

There is a castle known as Paleokastro, old castle, on the rocky promontory of Koryphasion; the Greek author and historian Pausanias circa 1200BC claims that this was where the palace of King Nestor stood. I promised myself years ago that I would find the bay and the castle that I was fairly sure was somewhere on the western coast of the southern Peloponnese. Fortunately, like me, Geoff is like a terrier with a rag, when he wants to go somewhere or find something there is no stopping him. After driving around for a while and getting nowhere, we asked a passing gypsy if he knew where a certain village was. He grinned and said, είναι εδώ, it is here! Hardly a village, crossroads and a few houses, some chickens and a chained dog. Nothing else. On we drove to an area of flooded wetlands and found a sandy track leading to perpendicular red cliffs and turquoise waters. Parking the car, we walked to the cliffs and there lay the Bay of Voidokilia, a perfect deep horseshoe curve led to a sandy sweep up the next headland and a grassy knoll. On top of the headland through dense undergrowth we caught glimpses of the crenulations of the old Frankish castle—Paleokastro. The Bay was separated from the magnificent natural harbour of Pylos by a wide sandbar of rolling dunes; stunted wild cypresses and clumps of pale seagrass combed by the fierce, cold wind which blew through the gap seemed to hold it together. We trudged around the curve through deep silky sand and up the headland but could not find a path to the castle; it stood remote and aloof above us hiding its secrets. Geoff disappeared with the camera while I sat out of the wind with the sun on my back and dreamed of returning to this enticing bay in the summer; the sea was so clean and clear and inviting we were tempted to have a dip but realised we had no towels.

"We could run around starkers and get dry," Geoff said with a grin, but we agreed as we put our hands into the freezing waves that we would not last long; the water does not warm up until June so we will return to this most beautiful part of this most beautiful world. Decision made—no swim—so we picnicked beside a stream that ran into the bay in the lee of the towering red cliffs that sheltered us from the biting wind, but it was so hot we had to strip off our jumpers and scarves to feel the sun on our skins.

Shaking off the lethargy that threatened to overtake us, we decided to find old King Nestor's Palace and drove inland and luckily, we called in at a tiny village with a most interesting museum and when we came out found we had a puncture. As is often the case with a newly purchased car, Geoff discovered there was no wheel brace so we borrowed one from a man from the electricity department, who it turned out, was married to a woman from the Mani! He was delighted to hear we lived there and when he had finished helped Geoff change the tyre, he vowed to seek us out to have a cup of coffee in the summer, and he probably will. As soon as there was weight on the spare tyre, we discovered it was flat. The museum curator said there was a garage *konda, pio konda*, close, very close, so we drove gingerly to the next village and found a garage with a workshop. The tyre was pumped up, an offer was made to mend the puncture, but we declined and decided to spend the night in Pylos and have it mended there.

At last, we were on our way to Nestor's Palace that I found to be somewhat lacking in grandeur; it seemed to be exceedingly small considering King Nestor was the third most powerful king of the alliance which laid siege to Troy. Homer speaks of the Palace of Nestor being the most important in the Mycenaean world—after Mycenae—but to my untrained eye and limited experience the excavated chambers seemed to be surprisingly undersized; the central hall had a huge hearth that left little room for anything else, much less a throne, and the waiting room next to it had a stone bench which would have seated only half a dozen visitors. Homer also tells of Odysseus in deep disguise, arriving at the palace and being offered a wooden bed in the 'echoing portico' which was the area due to all strangers, not realising that the man was Odysseus. The story makes fascinating reading and the photos of Piet de Jong's watercolours of the old king's palace depict richly decorated rooms in a luxurious palace, but the actual size of the excavated remains, appear to discredit his findings. Mention is made that de Jong was a talented artist but was not an architect.

We stayed two nights in Pylos, an attractive little port where the buildings follow the steep hill up one side of a large square dominated by spreading plane trees. There is a rather fine, three-sided statue commemorating the British, Russian and French commanders of the fleets that routed the Egyptians and the Turkish navies. The town lies against a bluff covered by the ruins of a Venetian castle known as Palaio Navarino where, in the last war the famous Battle of Navarone took place in nineteen-forty-three. Within the grounds of the castle that are beautifully manicured we found the museum of Pylos, full of interesting artefacts and old photographs and reproductions of paintings including those of female heroines much to my surprise and delight.

*

Evening after a most perfect day. I am running out of superlatives so I have looked at various sections in my Thesaurus to find 'peerless', 'matchless', 'faultless', 'unparalleled', 'divine'—and it has been all of those and more. It began as others have done of late, bright, cold and clear, every crevice and gorge and stone sharply outlined on the mountains and the air biting my face when I opened the windows. Initially we drove to Gytheio to the bank, the supermarket to replenish our village wine and grocery supplies and to buy odds and ends for Geoff's new project. He has greeting cards underway but needs ink pads to use as stamps for his cork images of towers and churches. We went into Georgios's shop on the waterfront and Petros was there, lively and cheerful and more Byronic looking than ever. He is normally in town over the weekends as he studies at the university in Athens during the week, so when I asked him why he was not in Athens he said he had decided to cut down on his classes as he could not be in both places at once and his father needed him in the shop. It would delay the finalising of his degree by six months but he was not unduly worried. I then asked what he would do when he got his degree and he said he would be working in the shop, and agreed when I voiced my disappointment for him, that it was indeed a pity.

"But," he said, showing unusual wisdom for so young a man, "I have been working on a project with some of the young unemployed in Athens and I realise that I am one of the fortunate ones and I owe it to my father." I applauded his admirable philosophy. We found the ink pads then bought two *spanakopitas* from our favourite bakery off the square and set off to explore new beaches south of Gytheio and when we got home, I wrote up my journal:

February and a magical day. The fields and roadsides are bright with a multitude of wildflowers whenever we go out and the last time we drove down the coast road to Skoutari, we picked a bunch of mauve and lilac anemones and now, several weeks later, they have been replaced by startling scarlet blooms. They are growing close to showy mustard-yellow clumps of gorse and other grass-like florets of bright yellow broom growing on long stems, the tiny flowers clustered round the shaft catch the sunlight and are almost luminous. The bushy plant with the mauve flowers on long stalks that I thought was honesty still looks like honesty so I must be right and there are hundreds more in a field, all in bloom. The valleys and slopes of the hillsides are scattered with the delicate white lace of almond blossom and the pink prunus is still in flower, although the pale green spring leaves can be glimpsed on the branches. The white and pink florets are exquisite against the indigo sea and the sky which today is azure, almost a summer sky. Further inland the trees stand in carpets of white, saffron-centred chamomile daisies interspersed with a starry flower that grows in patches like mauve shadows amongst the daisies.

A sandy track leads towards a long curving bay beside a fast-flowing stream that runs along the sloping sands and empties into the sea. Tall calamus canes grow along the southern end of the beach and we discover a well-made curved bridge spanning another stream flanked by a sloping sand dune. It is the perfect spot for a picnic, out of sight of unwanted intruders, warm silky sand within sight and sound of the sea and, most necessary, sheltered from the wind coming off the sea. The road across the old bridge peters out into bushes beyond which we can see a deserted campsite with tall trees close to the long sandy bay. It is fairly warm so we partially strip off our winter clothes—how good it is to feel the sun on our backs and pale limbs once again—Geoff's long legs which were chestnut brown are now freckled and pallid—and mine are unspeakable! We eat our spanakopitas with chunks of tomato, pull the fresh loaf apart with slices of Edam cheese and sip rosé as we lie back dreaming, feeling grateful as always, for our good fortune until the shadows begin to lengthen and the air to cool so we head home and as we round a corner on a steep hill Geoff says:

"Look lavender." I catch a glimpse of mauve and reply: "You mean rosemary, do you?"

"No! I mean lavender!" I jam on the brakes and reverse and there on the roadside is a small bush of flowering lavender, then I see another and as I pick a few long branches with their purple florets I inhale a familiar scent that takes me straight back to my mother's dressing-table drawers each of which contained a little muslin bag of dried lavender. How evocative are perfumes and fragrances, they can transport one in an instant, to years and times long forgotten. Round the next corner we find ourselves surrounded by more lavender bushes on both sides of the road and then, as quickly as we have driven into the lavender slopes, we leave them—there is not a single bush to be seen. It is *extraordinary how localised the lavender and many wildflowers are and how rapidly they disappear from the landscape. A brief, brilliant show and then over until next time.*

Later and it is evening. I have put the long sprays of lavender in a tall glass bottle and am drying a bunch to put among my clothes. Like mother like daughter. I have showered, brushed my hair out, sprinkled perfume on and changed into my white satin pyjamas and splendid turquoise kimono from Bangkok. It would be nice to say that I floated down the curving marble steps looking elegant, but it would not be quite true because even with the blazing fire which my beloved has, as ever, set in the grate, it is really cold. So, with my flowing silky sensuous nightclothes I am wearing heavy woollen knee-length bed socks of a rather unpleasant oatmeal shade, fluffy brown slippers and a huge black shawl which covers everything but my feet. The effect is lost but my love loves me anyway. He looks a trick in the evenings when he wears his elegant, black and gold satin dressing gown with the black lapels, also from Bangkok, it looks more like an elongated smoking jacket than anything else. On his feet he wears the same fluffy, fur-edged slippers as I do and an equally horrible pair of bed socks. Providing one doesn't look below the knees we might well be mistaken for a late eighteenth-century couple living in a Mani tower or a castle as we sit with our feet elevated on a velvet cushion, which we don't have, in front of the fire.

*

I must get supper; it is my turn to cook; we are having roast pork with rosemary, roast potatoes, onions and pumpkin with crisp runner beans and of course, apple sauce from a jar. Almost everything from the market and the meat always so tender. So English though I have never lived in England, I was born there and rapidly transported at the tender age of three months to the steamy port of Dar es Salaam on the East African coast. Geoff was born in England and emigrated to Australia many years after I did.

*

Sunday afternoon and we are absorbed by Mozart's *Bassoon Concerto*, although not my favourite instrument it is nonetheless beautiful, so velvety and smooth. It is still a joy for me to be able to listen right through a symphony or concerto without interruption. I have never had a CD player before, so this stretch of uninterrupted music is new to me except on the occasions when I am staying with one of my children in Sydney, all of whom have the latest in recording equipment. I am used to my cassettes that sometimes do not quite make it to the end because the cassette is slightly too short for the work. We are gradually ordering CDs from the UK but don't have a decent collection yet, although I brought loads of tapes from Crete and we still play them, even those that do not have an ending! We steel ourselves when we know that we are not going to hear the climax and wait for the Draconian cessation of sound and vow once again never to listen to that particular cassette. But we still do.

*

I have received a three-page letter from Bunty, an old friend who lives in Canberra, mostly about my adored Burmese cat, D'Artagnan, who is now eighteen years old. When I left Australia for Crete all those years ago, Bunty begged me to give him to her as she had fallen in love with him when I lived in Canberra; I was happy for her to have him as she was another ardent cat lover. I did not want him to go to a household full of children, only because he was used to living alone with me, and he was getting on a bit. Bunty tells me he has health problems and has acupuncture for renal disease, and she won't give him what she terms 'poisonous chemicals' to wreck his kidneys she says, so he is on homeopathy. She says she has never had a geriatric animal before and he is just the same as a human being! He is a surly old man like many old men, but he still kisses with his teeth, loves biting noses, fingers and toes. I was so grateful when she took him as he has been cossetted and cared for by this loving woman.

The sweet silkiness of the Brahms *Violin Concerto* performed by the brilliant Itzhak Perlman fills the tower house; outside it is still sunny with the cloudless skies we have been enjoying for over a week, but the air is cooling noticeably and Geoff will lay the fire when we return from our walk. Almost every day we discover new wildflowers, the scarlet anemones are out, the purple and mauve ones flowered profusely a few weeks ago but have now disappeared. We have had a spate of wild irises, delicate lilac with leopard yellow spots and earlier, wild jonquils with the most heavenly scent. The fields and roadsides are starred with white chamomile daisies and clumps of tiny mauve and pink flowers of *malcolmia maritima*, Virginia stock, so charming and along the steep road to the centre, more bright clumps are growing in cracks in the stone walls and from the base of a flight of concrete steps. They seem to thrive in concrete.

Golden gorse is in full bloom, not here in the Deep Mani but on the eastern side of this narrow peninsula where it is sunnier. The fruit trees, prunus and almond, are scattering their delicate lacy pink and white blossoms like a glorious confetti-sprinkled wedding in a natural rock garden with nature and not man as its designer; we humans have never been able to emulate nature's random choice of colour and design. Judging by the surge of growth, we might think that spring has arrived, but I have a sinking feeling that wild freezing winds and pelting rain will soon shred the lovely petals. When we are out walking, we occasionally see Maniot womenfolk in the fields and on the roadsides gathering *horta*. Interestingly it is not the peasant's or farmer's wives we meet but the elderly female who owns the smaller of the two grocery stores, smartly dressed with stylish hair, or the woman from the newspaper shop with her daughter Maria, and last evening we were greeted by a much younger person with masses of shiny brown hair, her arms full of *horta* and wildflowers. We smiled at one another with empathy, recognising a mutual love of flowers.

*

Following lengthy discussion, we have decided not to go to Turkey this year mainly because the planned long visit to Australia is more important, and we cannot do both. Plus, the political situation is in turmoil—but isn't it always? Perhaps we will go next year and just take a few long trips around Greece instead; I want to go to the Epirus region near the border of Albania, then show Geoff the fantastic monasteries at Meteora, across to Thessalonica then back via the Pelion Peninsula. We will keep the tower house during our Australian visit, so we have a base to return to. Then hopefully, we will set out to follow my craving to return to Turkey where I worked with the B.S.A's archaeological survey, and took a busload of mature students to a stunning Seljuk caravanserai. It was a truly memorable experience and I feel the urge to go back and record more of the caravanserais. It is such a pity we are not fulfilling our original ideas; I have a sense of loss and wonder if I will ever see Turkey again and if I don't, does it matter? Omar Khayyam tells us it does not matter and providing today 'be sweet' we have nothing to fret about—well—today is truly sweet as all our days have been but on reflection, I am not sure I subscribe to his seemingly hedonistic existence. There is a deeper meaning to life, and he warns us to take care, there can be consequences to life's decisions. The beautifully written philosophy of this twelfth-century Persian astronomer, mathematician and poet in *The Rubáiyát of Omar Khayyam* translated in 1859 by Edward FitzGerald is the version I prefer; I relate to the following:

> *The Moving Finger writes;*
> *and, having writ,*
> *Moves on: nor all thy Piety*
> *nor Wit*
> *Shall lure it back to cancel*
> *half a Line,*
> *Nor all thy Tears wash out*
> *A Word of it.*

*

CHAPTER TEN

A WILD ROCK GARDEN AND THE AMAZONS OF DIROU

To-day we went to the tiny white chapel that stands at the edge of the plateau down the road from us. It is our favourite spot, and it looks out over a second lower plateau where cows and goats graze and then the land plunges down to the sea. Around the chapel is a wild and wonderful rock garden full of wildflowers; we counted more than half a dozen different varieties growing between the grey and white stones. The scented air was pulsating with the drone of bees collecting pollen, butterflies hovered prettily and I found myself thrashing around in my brain wondering how I was going to describe this secret garden in my journal. What words do I use to portray the fragile, miniature bracts and curling tendrils of the many wild legumes that are in flower, dark violet sprays standing upright in the sun, or the tiny ivory petals of a smaller legume lying close to the ground, or those with the palest yellow blooms with their soft, fern-like leaves and the tiny spearheads of exotic mauve iris growing straight and soldierly out of the ground, or the now-fading clusters of electric-blue grape hyacinths swaying a little on their slender stems, or the clusters of exquisite starry blooms, miniature in size that start off amethyst then turn claret to plum, or the Lilliputian crocus-like flowers, whose petals are a waxy white on the inside and green on the outside? They too grow close to the ground and I have not seen them before. In between these treasures grow pools of cheerful chamomile daisies, bright yellow mustard flowers, bold and beautiful anemones that shout 'look at me' their scarlet petals glowing between the pastel shades of the other wildflowers, and the tall pinky-white pyramids of asphodel rising above them all. Asphodels—mentioned by Homer and poets throughout the ages catch one's attention throughout the year—they are one of the first flowers to show themselves as winter moves imperceptibly away.

On reading this I feel I should write nothing but simply remember the glory of the white chapel garden. My vocabulary is insufficient to capture its ethereal quality but I must try to describe it lest I grow old and forget these enchanted moments when my memory fails me. We took our painting paraphernalia and spent several hours sitting on separate rocks in the sun, trying to capture the scene; so many textures, contrasts and colours. The stucco white wall of the chapel, the blue of the sea, the headlands growing paler with distance, the bottle green leaves of an overhanging carob and of course the carpets of wildflowers. Back home now and I am not entirely satisfied with the pen and ink sketch that I later painted; Geoff's watercolour is perfect; he is so clever with shadows and shapes—but now Eric Copland's *Appalachian Spring* is taking over and I have to stop writing and listen to this brilliant piece written for Martha Graham. The composer, another one of our favourites, is mostly known for his inspiring Fanfare for the Common Man.

*

Today is the second of March and *Kathara Deftera*, Clean Monday, the day when Greek families fly brilliant dancing diving skimming racing kites with their children, and picnic on the hillsides. It is a public holiday and denotes the end of three weeks of festivities and is the beginning of serious fasting for many Greeks. *Carnevale* is an Italian word derived from the Latin *carne*, meat and *vale*, farewell. The English 'Carnival' is a traditional Christian celebration that marks the beginning of Lent, the period of forty days before Easter during which no meat is eaten. The festival reached its peak last night and we watched the most amazing floats on television from Rio de Janeiro. Glamorous girls in feathers and frills of enormous width and size with headdresses six feet and over and a varied collection of groups of dancers shaking and rolling their brown bellies, voluptuous bosoms and bottoms. I thought the whole show had lost its original spontaneity; it was no longer a fun street carnival, but a competitive 'outdoing of the other's float' procession. Spectacular certainly, but too contrived. We had planned to visit Patras where the festivities are reputed to be the best in Greece, but later decided not to bother.

*

A blue and gold day greets us as we prepare a picnic for a trip to Skoutari on the east coast of the peninsula; we drive via Kotronas, a cute little harbour on the other side of this peninsula. The scenery is spectacular as we tackle a windy pass where a bizarre shrine stands in the grip of the wind, protected by an iron cage cemented into the rock. The road twists and corkscrews steeply downwards to the inlet and its waterfront, deserted now with caiques sleeping on the beach for winter and mulberries pruned savagely down to their twisted trunks. How they survive this Draconian annual pruning I will never know, but survive they do and provide cool shade every summer. The Mani had a thriving silk industry that lasted until the early part of the nineteen-hundreds and the mulberries are the last reminder of those days.

Geoff points out Skopa, a tiny island now joined by a bar of sand and pebbles to the mainland north of the village, to which Patrick Leigh Fermor—commonly known as 'Paddy'—swam, forty years ago. The author and adventurer described the environment and the landscape so beautifully in his book; it is one of the many places I have wanted to visit, and we will explore further next time we come this way.

There is a new coast road linking Kotronas with Skoutari that follows the two mighty headlands in-between the two bays, it starts off as a track going up the hill south of the port then is rapidly transformed into a wide and wonderful highway with a sealed surface. We were a little incredulous at discovering such a fine road but within moments the surface degenerated into a rough track, it lost its width, and for a moment we thought that it was going to peter out altogether, but it continued in a half-hearted sort of manner along the cliff edge, fallen rocks littering the surface. It was as if the workmen had simply lost interest or the project had used up its budget and been abandoned. As we rounded the promontory a wild, wailing wind buffeted the car whipping up the waves in the bay into *blancs moutons*, white sheep, as the French so charmingly call our 'white horses'. Seawards the land fell away sharply and on the land side perpendicular cliffs rose above as if to push us into the ocean far below. The atmosphere was strangely inhospitable then I heard the barking of dogs and, in an instant, we found ourselves amongst a pack of what could only have been feral dogs, very angry ones at that. There were five of them, short and stocky in build with broad chests and big heads, heavy winter coats, their strong shape and large heads reminded me of hyenas for a moment. They chased the car barking savagely and snarling, baring vicious fangs and running alongside and in front of the vehicle as Geoff slowly accelerated. I was afraid that he was going to hit one of them, but at the same time we felt a little threatened and it took ages to shake them off. There were no shepherds or farmers within miles. I was glad I was not a hiker.

We found a spot on our beach out of the wind and Geoff painted while I read, lying on the warm sand. We paddled briefly, very briefly, in the sea that was clear and a gorgeous aquamarine and turquoise, but achingly cold. On the beach the temperature was perfect.

*

I am having problems being paid for my articles that appear almost weekly in one of the two English language newspapers in Athens; my first piece was aired late October and they have now published ten with Geoff's photos and our sketches for which, to date, they have not paid a single drachma. I've told them I am not prepared to submit any more until I am paid and I spoke to the editor who sounded like a Greek-American, well-spoken and apologetic. There had been problems she said. No, it was nothing to with the newspaper per se, which was a fairly new venture, it was doing well she assured me and she promised to deposit the whole sum within days. Ten days have passed and of course, nothing has arrived. I do not believe I will ever be paid, so a visit to Athens is looming.

*

I was coming down the marble steps from the bedroom in my heavy woollen socks that Francesca had sent me for Christmas when I slipped, lost my footing and came plunging down onto my side. It was if I had stepped on ice and luckily Geoff, who was in the kitchen nook, managed to grab me before I tumbled the entire length of the stairs. I was quite shaken; marble is so hard and sharp-edged and I ached all over for what seemed like weeks, fortunately my back appeared to be relatively unaffected by the fall. I have never seen such spectacular blue-purple-black bruises in my life.

*

Following weeks and weeks of amazingly warm and sunny March days the heavens have split asunder and we are being battered by rain, wind and sleet. It is undoubtedly snowing in the mountains as the air has that fresh bite to it. I can actually taste snow on the wind even though it might be miles away; Geoff does not believe me but invariably we discover there has been snow whenever I say I can taste it! We made our way up to the market through the rain and parked by the post office near one of our favourite stalls, but the truck and the congenial, plump little man who wears a black armband was not there. Instead, there was a pile of bricks and some drooping and very wet flowers and a few candles. It looked like a shrine. Later when I asked Iakovos what it was he told me the old boy had been driving his tractor and that it had upturned and killed him. His friends had put the little shrine there to mark his place in the square. I was so touched. We will miss him, not only because his tomatoes were small and red and the most delicious of any we buy, but he was part of our Saturday morning routine; we always bought vegetables and fruit from him first before moving on to the main square and the bigger stalls. Our other favourite is a square, blue-eyed Maniot woman called Vasiliki—a very grand name and she has a proud demeanour to match her name which means Queen. She looks ill most of the time and we have long conversations about her health, I think she suffers from rheumatism. She rattles off at great speed, with me understanding only half of what she says but she is not to know because she never stops to draw breath. She is the only person who sells pumpkins, the sweetest I have ever tasted and one morning she spent several minutes telling me the various ways she cooked it, and in return I gave her my own recipe for pumpkin soup which would surely win a prize at any gourmet competition. I grow sprigs of fresh rosemary, thyme and oregano in pots on the stairs and basil growing on the terrace and I sprinkle our soups liberally with all three, add garlic, carrots, onions and sometimes leeks then a spoonful of local sheep's yoghurt. Finally, sprinkle with parsley and serve with crusty, sourdough wholemeal bread hot from Milya's oven, just off the old square in Areopolis where the Greek War of Independence began all those years ago. Washed down with village wine, this soup tasting of herbs originally from the mountains is hard to beat. Vasiliki asked me to let her have the pumpkin seeds back and when I raved about the flavour of her pumpkins, she said it was because she never, ever, used *farmako*, chemicals, on her vegetables or fruit. But never she repeated, raising her bright blue eyes heavenwards. Greeks in general do not seem to eat much pumpkin although occasionally in mountain communities we see them drying on the roofs, but there is never anyone around to sell one to us.

*

One of our mysterious sea fogs is creeping in as I write. The great headland to the south has disappeared and the olives are shrouded in a spectral vapour which as I stand on the terrace, I can feel is damp and clinging, almost as though someone has walked over my grave. The silver-grey fog as thick as porridge gradually envelopes the ruined Mavromichalis tower then the golden crenellations of the tall tower higher up the plateau; the church with the two belfries is being consumed and soon the ravines, ridges and the crest of Agios Elias with its tiny white chapel will fall prey to the wraith of the swirling sea fog. We will be alone in our tower house with Mahler's solemn sound in our souls and a white and secret world around us; the mystery of living in the Deep Mani compels me to wonder if we will ever want to leave this place.

*

I realise I have not seen Flossie the foal nor her mother since well before Christmas; their rotund and smiling owner seems also to have disappeared. There is no sign of life around the spotlessly clean white house in the lane up the hill where he lives with an equally large but grubby woman, presumably his wife. I hope they reappear and that I see Flossie again. Animals mean a lot to me. Michalis the farmer tells us that his pregnant sow, Helen of Troy, will give birth next month, her teats are noticeably larger and she becomes broader in the beam as the weeks go past. She tries to rush up to the stone wall where we stand with our offerings, but her tether is so short she can't quite reach us so she stands restrained, squealing, snorting and grunting, ears alert. She and Menelaus are both very tame and it seems criminal to me to have her tethered so she is unable to come and get the titbits we bring her. Our walks take us in many different directions, one of them to the edge of this plateau where we look down over a lower plateau criss-crossed with stone walled fields, an old church and a few stone huts. We have been befriended by the shepherd's dog, a smiling creature with a shaggy thick coat, tan and white—she looks a bit like a collie. She lies along one of the stone walls dividing the fields guarding her flock of goats all day and when she sees us from afar, she comes leaping over the walls like an antelope, tail a-wag and almost turns herself inside out with delight, rolling on the ground with all four legs in the air in obeisance then leaps up and licks our hands. We share the pig's bread with her although she is not hungry, then she follows us, prancing around and making little sallies ahead of us, turning her head, tongue hanging, waiting for us to catch up but as we get further away from her flock she starts to hesitate and looks embarrassed. She wags her tail almost apologetically and eventually turns away to jump onto her wall where she settles down on guard once more and will not budge another inch. I find this quite amazing as she is alone with her flock but knows instinctively where she is supposed to be and will not abandon them, despite her obvious pleasure at being with us.

*

March the seventeenth and today Greeks celebrate the anniversary of the start of the Revolution in 1821 that culminated in ridding the Peloponnese of the Turkish yoke after three and a half centuries. The spot where the flag was first raised is marked in the cobbled square beside Taxiarches church, and today blue and white bunting flutters in the breeze. The Maniots in their finery are verging on the tiny square while policemen, smart in their tight uniforms direct the traffic away from the centre and I can feel excitement in the cold air. Fortunately, the sun is shining; yesterday it rained heavily with occasional fierce and destructive gusts of wind. A wooden platform with seats for visiting dignitaries faces the flagpole, the army band stands at attention, the young men in camouflage fatigues, excited children in national costume are arriving by the bus-load to celebrate the Mani's most momentous day. Areopolis's hero, Petrobey Mavromichalis, the leader of the Revolution, the most powerful man in the Mani, was also a member of the secret international organisation, the *Filiki Etreia,* that planned the Revolution. We considered waiting to see the children march and to hear the band but memories of the tiring hours I spent in eastern Crete in past years, waiting for these ceremonies to get underway, prompted me to suggest we went to Gytheio as planned and we could watch the celebrations there. But nothing was going on in

Gytheio and we realised that it was in Areopolis that the Revolution began—hence the major function here. Greece's official National Day, celebrating the start of the Revolution is on the twenty-fifth of March by which time the Maniots had been active for a week, so we will see the actual ceremony next week.

*

We delivered Geoff's first batch of greeting cards to Georgios in Gytheio; he was too busy to spend time with us, so we bought our usual village wine and a few groceries at the supermarket and headed east following the winding coastline through ugly flat country, saved only by bright groves of oranges still in fruit and the occasional purple splendour of the Judas tree that flowers before Easter. At Scala we turned inland still heading east, until we came to the ancient town of Geraki perched on a steep hill overlooking the vast plain of Lakonia. The road up through the town is steep and narrow, opening out into a square with a magnificent plane tree and a fountain, and then it curves sinuously between the tall buildings straight down the hillside until it meets the plain. Looking back, I could see cyclopean walls straddling the top of the rise—this was an ancient place full of history. In a lush field of olives standing in wildflowers we investigated the arches of an aqueduct which originally would have spanned the broad valley. Pretty country, grape hyacinths, poppies and pale pink asphodels abound, the air was bitingly cold but once again the sun was comfortingly warm though there were clouds about and I was happier in the car. The gleaming slopes of the Parnonas mountains that stretch down the eastern finger of the Peloponnese beckoned so we decided to go to Kosmas and find somewhere to have lunch, although we did have spinach pies with us. There had been a heavy snowfall and as soon as the road left the plain, we found ourselves in a silent, white world, the car tracks narrow between two high ridges of snow. The snow plough had been at work. High valleys, snow smooth and pristine, fell away from us on one side while on the other the conifers bowed low beneath their white mantles; these mountains are heavily forested and look more like central Europe than southern Greece to me. All sound was muffled and when we stopped the car it was as though we were the only creatures alive.

At the highest point—seventeen hundred metres—light snow was beginning to fall; flakes drifted past and melted on the windscreen and the mountains surrounding us lost their definition, softened by the snowfall. We reached the mountain village of Kosmas and looked down on the buildings; thick snow lay on the rooftops and the trees, everything looked so clean. "It could be Switzerland," we remarked at the same moment. In the square the snow plough at the ready throbbed quietly, it looked like a giant Darth Vader waiting for an electronic signal so it could charge the unseen enemy, but the driver was nowhere to be seen. We parked the car and I stepped out into the snow and felt the crispness and slight resistance beneath my boots, it was powdery soft to touch and lay thickly on every surface. We looked for signs of life— smoke coming from the chimney flue, a ventilation pipe sticking out of the taverna wall or lights—but the place was deserted except for one old man and a dog that barked at us for a moment then trotted away, leaving his footprints in the smooth surface. Siesta time and the inhabitants of Kosmas were asleep; we would not find our cup of sweet Greek coffee. Wandering round the silent square, huge flakes drifted down and touched my cheek softly. A jaunty snowman stood on a marble table between gigantic lichen-covered plane trees, deep layers of snow lay along the branches. A bizarre sight outside a modern restaurant of plastic tables and chairs with thick white cushions and tablecloths of snow, a giant *pithos*, earthen jar, stood half submerged in a snowdrift against a wall. A wild plum in delicate flower bent beneath its frosty cover and glistening icicles, some two feet long, reminded me of the miraculous scene in the movie Dr Zhivago when he and Lara took refuge in the country house and the icicles tinkled in the breeze. We did not dare stay long as the snow was coming down more heavily in blinding white swirls and we had no chains, so reluctantly we drove away, our tyres swishing and skidding in the slush and gradually descended through the wintry world of conifers, snow drifts and icicles to the flatlands below.

In the evening we went out to Xanthi's since neither of us felt like cooking and anyway we had nothing in the fridge. It was bright and cold with the sky full of stars but when we opened the door to the welcome of her taverna she looked up in dismay and shook her head as she stirred a large pot on the wood stove; she was not ready she explained—the taverna had been open all day to cater for the crowd of visitors who attended the celebrations and no doubt she was still serving lunch at six p.m. So the evening meal would be later than usual. Greeks traditionally do not even venture out for a meal much before nine or nine thirty, even in winter, but we have found that we tend to eat earlier when darkness closes in. We should go for a *volta*, stroll, or wait for ten minutes she suggested. We both knew what a Greek ten minutes meant and neither of us felt like walking around in the icy air or sitting in the empty taverna and by then it was after eight, so we came home and boiled an egg that we enjoyed with crusty bread slathered with thick yellow butter. We would try again tomorrow when she was better organised.

*

Next evening and the weather had closed in. As we left the tower house in the car, we found it was snowing, the wind lifting the lovely soft flakes as they swirled around. It took only a few minutes to reach Xanthi's taverna that stands in the main cobbled street with tall stone houses on either side, the lamp was swinging in the darkness and it was just like stepping into a film set. Snow and snowfalls are fairly new to me and I have always suspected that snow scenes look false when the flakes go whirling round at all angles, but they really do, they are so light the wind easily carries them hither and thither. Stepping inside the warmth of the taverna was a joy, Xanthi was not there but her husband and her teenage son, Yiannis, looked after us. The menu included *spanakorizo*, one of her specialities, a simple and flavoursome rice and spinach dish which we ordered amongst other things. Yiannis disappeared into the kitchen only to return a moment later full of apologies; there was only one portion left of the *spanakorizo*—his younger brothers had eaten the rest! We seemed to be doomed but Yiannis, after apologising profusely, suggested goat stew and presented it with a flourish; it was delicious! Tender morsels steeped in all varieties of wild greens, potatoes and onions and a hint of cinnamon I thought, accompanied with local bread in chunks and unashamedly used to soak up the mouth-watering juices; my oh my I was so pleased Yiannis's younger brother had eaten all the *spanakorizo*! It was not the first time I had eaten goat by any means, during my few years in Urambo in western Tanganyika, the only meat available in the local butcher's shop was goat and our *mpishi*, cook, certainly knew how to prepare and tenderise it in several different and most acceptable ways. The saga was over.

*

I leapt out of bed the following morning and opened the shutters to find the mountains drenched with snow shimmering like silk as it flowed down the contours of the high peaks and crevices. The storm had abated, the sun was shining and the sky was clear of clouds; perfect weather for doing something. After a cheerful breakfast of fresh coffee, porridge and hot brown bread from Milya's bakery, we set off on another *ekdromi*. I like that word; it calls to the gypsy in me; it means adventure and new faces and places. But today we did not go far, about five kilometres down the road going south, alongside the soaring bank of mountains covered in snow to the small and rambling village of Pyrgos Dirou, famous for a battle in 1826 between three hundred Maniot women wielding only their sickles and fifteen hundred Ottoman and Egyptian artillerymen arriving in galleys near Areopolis to threaten the Maniot rear. This to assist Ibrahim the Egyptian Pasha to rid the land of the Maniots which would enable him to cut the line of communication between the north and south of the Mani. These courageous women, all larger than life physically and using nothing but their sickles, drove the Ottomans and Egyptians back to their ships. Next day, so the story goes, they were joined by the few remaining men, most of them having gone north to concentrate their forces leaving the Deep Mani almost defenceless. The still outnumbered Maniots managed to repel the invaders, and only a third of the Egyptians survived by heading for their boats and lived to tell the tale; the remainder fell to the sickles of the furious and feisty females who are remembered as the Amazons of Dirou and there is a magnificent statue of a Maniot woman, head high, defiantly wielding a sickle in the village square where the Wednesday morning market is held. It is a stirring statue and a stirring story.

The triumphant strains of this warlike chorus were allegedly sung by the women as they fought. but I have to admit I was unaware of its existence while we were living in Areopolis. I understand some of the spirited Maniot women still sing this song on the anniversary of their magnificent victory over the invading Egyptians. I would so love to hear them.

O Turkish men, have you no shame
To war with womenfolk?
We are alone, our men are gone
To fight at Almira.
But we with sickles in our hands
Will lop off your heads like corn!

On my return home I went onto the Internet—good old Google—and found this defiant message sent back to Ibrahim Pasha of Egypt in reply to this message brought by envoy to the Mani demanding its surrender or else "he would pillage it." This was sent to him before the famous battle.

"From the few Greeks of Mani and the rest of Greeks who live there to Ibrahim Pasha. We received your letter in which you try to frighten us saying that if we don't surrender, you'll kill the Maniots and plunder Mani. That's why we are waiting for you and your army. We, the inhabitants of Mani, sign and wait for you."

It obviously does not pay to tangle with the inhabitants of the Mani peninsula who are still considered by many to be the direct descendants of the warrior Spartans. No doubt future research may deem this belief to be questionable, but I want to pursue this subject when I can.

This village is incredibly old with winding, high-walled lanes, invasive Frankish figs pry into deserted and crumbling stone buildings and many towers, some restored and occupied others in ruins, courtyards hold sun-loving lizards, primitive ninth-century barrel-vaulted chapels and naturally, a fully restored Byzantine church. We spend a rewarding few hours photographing, exploring and discovering new wildflowers and as always, finding abandoned towers we would like to restore and live in. Such dreamers are we. On the outskirts we come across an outcrop of white marble in a field of multicoloured wildflowers; colossal slabs and curved rocks as big as a house lie on the ground and we think at first, that we have found a partially buried, ancient chapel but it turns out to be an entire hillside of marble erupting out of the ground. Some has been mined and we see the straight sides where some instrument has been used to cut huge slabs away; the remains lie there forgotten in their bed of flowers. Nearby, the tallest watchtower stands in good condition—unoccupied—with its own small church attached and behind the tower, we discover a huge square cistern like a swimming pool cut from marble and full of weeds and creepy crawlies.

*

The gods are angry about something; it is the twenty-fifth of March and Greek Independence Day. Since midnight, a ferocious gale has seized us in its grip and we are in the throes of a torrential downpour with rain flying horizontally past the windows while savage gusts like mini-hurricanes, thud into the walls of this tower house. I know now why the inhabitants of the Deep Mani built their towers with metre-thick stone walls, not only for protection from their feuding enemies but also to withstand these gales that come thundering through the gap in the mountains, ripping up everything in sight. Stephanos told us of a scary episode he experienced while driving during one of Areopolis's famous windstorms; an old Volkswagen body that had been lying on the roadside for many years was suddenly lifted up by the wind and propelled towards him down the road at great speed. He only just managed to avoid being hit by driving off the road into the bushes and on the same day, a bus was completely overturned on the escarpment to Oitylo. We will not be going out today, although Geoff has just donned his wet weather gear to collect more olive logs for the fire and to unplug the drain hole on the terrace that is blocked up with leaves and rubbish hurled in by the elements. I love *real* weather, I really do!

*

CHAPTER ELEVEN

A HIDDEN BYZANTINE GEM

On our way back from an abortive trip to Gytheio to see Elias the lawyer, who was not in his office, Geoff turned down a strip of road on the outskirts of Areopolis that led to the hamlet of Kouskouni crouched beneath the looming mountain. Wildflowers of so many varieties on either side of the road, poppies shouting red, yellow Jerusalem sage vying with gorse for brilliance, tall white flag irises, ivory cistus with yellow centres; the pink variety smothered in a thousand buds and about to bloom. Long sprays of purple sage lined the roadside and the air was heady with its pungent aroma and masses of oregano grew from crevices in the stone walls along the roadsides as new green shoots sprouted on thyme after its winter sleep. We parked beside a walled mausoleum with a plaque dated '28.8.87' in memory of the sister of someone called Eleni Stavrolaimous, but I was unable to understand the rest of the inscription.

Turning towards the Bay of Limeni far down beyond the stands of olives along the narrow coastal plain, we found to our astonishment and delight that we were looking down onto a small Byzantine church of red-tiled roofs hiding against the cliff on the edge of a deep gorge. A precipitous drop to the valley floor, tree-covered with cypress and local oak fell away from a stone wall surrounding the church, stone steps zigzagged sharply down the porous rockface past yawning caves gouged out by water. Dark and secret grottos harboured maidenhair fern, wild parsley, shy mauve cyclamen, a waxy white flower, star-shaped and thick carpets of moss. I heard a blackbird and the soaring, falling notes of a nightingale above the faint sound of the crashing waves far below. It was a wondrous place, silent but for the birdsong. Shrubs, small trees and vines covered the rising slopes above the church as far as the eye could see and along the cliff-face, many caves mostly hidden in foliage; I learned later these were once inhabited by hermits. A delicate covering of spring leaf was just visible on the deciduous trees, although mostly the trees were evergreen oaks, their acorns lying thickly on the ground. On a sunny slope beside pale yellow mustard flowers, scarlet poppies stood above their beds of white chamomile daisies, and an ivory-tinted head of florets on a long stem suggested wild onion, and I glimpsed sky-blue irises on stiff stems. It was cold and damp in the shadow of the hill so we decided to return the next morning to sketch and paint when hopefully, the sun would be on the church. But I suspected that I would be unable to capture the magic of this secret place.

Next day and we are painting the little church; the sun though weak, has obediently peeped over the cliffs behind us and the red roof tiles on the various roofs that are at different angles, are glowing. Geoff sits below me level with the church, legs outstretched, totally absorbed while I am much higher up on the steps in full sun with a sweeping view of the gorge, the valley and the bay of Oitylo that includes the narrow coastal strip with its scattering of red-roofed houses and another domed church dwarfed by distance. The bay curves and stretches far to the Northern Cape and today the sea is calm and flat, no sound of waves. Past Nea Oitylo and across the gorge, the Monastery of Doukoulo sits halfway up the bluff, very Italian looking with cypresses pointing darkly against the hillside. I am quite pleased with my painting after all!

April, and the warmest day so far this year. The temperature has risen to twenty degrees Celsius and we are celebrating the change by going for a drive into the plateau villages and hamlets of the mighty headland known as Cavo Grosso, the Great Cape, that bulges out into the ocean for ten kilometres between Mesapo and Gerolimenas. These towered settlements seem to be untouched by this century apart from the ubiquitous television spires and our presence barely noticed by the locals, possibly due to our Greek number plates. The countryside is a-glow with a profusion of wildflowers and shrubs: Judas trees in purple bloom—the name and the colour supposedly signify the blood Judas shed over Easter. The blossoms mingle with the brightness of gorse on the hillsides and road edges as if some discerning and sensitive gardener has been given the task of beautifying the drive. On reaching the southern end of the Cape we follow a narrow road down a cliffside pulsating with golden gorse, broom, wild mustard and Jerusalem sage with its soft grey leaves, and now the aromatic purple sage, blue periwinkle and new saffron shafts of Aaron's Rod which goes by the ugly name of Mullein. It is as though all the shades of yellow are competing with one other.

We stop at Yiannis and Spiros's hotel in Gerolimenas and are greeted warmly by the brothers whose names I always mix up; I cannot tell them apart unless they are standing together. We order *kalamari* and *horiatiki salata*, squid and Greek village salad, with retsina and sit at our old spot by the harbour wall enjoying the sun. Seagulls wheel and call, pale against the sheer sides of the cliff; a few fishing boats are in the bay, most of them still beached as it is a bit early in the year for reliable weather. Yiannis talks to us, cynical as ever, but when I ask him if he is happy, he replies:

"My wife loves me she tells me. My two children are at university and of course I have many expenses. But I think I am content."

Geoff asks whether university in Greece is free and he snorts and says it is supposed to be but there are always shortages of books, so he does not think it is free. I ask if students work part-time to help with expenses and he explains ruefully that it is not possible as unemployment is so high in Athens. I remark that hopefully, he was making a good investment in his offspring and that the children will look after him in his old age as he in turn, is caring for his aged parents. He looks a bit askance at my statement and is not sure that things are the same any longer; children have lost their respect for their elders he says, and he blames the influence of too much American television. I have noticed that Greeks in general have no time for Americans; they distrust them and accuse them of manipulation and double standards.

*

On the way home we stop once again to see the donkey with Flossie, her fluffy foal. I clamber over a stone wall to stroke the youngster; she approaches me cautiously then gambols back for a quick pull at her mother's teats, but she is having none of it and keeps nudging her baby away each time. Flossie stands back in surprise perhaps—her outsize ears so expressive, always in motion—but she remains unsteady on her long legs with hooves so tiny, about the size of milk bottle tops. She is curious about me but not quite brave enough to stand still while I stroke her—and I find it difficult to drag myself away. I adore her. I discover a female donkey is called 'a Jenny' and I wonder why?

*

Hans rang and asked us over for a coffee so we walked up the lane to his tower house where he and Iakovos met us at the gate in the high wall; it is always locked in true Maniot fashion. We were chatting upstairs in Hans's living room-cum-kitchen when someone said something about our computer. I had noticed a laptop sitting on the table and suddenly I realised it was our computer! Had they brought it back from Sparta for us? Yes, they said, they had been in Sparta and had decided to visit Tasos who was, for once, in his office. He apparently told them that our computer was not in the office and he would have to go and get it. They then mentioned casually that they would bring in the police if he did not return with it immediately, fearing he would do a runner! Unbelievably he was back within half an hour with the computer which he said had been mended. I smothered the boys with hugs and kisses, speechless with gratitude and raced home to try it out. It seemed to be fine. Is this really the end of the saga after four months of hassle and ill humour and tension which ridiculously, more often than not led to silly arguments between Geoff and me? We'll see.

What we have decided is that we need a receipt from Tasos

recording exactly when we bought the computer for the purposes of the warranty, also to extend our six-month's access to the Internet for which we paid sixty thousand drachma that includes the four months it has been out of order.

To follow up on this subject, we are off to the central west coast and hinterland of the Peloponnese via Sparta where we will attempt to get Tasos to sign a document I have drawn up. On our arrival Geoff went in to get his signature as I had decided I never wanted to see the wretched man again; some fifteen minutes later Geoff returned looking a bit hang-dog to say Tasos would only sign the extension of the Internet contract and had flatly refused to sign the receipt. Enraged, I stormed in, he was slumped along his desk with his head in his hands in an attitude of total despair. I ignored his plea for pity and asked him why he had refused to sign the receipt and told him he was a disgrace to his countrymen and that I had never, during my nine years in Greece, been treated in this manner. I demanded that he sign the receipt. He refused and gave me the same story he had given Geoff, that his receipt book was with his accountant and he would send it to us 'next week'. I snorted and suggested he was not telling the truth and asked why he refused to give us his signature, was it because the computer he had sold me was stolen? He didn't reply—he never does—and shook his head, sighed deeply, and slumped lower behind his desk. I then announced that I intended to sit there until he did sign even if it took all day. He thought for a moment then said, "OK, Valerie," and passed me a piece of blank paper and a pen on which I wrote the date of purchase and computer details which he signed without a murmur. End of story, I hope!

*

We are in Kiparissia on the central west coast of the Peloponnese in a hotel by the sea. After a rest and a shower, we find a *psarotaverna* overlooking the sea and choose our fish. The Greek salad came with the bread and *tzatziki*, then we waited and waited; where was the fish? We were becoming slightly irritable when our waiter turned up with one portion of three small fish. Overcome with embarrassment he explained in excellent English that the larger fish we had also ordered had disintegrated during cooking and was no good. Was there anything else we would like? Geoff, ever the gentleman, refused to share my small portion and chose *souvlakia*, a popular Greek fast food consisting of small pieces of all kinds of meat and occasionally fish or vegetables, generally eaten straight off the skewer. He ordered chips of course, which I shared of course—no one can resist Greek chips when freshly prepared, however we had to wait for these as well but they were very good. When the bill came, they only charged us for the *souvlakia* and wine, and apologised yet again for the fish debacle.

Next morning following breakfast we drove up to the fortress high above the town, it was very hot and I was over-dressed, and uncomfortable. Not much remains of the castle although the outer walls are rather fine, wildflowers abound and I watched a bumblebee moving like a Lancaster bomber from poppy to poppy, many of which folded downwards under his weight, briefly trapping him. He became quite flustered and eventually reversed out covered in yellow pollen, buzzing loudly to try the next one. Lemon yellow and white butterflies floated lazily around as we looked down on the old red roofs of the town while in the soaring pines, blackbirds carolled as if their hearts would burst.

A spectacular scenic drive into the mountains left the humid coastal plain behind, we were on our way to Karytaina high in the mountains. We stopped for a Greek coffee and as the engine faded the sound of rushing water filled my ears. The tiny mountain hamlet of Lepeos has a central square that stands against a steep cliff down which races a mountain stream—a river almost—through stone channels then flows under humpbacked bridges, past the stained walls of old houses that stand in the rushing water then under the road and into a green valley. Patches of white arum lilies, yellow daisies and purple irises cling to the edges of the channel, and high above, gigantic plane trees in spring leaf spread their branches.

I watched two tinkers at work. They were both wearing heavy

gloves and boots as they sat by the stream and polluted the water with various chemicals. One, using makeshift bellows, was fanning a small fire and melting tin solder to resurface copper pots and containers from the village. The older of the two was scrubbing the mended utensils with some kind of foul-smelling acid then dipping them into the running water. I wondered how the people, livestock and crops fared downstream. They were very friendly and said they came from Pyrgos on the coast and travelled round the area mending broken containers. They asked if we were German and as always, were delighted to hear we came from Australia. The Greeks know about the German/Italian occupation of Crete and the major role played by the Australians, New Zealanders and the British in ridding the island of the enemy occupation.

As we approached Karytaina we stopped the car to photograph the castle that stands supreme on a high plateau rising out of the great gorge of the Alfeios River, a perfect place for a castle. An old shepherd with his dogs stopped by the car for a chat. And chat he did! I understood most of what he was saying; he was seventy-five and how old was I? How many children did I have? I hesitated to say we had eight between us so said "four!" Bravo, he enthused. He had six but they had all gone away and he was alone as his wife had died and if we were staying nearby, we should come and have coffee with him, and he pointed to some quite substantial houses on a green plateau across the ravine above the river. I thanked him and said we were not staying, but intended to climb to the *kastro*, castle. It was a fine *kastro*, he said proudly, as if it belonged to him, and perhaps it did in a sense. We parked the car as far up the hill as we could drive and climbed the old steps and path to the remains of the crumbling castle where only a few of the battlements were standing. A brave Greek flag fluttered on top of a terrifying bastion with nothing between me and the vertiginous drop to the old town below, and it was also scorchingly hot. I felt slightly dizzy.

Next day we drove on to the mountain village Andritsaina known as 'The Switzerland of Greece'. It really does resemble Switzerland with its traditional architecture and chalet-style houses, steep hillsides and plunging ravines and is quite charming but lacking in a choice of accommodation at this time of year; we were the only clients at the one hotel, a barn of a place run by two elderly women. In the evening we ate in a tiny and most attractive taverna in one of the side streets, avoiding the more touristy bright lights in the main street. A Dutchman with his young son came in and we started chatting, he was taking his son around the Peloponnese on a motorbike 'because he had turned sixteen' which I found most endearing.

*

While driving round the Deep Mani with our visiting friends from Australia, Jane and Mike, whom we met off the hydrofoil at Monemvasia, we crossed the peninsula just above Vatheia, and through the pass we came across hundreds of astonishingly tall candelabras of yellow flowers emerging from long thick spikes; they looked like giant asparagus. Jane thought they were fennel, and although the frilly leaf looked like fennel, it had no smell at all. It resembled a miniature, yellow sisal which I knew it wasn't of course. Later I found out it was in fact *ferula communis*, a giant fennel, she was right. The giant candelabras were spectacular as they rose above the rounded clumps of euphorbia whose lime-yellow flower heads were metamorphosing into to a russet-red colour and looked quite autumnal across the hillsides. Purple Judas trees were still in flower although the green leaves of spring were starting to replace the blossoms.

I am fond of Jane and recognise a true kindred spirit from the old colonial days. Her father was the governor of Tanganyika when my father was municipal secretary, among many other titles. Jane and I are quite alike and I often see myself in her, so does Geoff which is amusing. I admire Mike for his enthusiasm and unbounded physical energy which is unhampered by a gammy leg from early polio. We did enjoy seeing them and showing them around although it was for only three days. They stayed in the GNTO's converted tower house in great style in a huge en suite with full-sized bath, heating, huge towels, you name it they had it, plus a full breakfast. It wasn't cheap she said, but the Deep Mani is expensive and the locals intend to keep it that way in an attempt to keep out the riff-raff—I hope they succeed. During their visit we drove them all over the Deep Mani, took picnic lunches and ate in tavernas in the evenings—it was a fun time and surprised Jane, who had told me that when she was recently in Aegina, her friends told her the Mani was dreary and an awful place to visit, whereas she and Mike were fascinated with the region and loved its drama; they felt it was much like the Scottish Highlands. There is also a similarity in that the Scots too were feuding and fighting, clan against clan for centuries, just like the Maniots, right to the end of the last century. They were returning to Athens to join a tour led by Margaret and Gough Whitlam, Labour ex-prime minister of Australia and his wife.

When they left by bus for Athens, I was sure that I was going to see them again quite soon, but I had no idea where, so the thought was ridiculous—but I knew it was not. The day after they left, another friend arrived several days earlier than arranged, so we did not have a breather which we found quite difficult after our normally quiet existence. She stayed a week in the Tzimova guest house in our old room off the courtyard and was extremely comfortable. We explored the Outer and Deep Mani and returned to Olympia which she was longing to see, and as we were about to leave the museum, we bumped into Jane and Mike! Once again, my hunch proved to be accurate, I was convinced that we would see them again. They were enjoying being guided by the Whitlams and we had a close look at the couple as they walked by; goodness how old they have become, and I had forgotten how enormously tall they were.

*

CHAPTER TWELVE

GREEK ORTHODOX EASTER

Good Friday and the Church of Taxiarches was a-bustle with the local population going in and out, crossing themselves with the hand then resting momentarily on the breast in final acknowledgement. In they came, the women chattering and exchanging greetings not in muted tones as one might expect, and not as vociferously as normal, but noisy still. They moved with reverence to the altar to kiss the flower-covered bier representing the body of Christ following his crucifixion; the children were pushed beneath the coffin and through to the other side and those that complained were severely chastised. Further commotion. The excited crowd then piled out into the cobbled square to continue their gossip at greater pitch which almost, but not quite, outweighed the microphone tones of the priest's monotonous chant. These services drone on for hours with the congregation changing all the time although the very elderly and the pious sit quietly in the pews watching the goings on, dark eyes sharp beneath their black headscarves. It is not surprising the services are so relaxed for no Greek could possibly stay still or silent for so many hours of reverence. All the women were dressed in black tonight for it is a serious occasion, this remembrance of Christ on the cross. We wandered around the square avoiding the screeching, racing children, some noticeably young ones, many of whom were setting off fireworks, but the occasional muffled boom told us that not only fireworks were at work tonight but also dynamite. It reminded me of the little English-Greek boy in Kroustas, a mountain village outside Agios Nikolaos in Crete, who, two Easter's ago was helping his older friends stuff dynamite into a length of piping and it exploded and blew most of his hand and fingers away. There are always tragedies over Easter as the Greeks are obsessed with the noise element when they are celebrating anything, and it starts young. I can hear gunshots too. They also occasionally go astray and at the risk of sounding irreverent it is often not only Christ's death that is mourned at Easter but that of the recipient of a stray bullet fired by an excitable Greek. A photographer was recently shot at a wedding somewhere in Greece that rapidly turned into a tragedy.

We bumped into Stephanos and his brother-in-law as we walked home down the steep high-walled lane that leads directly from the square to our tower house. I could not help noticing they had been drinking, they were both relaxed and decidedly merry; would we come to share their Easter lunch tomorrow they asked, to eat lamb on the spit? Of course, we accepted with delight and hands were shaken several times, laughter shared. Stephanos had brought Yiannis, his father home after a three-month absence in Athens during which time he had undergone an operation on his lung for cancer. Yiannis, still a big man, has lost a good deal of weight and looks fragile and unsteady but the yellow-grey pallor of his skin has now been replaced by a healthier, pinkish tone and his high blood pressure has been reduced.

Stephanos told us the procession carrying the bier would come past our entrance after the service and we planned to join in; it would come soon he said and gave a laugh, "well within an hour or two," he added. We know about Greek times so we made a Greek coffee and watched television, but of course being Easter, the channels were showing mainly biblical films, old and badly acted, or church services. Not quite our viewing choice! There is no escaping this most important religious festival.

When the service finally ended the bells rang out and we heard the priest chanting as the procession came down the street towards the two little chapels at the entrance to the property. I could also hear the tired spaniel howling his head off outside the Tzimova guest house; he will suffer from nervous exhaustion before the end of Easter I am certain. We could smell the incense and hear the firecrackers getting louder and louder as they came nearer, the priests stopped and chanted more loudly for a moment and then moved on up the laneway. Joining the crowd of several hundred well-dressed Maniots all holding candles, we followed the bier led by several priests in their richly coloured robes and tall black hats. The procession wound round the narrow-walled lanes of Areopolis lit by scores of candles on walls and niches and each time we came to a Byzantine church or a chapel—and there are many around the town—the priests stopped fleetingly to chant. They moved slowly, with solemn dignity, enveloped in the clinging aroma of incense as it mingled with that of the candles and the smell of cordite as firecrackers went off in quick succession. The stone houses and towers in the Deep Mani are approached through courtyards with massive wooden doors that are always closed and locked so one can never see into their gardens. The Maniots are a very private people quite unlike other Greeks and many of them live in great style with beautiful traditional furnishings, fine rugs and *pithoi*, earthenware pots, and have a passion for flowers. Just for this one evening all the courtyard doors and the entrances into the houses were wide open, candles lit and lights ablaze, gigantic vases of decorative leaves and flowers and pots of freesias stood at the open doors. It was obvious the womenfolk had spent weeks preparing their showroom for the eyes of those in the Good Friday procession and it was immensely satisfying to be able to have a glimpse of their paved courtyards, spring gardens and the interior of their homes for a change. Proud homes for proud people.

The Maniots, both men and women are in the main a large people, most of the men are well over six feet, more than two metres in height, big-boned and broad as well. The women are also often tall and broad of shoulder—occasionally somewhat authoritarian in their appearance and demeanour and it felt as if we were walking among the giants of Homer's time, the Laestrygonians, through these medieval streets. I felt dwarfed by the people around me and Geoff looked short, which he is not. I was a little apprehensive in the very narrow lanes because, as always, young boys were setting off not only firecrackers but alarmingly big explosives, the shock waves resounding along the narrow laneways contained by the solid stone walls. The small children did not seem to be put out by the crackers as they danced along holding the hands of their *yiayias*, grandmothers and parents and I wondered how my little granddaughter Alexandra, would have fared had she been with us, holding our hands; I kept feeling that she and Francesca should be with us. It was a most moving experience, and I can imagine that were one religious it would have colossal significance. As it was, I felt that I was part of history and of a pageant that had gone on since the arrival of Christianity in the ninth century; and although the mighty Maniots were feudal and warlike, they had always put down their arms and grievances and behaved peaceably during the Easter festivities, and for centuries had walked along these same lanes with the same ardently religious fervour that I saw on the faces of today's inhabitants.

On Easter Sunday we crossed the garden to join Yiannis and his family for lamb on the spit that Panayiotis, one of his sons-in-law was cooking. His two young sons, Yiannis and Stephanos were a lively pair, excited about Easter and it was nice to have children around us for a change. Maria, Yiannis's daughter did not speak a word of English so I got an earful of the local lingo which was useful and I managed to respond fairly intelligently, I think. Stephanos lives in Gytheio but having seen him last night absolutely plastered out of his mind we wondered whether he would make it to the family get-together. They phoned him well after midday and he turned up looking quite ghastly and without Susie his wife, who, he said graphically, was busy throwing up after last night's excesses. So, we broke our red-dyed hard-boiled eggs against those of the boys and feasted with a reduced family on an entire succulent lamb, brown and crisp from the spit redolent with rosemary and other flavours I could not identify, with potatoes in lemon and herbs, bowls of colourful crisp salads, chunks of village bread for dipping into delicious *tzatziki*, that refreshing side dish of sheep or goat's yogurt with grated cucumber, loads of garlic and chopped mint.

Hours drifted past as we became enveloped in the generous company of our Maniot friends as we sat around the table on the covered veranda, the surrounding shrubs in pale spring leaf, the square shape of 'our' tower house beyond and big black dog Azore, tethered mercifully, watched us tail a-wag but mainly asleep. Copious amounts of light village wine were heartily imbibed as we clinked our glasses and the usual *stin yiamas*, to our health, was called out with glasses raised. An ancient belief decrees that the five senses should be recognised when drinking wine: sight, sound, smell, taste and touch—with eyes meeting.

The afternoon ended up with a glass of fortified wine of "a very special vintage" proudly announced by Stephanos, glassy-eyed by then; it was indeed quite delicious and made waking up after our very late siesta almost out of the question.

*

CHAPTER THIRTEEN

HAVE I EATEN HELEN OF TROY?

A few weeks ago, Michalis the farmer moved our favourite pregnant sow whom I have named Helen of Troy into what used to be Menelaus's paddock—but our boar friend has disappeared and Michalis has freed Helen of her tether; I was astonished at the speed with which she thundered up to us when we called, worried that she might abort her young. She was colossal and her teats so swollen I felt certain it was about time for her to give birth, then she too disappeared, and I naively thought she had been taken to another pen to produce her litter and would soon reappear with lots of little pink piglets. But no. The paddock remained empty and we missed her communicatory grunts and snorts; the way she used to stop and think when we spoke to her, and how she registered faint disapproval when she had finished the bread and realised that all we had left were vegetables. Her reactions were almost human. When we next saw Michalis I asked him where she was. He said she had had twelve piglets, lain on ten the first day and on the last two the next day. He smiled sadly and I was horrified and asked him what happened to her. Another smile—fainter—and his graphic body language intimated that he had slit her throat because she was a bad mother. I found this most upsetting as she had become my favourite pig friend of all time. Last week we joined some of our human friends at Nikos's taverna where I happily ordered roast pork and was enjoying it when suddenly an awful thought struck me, and I can hardly bear to write the words. Could it have been Helen of Troy I was enjoying? I may never eat pork again!

*

We have just found out why the phone has been cut off for a week; the bill has not been paid but we've never seen it! One hundred and sixty thousand drachmae is a bit of a shock, but it was installed in early September so the cost is hardly surprising. We have had my second grandson's birth that of course involved many overseas calls, plus other birthdays in both of our families, plus Christmas; also we have used it for the Internet on the occasions we have managed to make contact with it. Stephanos just kept saying he had received no bill for us, so we stopped asking, which was stupid. Obviously, it had to come eventually, so wham! It is only money after all.

Ah well, I decided there was no point in thinking about all of this, so I found some inspiring music instead. Richard Strauss wrote the first of his 'serene and transcendent' *Four Last Songs* for soprano voice when he was a boy of six and wrote the last one a year before his death in 1948 at the age of eight-four. This evening Lucia Popp's sublime voice is making me tingle as once again I am transported to somewhere else, somewhere indistinguishable my pleasure is so profound, only more so now that I am no longer alone

*

I have coughed and wheezed all through the night so am going up to the clinic to see if I can get something for it. Jane gave me a puffer for the asthma that struck so savagely the night after she and Mike arrived from Australia. I have not had an attack for at least four years but have been unbearably allergic for the past week, pollens from flowers and trees used to affect me but not of late—or so I thought—but recently my eyes have almost driven me crazy with irritation and I have sneezed endlessly. But now breathing problems? I simply cannot get my tight chest to loosen up despite deep, slow in-breathing to expand the intake of air then holding, breathing out gradually until the entire rib cage collapses—that plus positive calm thinking used to help—but now nothing does. On second thoughts, looking outside I wonder if a gentle swim might be more beneficial than a visit to the clinic. I tell myself it *will* be more beneficial but my wobbly legs refute the idea and I go to the clinic instead!

*

It is mid-May. I am better and this was our first swim of the season and it was delicious. We were the only people on the beach and although the water was cold, we went in twice, mind you the first time it took a while to adjust to the biting temperature and we were both gasping for breath—I thought I'd been really stupid but kept going, wheezing away. The sandy bay at Oitylo remains shallow for a long way so initially the water felt almost bearable, but as I waded out into the deep the iciness gripped my legs and the dive was quite painful. I found I could only do backstroke with any efficiency and when I tried the crawl, I started coughing so left the water and lay on the inviting warm sand to do some slow, deep breathing for a while. The next time I took the plunge my breathing capability had increased by at least fifty per cent but I felt a little wobbly so I again retired to the sand and sun until I could feel it soaking into my bones, rapidly joined by Geoff who also is not keen on cold immersions. When we got home and after a salad lunch, we lay on the upper terrace and soaked up a bit more sun and vitamins. I felt wonderful for the rest of the day, not in the least bit sluggish, less allergic and my back was not as stiff and painful as it has been. How could a little exercise do so much good? I don't know but it does, and we have both taken on more of a tan, although we have acquired quite a good colour from sitting on the terrace when weather permits—studying Greek, writing and painting—including al fresco breakfasts and lunches as we follow the sun. Fantastic!

The day following our first swim of the year I woke up without a sign of sciatica down my legs, Geoff too, found that his back was less stiff so naturally, we went for a longer dip today and this time we swam quite a distance to the first white house across the bay; the second white house was our goal last summer and tomorrow, after a visit to the market, we will swim a bit further. My breathing has improved and I have not wheezed much at all.

*

It is a wonderful golden-blue day, warm, full of birdsong and the scent of roses. The entrance to our terrace is festooned with the offerings of a glorious red rose, a single variety with a yellow centre; there must be over a hundred blooms, so simple, honest and spectacular and the perfume is delicious especially on hot days. The pot plants on our terrace are all in flower, petunias and geraniums of many shades, mostly grown from the cuttings which I brought from Crete, one a most unusual salmon pink. The wild lavender is blooming, the self-sown poppies in pots are shouting their scarlet brilliance with the first nasturtiums in serious competition, the maidenhair fern from under a damp bridge in Skoutari is thriving and thyme and mint grow inches per day. The wild vine we are training across the terrace to hide the junk at the end of Yiannis's drive, is climbing at an astonishing rate; one can almost see it growing. I check the pots several times a day and I am sure they know they are loved and nurtured—therefore they respond so ardently.

*

And who has returned to his nest with a vengeance? Ugly old ginger tomcat, Kokkino, with his dirty nose and scruffy fur has taken up residence and now sleeps on a mat on the stone bench on the terrace. After we went away for three days last month, he evidently decided we had left for good and did not make an appearance for several days following our return, then he was most offhand and quite unfriendly and I was a bit upset as he had become so tame, but he is now very decidedly part of the household, although he disappears at night and during the day at odd times and is never hungry. There are loads of briefly visiting cats, white ones, white and striped ones, black with two eyes, black with one eye, a sleek, thick-pelted grey creature that I am sure is a blue Burmese and a variety of ginger females to whom Kokkino does not take exception—but he dislikes the foraging males and becomes seriously territorial when they appear.

*

I have been discovering more about the origins of the Taygetus mountains; depending on which book you read their original name, Taleton, was Doric. Currently the word stems from Taygete who was either one of the daughters of Atlas, or a member of Artemis's entourage. The mountain was sacred to the Olympian twins, Artemis and Apollo, although more recently Artemis's entourage disguised themselves as forest *neraidhes*, nymphs who dance on moonlight nights and, should any shepherd be unfortunate enough to glimpse their carousing, he would be thrown to his death from the mountaintops. The shrines at the various summits of the range were dedicated to Apollo but, following Christianity, were rededicated to the *Profitis Elias*, Prophet Elijah. The name day is celebrated annually in July which was when the mystery of the white stones took place last year. The Taygetus limestone range is a hundred kilometres long and is one of the most popular hiking areas in the whole of Greece and its ravines and crags and gorges attract many walkers. We occasionally see them arriving at tavernas and rent rooms looking quite exhausted and at the end of their individual tethers. I do wonder why they do it but obviously the glories of the mountain hikes make up for the exhaustion at the end of each day.

Recently we met Ruth and Georgios who are walking tour guides and last night we went to dinner with them in their old Mani tower house that they are gradually restoring. I gather Georgios is a Maniot and his English ex-teacher companion Ruth, has given up teaching to take elderly Americans and others around the Mani and in Crete. In the summer she moves to Scotland and does the same thing, thus avoiding the Greek soaring temperatures, and the humidity. He is the wildest looking man I have ever seen, not like a Maniot at all with his short, stocky figure and very blue eyes and wild curling prematurely white hair, which falls over his forehead with abandon. He has a lovely open personality, quite different to that of the locals who are initially rather shy and quiet, this might be partly due to the fact that he has lived in Holland for a lot of his life and worked on oil rigs and ships; he seems to have done everything—unlike most men of the Mani—and is, therefore, somewhat more northern European than Greek. He introduced himself and Ruth to us months ago as he works with Stephanos and is to be seen in his red jeep, rushing around and usually in a state of nervous tension caused entirely by the Greek workmen he must employ to do the renovations on his house. He says the only reliable workers are Polish but Stephanos employs them all so they are seldom available, so Georgios has to deal with his own people and they drive him mad with frustration. He says they have no idea of aesthetics although we would question that; in Geoff's opinion as a retired architect, the restored buildings in the Mani are superbly built, using old stone and little mortar.

Georgios was born in the old and virtually abandoned village of Omales that lies a few kilometres down the hill south from us, towards the Bay of Dirou where we sometimes went last summer on warm evenings. It is a silent and beautiful spot on the side of the hill with cobbled paths that meander between rather desolate stone cottages, one or two tall crumbling towers, a little white church with a bell tower, walled paddocks full of Frankish figs, huge, gnarled olives and, rather bizarrely for a Maniot village—a fine stand of young eucalyptus trees. Who could have planted them I wonder? There were many eucalyptus trees in Crete but these are the first I have come across in the Peloponnese. The only person we ever saw in Omales was an old shepherd, friendly and curious, as they all are. At that time there was one ruin under restoration, it belonged to a *very* rich fish taverna owner from Limeni he told us—designed by courtesy of Stephanos of course. It was a fine mansion of three levels each with its own high terrace and long bright rooms with, of all things, a jacuzzi off the huge upper bedroom. A hideous red brick barbecue stood out like a sore thumb in the otherwise pleasingly contoured and terraced garden whose privacy was ensured by a high stone wall encapsulating several gnarled and twisted olives. Lower down the slope we noticed a brand-new tower mansion, rather too clean and pristine for my liking, and to my surprise we could hear sounds of merriment and the splashing of water. A swimming pool in the Mani? Surely not!

The remainder of the stone cottages and buildings were in a state of total disrepair but while looking around—one of the tower houses took our fancy—we went in through a rickety gate and up old stone steps to a flat roof that looked out over ancient walls and rows of olives, glowing grasses and dried candelabras of asphodels to the misty blue of the far horizon. What a perfect place to live! Geoff's creative brain was ticking over I could tell, and we were both fantasising about living there, spending our cicada-filled evenings on a private terrace soaking up beauty and tranquillity, the air redolent with the aromatic scent of hot eucalyptus leaves, dried thyme and oregano. But we made no enquiries. It was just one more barely mentioned plan, half joking but for me at least, with some basis of truth.

Georgios's land lies at the southern edge of this village, one cactus-filled field away from the tower house we had looked at several times last year. How strange I thought to myself, that we should be talking to a man whose family owns the entire village, and who is now restoring a place next to the one we had dreamed of buying last summer. I have always found that fate has curious methods of forging links; was this a link or just a twist of fate leading nowhere or somewhere?

The walled courtyard surrounding their stone house is cobbled with uneven stones and is approached by a fine stone archway and gate that leads down an ancient *kalderimi*, cobbled donkey path, through shimmering olive groves down several plateaux where cows, goats and sheep graze, to rocky cliffs that plunge three hundred and fifty metres down to the churning sea. The house is solidly built on several levels with outer stairs, the ground floor rooms were once stables, and have beautiful barrel-vaulted ceilings, the rough stone walls are painted white and the ceilings have been attractively restored with tightly fitting bamboo poles behind heavy wooden beams. Georgios has used the old worn roof tiles by first layering the roof with new tiles then placing the old ones on top of them, so the effect is of an old, lichen-stained roof but underneath is, in fact new and waterproof, which the old one was not. They now have running water and electricity, and flushing loos at Ruth's insistence, and even a bath in a tiny, curved room with rather alarmingly exposed pipes. The atmosphere is most pleasing and quite quaint and when they have completed the restorations, which will take time as there are financial restraints, it will be a handsome and comfortable place in which to live. Upper stairs lead to a flat roof that is to be walled off for a private high terrace looking over a sweep of bays and mountain promontories to the north and south. It is so peaceful this home; filled with birdsong, the occasional bleat of a goat and the bored hee-hawing of a tethered donkey.

Our urge to buy and restore was rekindled and we spoke to Georgios about the possibility of purchasing the property next to his, which of course belongs to one of his relations, or rather many of them. He told us that it was almost impossible to buy property in the village since it is owned by up to half a dozen family members who can never agree with one another. Even the Greeks have tried and failed to get any sense out of the multiple owners; this is the problem with buying property all over Greece as we know. The few restorations in the village belong to Maniots who mostly live in Athens and want somewhere for their long summer holidays. The rest of the year the houses remain closed.

*

I know my friends must think I am inordinately lazy, I've written to no one for ages, but I have been working quite hard on travel stories and of course with you, dear journal. I recently submitted another new story on the delights of the southern Peloponnese out of season to a magazine in Australia so must wait until I have their response before sending a new subject, a tricky subject—although superbly caught on Geoff's camera—on the wildflowers of the Mani based on my journal which may or may not be a good idea. I am not a botanist, and my life is one of learning then trying to remember the Latin or Greek names of the myriad new flowers, trees and shrubs I am encountering almost every day. I don't feel sufficiently informed to write about them so I will add an 'apologia' for any errors. Maybe that will suffice. If I were writing about the tropical flora of East Africa, I would be better prepared no doubt. Anyway, I have approached several glossy magazines in Australia and one in the UK and await their response; I desperately need an agent to free me from the administrative side of being a writer.

The other reason for my tardiness in writing any letters is the vagaries of this computer that now and then goes berserk and will not allow me to use the mouse arrow to exit, so I must keep booting it up, not a good idea. I have found this last two days however, that using the internal mouse seems to be OK, perhaps the external mouse is the problem? Who knows, not yours truly. The modem was due back today from Athens where it was sent for repair/replacement as it was faulty, but it did not arrive, surprise, surprise! One day we will have a functioning computer seven months after purchase, but I am not counting on it.

Later—update on modem—the ACS's courier service came yesterday which was a Sunday but could not find Yiannis's house at the address we gave them for some extraordinary reason, so back they went to Gytheio and when I chased them up, they refused to deliver it. I protested, surely that was their job I said firmly, they finally agreed to deliver the parcel tomorrow if I promised to be at home. I speak enough Greek to wrangle with these chaps who invariably end up being polite after an initial stance of non-cooperation.

*

CHAPTER FOURTEEN

IN HOMER'S FOOTSTEPS

Our journey—where do I start? One of the most exciting moments was standing in a cave just off the island of Lefkas, known also as Lefkada, south of Corfu, which is now connected to the mainland by a causeway due to silting up of the narrow sea passage. A nearby cape has been known as Cape Skilla for centuries and Tim Severin in his book, *The Ulysses Voyage*, believes this cave might well have been Scylla's lair from Homer's *Odyssey*. It is now a chapel to St Anthony, that figures since the Christians in order to suppress pagan worship, always built their churches and chapels on the same sites. The chapel is in an ancient cave halfway up the steep slopes of a spider-infested mountain called, since ancient times, Mt Lamia, which means 'Mountain of the Long-necked Devouring Monster'. Geoff opted to go ahead with a stick breaking down the webs of early morning spiders and the terrace in front of the cave was laced with webs—it was quite spooky although the bright early morning sun on the lagoons and reedy waterways below was spectacular in contrast to the gloom of the cave. The site is graphically described by Homer who probably lived in the tenth century before Christ, he is the earliest surviving Greek writer and was supposedly blind, yet his descriptions of the places are so physically recognisable in the twentieth century. Worth reading is Homer's description of Scylla's cave which the goddess Circe gave to Ulysses as she released him after a year's lovemaking and good living:

"... two rocks, the higher of which rears its sharp peak up to the very sky and is capped by black clouds that never stream away or leave clear weather round the top, even in summer or harvest time,

no man on earth could climb it but half-way up the crag there is a misty cavern facing the West and running down to Erebus, (land of the departed spirits) past which you must steer your ship. Scylla has twelve feet all dangling in the air, and six long necks, each ending in a grisly head with triple rows of teeth, set thick and close, and darkly menacing death."

The cave, although I think the word 'lair' might be more appropriate, is approached by a small, roofed platform that juts out over the hillside and supports an outsized cross that I noticed from the road, a large bell hung from a metal beam. Fat, round spiders sat in diaphanous webs that festooned the balcony beams and I thought wryly the ancient cave may have been a dangerous place for Bronze Age galleons and that today's spider-ridden chapel could be equally alarming for arachnophobes. A wreath of dried flowers and grasses hung above the wooden door, a legacy from the first of May celebrations most likely. We opened the door with the rusty key hanging on a nail and stepped inside the malodorous cave and waited for our eyes to become accustomed to the gloom. The accumulated stench of centuries of mould and candle grease and human sweat was quite overpowering, the cave was still a cave with rough and pitted walls gouged out of the hillside and nothing had been done to alter it in any way. It was small; Severin says the highest point was fifteen feet, twelve feet deep and about thirty feet wide, faded frescos of saints lined the uneven surfaces and ikons hung from rusty nails including one of St George and the dragon which one sees in every Christian church and chapel throughout Greece. Ulysses, preoccupied with avoiding the swallowing whirlpool Charybdis caused by the convergence of conflicting tides, forgot Circe's warning about Scylla and, as his ship passed beneath Mount Lamia, the she-monster struck. As Homer says:

"...and snatched out of my boat the six ablest hands I had on board. I swung round, to glance at the ship and run my eyes over the crew, just in time to see the arms and legs of her victims dangled high in the air above my head... Scylla had whisked my

comrades up and swept them struggling to the rocks, where she devoured them at her own door, shrieking and stretching out their hands to me in their last desperate throes..."

I could not wait to get out of the evil-smelling cave; not only was it physically repulsive but I sensed something deeper, something threatening in the atmosphere. The presence of centuries of fear leaving an imprint on the landscape. Looking seawards to a calm morning, no waves breaking over the two-mile-long reef known as Plaka Spit which is only a foot or so above sea level and ends in a tiny atoll, I noticed a small house on the point; does it get swamped every time there is a high tide, or does the entire strip of land float when the sea comes in? Down below me the road to Levkas ran past the silted-up lagoon that lay engulfed with reeds and marshland where fishermen catch eels in large quantities.

I stood on nearby Siren's Beach at the tip of Yrapetra Point and could see the faint remains of the three tumuli on the beach recorded in an Admiralty Chart by a surveyor on Captain Spratt's voyage in these waters. Severin postulates these tumuli could have been the three ancient burial grounds where the Sirens buried the bones of the seafarers they lured with their sweet voices, lyre and flute music. Once captured, their homes and families were forgotten and they remained until they died. It was easy to imagine the Siren's seductive voices drifting across the waves but Ulysses had been warned, and he instructed his crew to tie him to the mast, having stuffed their ears with wax so they could not hear the voices and although he tried to persuade them to release him, they ignored his pleas Thus he managed to both hear their voices and escape their clutches. It was said that this evasion ended the power of the Sirens who then committed suicide by leaping off the high cliffs at the south-west end of Levkas. The female poet and lesbian, Sappho, also ended her life there and the point is known as Sappho's Leap; I understand the site is a favourite venue on the lesbian's list of places to visit. Ulysses went on to face another set of terrifying tests of his strength, but also had a good time wining, dining and making love to various seductive goddesses for years on end despite his desire to get home to his wife Penelope, which of course he eventually did. He then very nastily killed off all her suitors one by one, who had been plaguing her during the twenty odd years of his absence.

We stayed several days in Lefkas in rent rooms in an attractive old house near the port that is a lively place well supplied with tavernas and eating places. A placid lagoon and yacht basin offer a more tranquil scene. The fine castle guards the narrow entrance to the harbour and marina now crowded by a sea of masts as contestants of the annual yacht race stopped by for the night; the little harbour was positively jumping with activity. We drove to the southern end of the island to Vasiliki, a quiet and charming seaside resort. Aquamarine shallows, shot silk surface of the bay, anchored craft at their moorings in a sheltered harbour, white buildings, trees rattling with the castanet sounds of *tzitzikia*. Masses of yachts for hire, plenty of sailing in these waters; windsurfers like playful butterflies skim across the surface and occasionally get their bright wings wet. We had our first dip into the Ionian Sea after a picnic beneath an olive tree on a rough track that clung to the edge of a deep ravine above cobalt waters. Wonderful colours and views—a mountainous island on the southern horizon—could it be Ithaca? The name conjures up such stirrings.

Back home and dawn on the upper terrace, I wake beneath an apricot sky. All around me an artist has been at work and the world is awash with colour, to the west a tired moon hangs askew over the sea that lies like glass; not a breath of air disturbs the surface. The waking birds are jubilant, but Geoff is oblivious to their chorus and sleeps on beside me, relaxed and breathing so quietly. I love his profile and his strong, brown hands, his slender artists' fingers. We have been in the Deep Mani exactly one year and tonight we will celebrate. Nothing unusual—we do it all the time. We will have our meal on the terrace by candlelight, the fragrance of petunias in the air and the incessant ring of cicadas competing with the majesty of Mahler and above us a sky full of stars.

*

CHAPTER FIFTEEN

ZAGORI LAND BEHIND THE MOUNTAINS

We are in Xenonas Zeus, the only guest house in the tiny hamlet of Mikro Papingo, in a beautifully renovated building which stands beside the only tavern in this remote mountain settlement. The day was closing when we arrived and it was raining gently, concealing the outlines of steep forested slopes, gorges and valleys and a suspicion of a magnificent mountainous landscape, but a suspicion only through the mist. We were given a comfortable en suite in a traditional stone house with wooden floors, rugs, panelling on the walls, two double beds on raised platforms with a fireplace in between, also with central heating. We dined in the tavern-cum-bar that produced a small but select menu of home cooking, the taped music was good, and the local wine was decidedly quaffable and the feel of the fire most comforting although it was not cold, just damp. The tavern belongs to the guest house and is run by a floating population of young men who also act as guides for hikers wanting to explore the higher peaks and more remote areas of this region. Replete with good living we slept soundly in our cosy quarters; I was aware of the damp mists closing in outside and heard the liquid circles of an owl's cry in the distance and wondered if its feathers were wet.

In the morning I woke early and looked out of the small window into a secret world of drifting, billowing cloud. The tiny stone village of Mikro Papingo, Little Papingo, had vanished! Following a delicious breakfast of boiled eggs, fresh bread complemented by thick white slabs of home-made butter and local honey, we followed the winding path through the morning mist to the end of the village. The small houses and cottages are built entirely of local slate, undulating grey roofs fell away below us in graceful curves and shapes pierced by large chimneys; wonderful shapes to draw and I went back to our room to get my sketchbook while Geoff took photos. Most of the cottages were in a state of collapse; Kostas, our bearded waiter who worked as a guide during the day, told me that Athenians were buying property and spending their summers in the village. Finally, the first rays of sun pierced the mist and it cleared gradually to reveal the rounded buttresses of Astraka, at two thousand four hundred and thirty-six metres they are the highest point on the plateau. I had to crane my neck, yet still the rocky towers rose higher and higher until they obliterated the entire northern sky.

The shepherds still graze their flocks on the plateau in the summer, but they no longer walk as they still do in Crete. While we were driving up to Papingo, we passed ten huge trucks with double-decker platforms holding sheep on the top level, goats on the bottom with several horses and donkeys and shepherds' dogs at the rear, all looking at us with great interest. They seemed to be enjoying the trip I thought; the twentieth century mode of migration is on four wheels and they return to the coastal plains in November for the winter. Our drive yesterday was along snaking roads through spectacular wild country of densely forested mountains and valleys with occasional patches of high green pastures. Up and up the road curled and twisted, flanked on either side by miraculous wildflowers—scarlet poppies, yellow Jerusalem sage, swathes of coral-coloured orchids, love-in-a-mist, graceful ladies' lace, snowdrops and lilac campanula leaning towards the sun. Below the dark conifers lining the road, the hillside plunged into steel grey gorges where icy rivers flowed and the sound of rushing water filled our ears when we switched off the engine. We had not stopped in the cobbled street of Megalo Papingo, Big Papingo—which is not big at all but had headed for Mikro Papingo, a smaller more solitary hamlet perched a few kilometres further up the mountain. The road came to an end by a wall, so we parked beside a narrow church dated 1808—1810 with a roofline of grey slate over cloisters that ran along one side of a tiny square, shadowed by a gigantic plane tree.

Yesterday as we stood in the drizzle a shaft of late sunlight lit up the bell tower on the edge of the hillside where below us, grey, slate-roofed stone cottages jostled for position as they ambled along the curve of the hill. No indication of a guest house anywhere, no signs or arrows but an electric light bulb was on, presumably to light the way, the only way into the walled hamlet through an old gate leading to a flagged pathway that wound through cottages drenched with rain. It was quite cold and the village was wreathed in the palest pearly mist as if it were floating above the hillside, disconnected from the earth and it appeared to be deserted. Further around the arm of the hill I could see several fine mansions and terraced gardens hiding behind stone walls with free-standing entrances like old coach houses; massive wooden doors led into courtyards covered with rustic pergolas which, in summer, would be smothered with grapes, the buds just beginning to swell.

We were in the Pindus Sierras in the Epirus region of north-western Greece bordering Albania in the Zagorohoria, a region that covers some thousand square kilometres known as the Villages of the Zagori. This remote mountainous region which is also the Vikos-Aoos National Park encapsulates some forty-six traditional villages many of which are barely populated and are in a state of collapse. In the ravines, graceful, humped stone bridges built by Greek engineers and stone masons in the eighteenth and nineteenth centuries span fast-flowing rivers, many are no longer in use but mercifully they are being preserved. The Zagori, due to its remoteness, managed to retain certain autonomy under Turkish rule and the region flourished economically and culturally and several of Greece's main benefactors came from this area. Those settlements under restoration are enchanting and quite unspoiled; many of the walls in the mansions are painted with folk murals both inside and out and, in the profusion of old churches, striking wall paintings and carved wooden iconostases from the seventeenth century are to be seen. We visited several of the villages, many are indeed almost deserted, cobbled streets wind uphill between tumbledown slate cottages, paved squares sit beneath shady plane trees, water gushes from carved stone fountains and races down channels on either side of the lanes. In each tiny hamlet there are the ubiquitous *kafenia* with plastic chairs where solitary *yia-yias* in black serve Greek coffee, thick and sweet, ever-friendly, ever-curious, many have families in *Melvourni*, Melbourne and were delighted to hear that we come from Australia. *Australie, poly orea anthropoi*! Very good people Australians! They proclaim with one voice.

I was hoping to see some Sarakatsani nomads, these strange, independent herdsmen and their flocks who were until quite recently, the only true nomads of Greece; their journeys stretching from southern Albania and as far east as Cappadocia in central Turkey. They alone had no permanent settlements, no villages of their own but built conical reed huts on the plains in which to house their families for the winter, moving to the high plateaus in the spring to follow the grazing. I read in the brochure that in a pine forest clearing near the village of Gytokampo on the north-west side of the Astraka Plateau, one can see reconstructed traditional huts at the Sarakatsani *stani*, sheepfold and in the summer, it functions as an open-air museum. Unfortunately, we ran out of time and did not get there, but next time we will. Most of the villagers in the high country are Sarakatsanis, our guest house owner was a Sarakatsani, he told us that he had become middle-class although his parents were still nomad shepherds who migrated to the coast each winter with their flocks but lived in a house in Mikro Papingo.

The Vikos Gorge, known as the Grand Canyon of Europe is twenty-five kilometres long as it cleaves its way through this landscape; it is a favourite haunt for hikers and it takes five to six hours and some stamina to trek the full length, although the terrain is not too difficult. Geoff took off for a shorter hike along the ravine and I drove the car four hours later to the hamlet of Vikos to meet him. As I negotiated the cobbled streets of Megalo Papingo, a young man, smartly dressed in red cords and a blue T-shirt hailed me. Would I give him a lift to the *potamo*, river, many miles down the mountainside? Yes, of course I would. He hopped in and offered me a cigarette, when I refused, he smiled and put the packet back in his pocket despite my protestations that I did not mind him smoking. A gentleman shepherd. He was a most attractive individual with bright eyes and a clear, glowing skin, perfect teeth and when I asked if he was a Sarakatsani shepherd he said he was and showed surprise at my question. He told me his family had lived at Megalo Papingo *panda*, always, and their animals were now on the Astraka plateau and he was going up there soon. He added the air was pure and clean on the plateau and the milk, cheese and yoghurt from his goats was *poly orea*! I should come and visit his family. I said I would if I was able. I left him at the bridge crossing the Voidomatis River that is the most extraordinary clear malachite green colour; its banks are shaded by willow, birch and juniper beneath massive plane trees and other deciduous giants all in pale spring leaf. An idyllic spot enhanced by the murmurings of shallow rapids and I am sure I heard a nightingale.

That evening at dinner in the cosy tavern with good jazz, I asked Kostas if he knew the reason for the amazing colour of the Voidomatis River. He believes it is because it is the purest water in Europe, fed directly by the melting snows and unpolluted by man. He also told me that this was bear, wolf and wild boar country and when I told him that Geoff had walked alone halfway down the gorge, he laughed and said the bears were harmless but quite cheeky. Once, when he was swimming in the river, he watched one steal his sandwiches but said he didn't mind, the bear was obviously hungry. Whitewater rafting and kayaking are popular sports on both the Voidomatis and Aoos rivers, the latter rises in the west and cuts across the northern borders of the national park past the mountain town of Konitsa. This region is well known for its therapeutic springs, sulphurous spas and superb mountain walks; precipitous cliffs challenge rock climbers while hikers follow the racing waters through the lonely gorges. The walking season is from May to September, and Mikro Papingo is one of the starting points for hikers intent on scaling the towers of Astraka to the spectacular waters of Drakolimni, Dragon Lake. The campsite at this heart-shaped lake is reputed to be the coldest in Europe. It takes six hours from the village to reach the summit of Mount Gamila, at two thousand four hundred and ninety-seven metres. This is gloriously wild and unspoiled country barely discovered by tourists.

Next morning and the air is bitingly cold. The tiny grey slate settlement of *Skala Vradetou,* Stairs of Vradetou sits on top of the world above a tortuously winding road rising sharply from the shadowy depths of the Vikos Gorge. The hamlet lies ten kilometres beyond the snowline and we drive through bare mountains seared by icy wind and weather, yet as we climb we are rewarded by a startling patch of royal purple violas, just the one clump with each flower turning its hopeful face to a reluctant sun. A spectacular and ancient *kalderimi*, cobbled path, the old approach to the village zigzags up the vertical mountainside and while Geoff negotiates the steep ascent by foot, I am drawn by the wonderful sound of bells and chat at length, with a bespectacled shepherdess in a long skirt who is guarding her flock as they range knee-deep in a multitude of wildflowers.

*

We spend a night in the city of Ioannina that was the stronghold of the barbarous, though cultured, Turkish ruler Ali Pasha and went in a boat to Nysi an island, in the middle of the lake where he fled when his own people turned on him. He was reputed to be quite mad and suffering from delusions of grandeur, as he planned to secede from Turkey and create his own state combining with Albania, when the ruling sultan decided to put a stop to his dangerous antics. There is a museum in the little house where he was shot and then beheaded—lucky for him it was not the other way round! We dine on fresh trout to the whine of a million mosquitoes with our feet almost in the lake and then take the little boat back to the twinkling lights of the mainland and our rent rooms. Chugging through the dark it was not difficult to visualise his assassins arriving stealthily, tying up their boats in the reeds then attacking the house where he was awaiting a pardon—but got the bullet instead. He was shot from below the wooden floorboards and his death prompted the movement leading to the uprising.

*

CHAPTER SIXTEEN

BRYON HERO OF THE GREEKS

We decided to follow in Byron's footsteps as we travelled southwards from Ioannina along the coast road to Astrakos which sits in a hot, flat valley at the base of a deep inlet. It is a curious place with a strange and somewhat forbidding atmosphere; scruffy yet with a surprising number of tavernas with bright awnings, huge lamps along the quay and I saw with sinking heart, a taverna called Byron Bar run no doubt, by some seedy Englishman or maybe a German with a bald head and sparse ponytail. There are many alcoholic ex-patriates in Crete making a quick buck—opportunists to the last—however, I was surprised to find a bar with an English name in this desolate fishing port. Gypsy women, colourful in maroon dresses to their bare feet, tinkling bracelets and earrings, white scarves with silver thread around the edges, selling long ranks of garlic and in the harbour, wide fishing boats with twentieth century equipment at anchor; radar, huge winches and the crew resting with their feet on folded nets—eastern music from a portable radio. We spoke to a man of dark complexion with a seasoned skin, he said they were Arabs who had always fished in these waters. I noticed that the benches along the grubby waterfront faced the town not the sea—Greeks are more interested in people than in vistas. As we left Astrakos we passed a shipbuilder's yard with men working on the skeletal bones of a huge wooden hull— and further south thriving fish farms along this otherwise unrelentingly barren coastline.

And so, to the dreary hot little town of Missolonghi where Lord Byron, poet and hero of the Greek War of Independence, exhausted and depressed, died of some mysterious ailment in 1824. It is thought he might have contracted malaria and the cure at the time, bleeding, would most likely to have been performed using unsterilized equipment, could have led to sepsis. A confirmed Hellenophile, he revered the Greeks' free and open frankness when he travelled through parts of Greece as a young man and his lengthy poem *Childe Harold's Pilgrimage*—one of my father's often quoted favourites—brought him fame and fortune. His other poems, in particular *The Prophecy of Dante* that referred specifically to the Italian problem, denounced tyranny and spoke out for the oppressed; his reputation as a champion of liberty prompted an invitation to join the Greek insurgents in their struggle for independence from the Turks. He enlisted with a regiment to which he advanced large sums of his own money, mainly to prevent them from changing loyalties, as they were unable to find sufficient funds from other sources. His presence in Turkish-dominated Greece brought the plight of the Greeks under the Turkish yoke to the attention of the western world and this, in turn, sparked financial and practical assistance that gathered the disparate forces of the Greeks, and culminated in the War of Independence and the final expulsion of the Turks following four hundred years of rule.

Greeks still worship Byron mainly as the hero of the Greeks and many children are named after him; I went to boarding school in the obscure highlands of Tanganyika and knew a Greek boy called Byron and a Greek girl with whom I became friends. I cannot remember her name, it might have been Εύα, Eva in Greek or Eve, sometimes short for Evelyne in English, but I can see her clearly; a wide and smiling face thick, curly honey-coloured hair and dark brown eyes. There were many Greeks in the school, and they all knew about Byron and his involvement in the fight for independence. Their parents had tobacco farms on the plains beneath the little plateau town of Iringa, in the southern highlands of Tanganyika.

The Garden of Heroes is a well-kept park with multiple statues and memorials of Greek resistance fighters and in pride of place, there is a full-length delicate statue of the poet, depicting him as the sensitive, rather small man he was, physically insignificant with full-lipped, effeminate features. Born with a deformed foot, he limped but was known nonetheless, as the "playboy poet" his reputation due to his popularity with the fairer sex. The white statue, reputedly made of china, was filthy and streaked with bird droppings which I felt sure would have amused him; larkspur grew around the base and birds felt at home on his head and shoulders. His heart, that I did not wish to see, is apparently in the museum by his request although his body is in Westminster Abbey. Outside the entrance to the Garden of Heroes there is a new bronze statue of him in partisan gear with a bristling Greek moustache. I wonder did he have one. This statue depicts him as a huge, aggressive man with handsome, clean-cut features and a fine patrician nose which he did not have; he had a beautiful and small nose as the earlier statue has captured to perfection. He is standing with legs akimbo in true *palikari,* warrior, fashion. I know he dressed in the Greek garb of the time, that was frightfully dashing and romantic, swirling cloak off the shoulders, waistcoat, boots and an embroidered shirt and so on but I am sure that the man portrayed in the latest statue, is not the real Byron. We left as soon as we could. Missolonghi is a depressing hellhole of scorching heat even in early June. It would be an awful place to die, but even worse to live in.

Home again and I am reading all about our trip from my notes. I find it so exciting following historical and mythical trails; it makes travel so much more meaningful and Geoff is the most enthusiastic partner. His photos are improving in leaps and bounds as he becomes more confident with the camera, and we now have a varied and interesting collection to illustrate the travel pieces that are being accepted surprisingly well.

*

Summer siesta is often interrupted by gypsy vans with blaring loudspeakers calling out their wares: *karpouzia, peponia, orea* or *karekles, trapezia* as they wind their way down the narrow laneway past the two churches at our front gate. The sound is badly distorted and only a practiced ear can tell what it is they are selling—I hear *karpouzia* but we can get melons, watermelons anywhere so we ignore him. Our friend the fishmonger from Mesapo, also drives round but his tone is more muted, less intrusive. He is not a gypsy but from a family of seventeenth and eighteenth-century pirates and we know him quite well now. Too much energy is required to raise ourselves from our siesta and chase him down the stifling high-walled lanes to buy his fresh fish—although I know it would be worth it if we did.

In the still heat of the afternoon I hear the soft interjection of a dove—*coo-coo, coo-coo,* a velvety, throaty call. The familiar sound invades my siesta-befuddled brain and transports me back to my childhood days in Dar es Salaam, to steamy afternoons with my mother, prostrate by the heat and humidity as she rests on a white sheet beneath a purring ceiling fan. The bedrooms were in the upper storey of our old German-built house that stood at the corner of the Botanical Gardens; the address was 21 Park Road. I slept above the treetops in what was known as 'the cage' a netted and totally enclosed wide veranda that wrapped around the large rooms to keep me and, in a spacious high-ceilinged inner room my parents, safe from mosquitoes. From my bed I could just see the glistening ocean, past the palms and giant flamboyants, to an intriguing fairy-tale building with several delicate spires that was used as the nurses' quarters. To my child's eyes, it resembled a small Disney castle in a film. An afternoon nap was mandatory in that tropical climate and I have kept up the habit all my life and instilled it in my children during their early years. They were all avid readers during siesta and I believe those early years may have accounted for this most excellent habit; their beds from cot-stage upwards, were always littered with books which they would read if they did not sleep.

This summer we have bought ourselves swimming masks and I use a snorkel. I have no idea why we did not think of doing this last summer as the underwater world is always so fascinating. Unfortunately, Geoff is unable to use a full-face mask because his moustache lets the water in, so he wears goggles. The ocean bed is a treasure trove of different weeds ranging from lime to vivid green, lilac to deep purple, pale yellow to orange, and in the deep there are pastures of a long green weed, slender leafed which sways to and fro with the currents. Shafts of sunlight reach into secret corners disclosing bright orange starfish and a brilliant tangerine coloured mossy plant that grows on the underside of rocks. White patches of sand lie between the jagged rocks that resemble miniature mountain ranges with fish instead of birds, flying between the peaks. There are many varieties of fish, including a school of electric blue fingerlings which hover against a jutting rock and seem not to move from this safe place. Deeper, in the darkness of an underwater cave, translucent orange fish resembling goldfish skulk in the shadows; they avoid the light and never venture further afield.

Yesterday, late evening we went snorkelling with Iakovos and he showed us the remains of a sunken fourth century BC galleon in Limeni Bay, a short distance out from where we swim off the rocks. There are literally hundreds of amphorae on the seabed, some still undamaged and standing upright so that one can make out the outline of the galleon by the way the amphorae sit on the ocean floor. An amphora is a jar with two vertical handles, most often ceramic although examples in metals and other materials have been found. The name derives from the Greek *amphiphoreus* meaning 'carried on both sides'. Used in antiquity for the storage and transportation of wine, honey and olive oil, it is thought the vessel had probably loaded up in Limeni harbour—once a major port in the southern Peloponnese—and had barely left the harbour before it sank in quite shallow water a few hundred metres from the shore. What made it sink I wonder? Iakovos told us that the vessels transported amphorae in sand to keep the jars steady and possibly during a storm, the sand had become soaked and heavy and the waterlogged vessel went down. Sunk like a stone so close to the shore. Were the many rowers able to swim? I cannot bear to think of what might have happened, yet the ancient shipwreck keeps entering my brain like some unwelcome visitor.

We swim mainly in the late evenings after the burning sun

starts to sink and the summer holidaymakers are heading home; then we have the rocks to ourselves and the sea becomes quiet as it cools and settles in for the night. It is a peaceful time, and it freshens us up for the sultry evenings, the meal preparation and the still, humid nights. The most interesting creatures we have found beneath the surface, are the Cuvier sea hares that we discovered quite recently as we were sitting on our special rock in the bay. Geoff called my attention to what looked like three lumpy bits of black weed on one of the rocks just beneath the surface, which was covered in a bright green weed. At first we thought it was a kind of seaweed, and then the lumps began to resemble outsize slugs with two loose, wavy mantles on their hunched backs that flowed to and fro with the movement of the water. Nature's camouflage is truly miraculous. Looking more closely, we saw the lumps had two little horns and an obvious front end from which they appeared to be eating the green weed and moving very slowly forward as they grazed. They were jet black with a scattering of silver on their backs, a bit like the glitter one sprinkles over Christmas trees and the group appeared to be a family of three. The largest was a good twenty-five centimetres in length and the next, probably a female, was a little smaller. The baby, feeding all alone was about half their size. The trio resembled a family of underwater rabbits, a beguiling sight and we were surprised that we had never seen them before. The speed with which they cleared the rock of seaweed was as effective as that of their relations on land, they grazed voraciously and it took several weeks for the weed to grow back again. A few evenings later we were snorkelling in the deep and saw more of them feeding, their graceful black frills swaying with the tide. The boys have a book on sea creatures that tells me they are called *Aplysia depilans,* Cuvier sea hares, a genus of medium to large sea slugs, specifically sea hares. This variety occurs in the Mediterranean and is distinguishable from other sea hares by its black mantle. Their habitat is shallow waters.

*

August—and Greece is having one mighty heatwave; in Athens it was forty-four degrees Celsius and here it was forty degrees, so we resorted to the cooling system but, when we switched it on, we heard a persistent dripping and discovered a huge wet patch on the couch and water was coming down the wall from the unit. We called our gentlemanly Polish electrician Yatzek who had a look and found the outer pipe had beeswax and honey in it! Now it works thanks goodness, and we are living in a kind of timeless, cool and spaceless element with the shutters closed, lights on and the hum of the air conditioner, a bit like spinning in space I would think. Outside, after three days of calm a stinging hot wind is blowing; the sirocco from Libya with accompanying gritty sand is churning up dust and tossing the olive branches around. We will drag ourselves out for a swim in a tepid sea after eight when the heat goes out of the sinking sun.

Later at night and the news on the television is alarming with high winds and fierce fires raging, many in the southern Peloponnese. The temperatures are higher than ever, hovering around forty-six degrees and will be the same for the next few days. Last night the mountain range was ablaze with colossal flames that lit up the sky and we watched until two in the morning as the fire raced at a determined speed up the slopes. We were fearful that if the wind changed it would come straight to Areopolis and to us as we are on the southern edge of the village, next to olive groves standing in high dry grass that would have gone up like a tinder box. This morning on the way to the market we drove through a scorched landscape of blackened olives and cypresses and discovered the fire had leapt across the main road towards the town but was evidently put out before it got away. We do not know how many villages have been burned further down the Mani peninsula but I hope they escaped; fortunately, the blustery, burning wind has dropped today and it will be easier for the fire brigades and their excitable helpers to keep control of the blaze. The sky is full of smoke and the air smells of burnt grass and I dare not think of the animals that have been killed. As usual it is the arsonists and land developers who are mostly responsible, not the elements. There have been three thousand separate fires recorded this summer in Greece. Most of them deliberately lit.

CHAPTER SEVENTEEN

AN EVENING WITH SOPHOCLES

We have arrived at Nea Epidaurus, New Epidaurus—an attractive little port where the Flying Dolphin hydrofoil comes hurtling in on its outstretched arms then sinks as if exhausted into the calm sea of the bay to disgorge and collect passengers. We are staying in the Posidon Hotel, and it is extraordinary how the spelling changes in Greece! Seldom do I find a map or a signpost with the same spelling as the next one and I certainly have never seen Poseidon spelled without the 'e' like this before. It's blisteringly hot, steamy too however, our spacious room is air-conditioned with a balcony overlooking the marina with chairs and tables lined up that are full each night; jazzy sun umbrellas and awnings cast shade but the sun is burning hot beneath them. I can hear the slip slap of the waves against the boats moored along the harbour that stretches a good distance around the curve—and I counted eleven ocean-going yachts of substantial size with soaring masts and fluttering flags from France, USA, Italy and Holland. A very smart launch moored nearby is obviously Greek and I can see a large table set for dinner on the lower deck, smartly dressed people moving about, children leaning over the railings.

Evening, and it is half past seven and we discover at the ticket booth at the entrance to the Ancient Theatre of Epidaurus that the tickets we thought we had reserved are not reserved at all. The woman tells us that it is not possible to reserve seats over the phone as plastic card style of payment is not acceptable, yet last week Geoff spelt out his name to the female voice on the Athens 'Reservations number', told her that we were prepared to pay for the tickets and she said we could pick them up at the Epidaurus booth. We naturally assumed we had reserved seats. But no!

Luckily there is plenty of room, so we purchase two five-thousand drachma tickets and join the small queue at the inner gate that rapidly grows to a substantial mass of people, some also carrying cushions. Just before eight, the gates open and we are propelled forward past the gate keeper who I notice is confiscating plastic bottles of water and throwing them into a nearby bin with a resounding noise but totally ignores all the haversacks and carrier bags people are carrying. I suppose he has his reasons.

We have the most perfect stone seats with curved backs to fit one's shape, most of the backs of the seats have crumbled over the centuries, but we find two intact in the centre and towards the top where I want to sit high up and test the acoustics once again. Armed with cushions, a bottle of cold wine, fresh figs and grapes, appropriate for a special night of excitement while in the pit of my stomach, the knowledge that people like us have been sitting in these same seats since the fourth century BC waiting to hear these same words spoken, thrills me. I find it hard to believe that I am finally to experience a Greek tragedy at this most ancient place—yet here I am about to see Sophocles's *Electra*, another dream come true and to be able to share this with my man makes it absolutely perfect. The complicated play was written by the ancient Greek playwright, Sophocles, presumably around 410 BC or later. It is based on the story of Electra and her brother, Orestes, and the vengeance they take on their mother Clytemnestra and stepfather Aegisthus for the murder of their father Agamemnon, in the aftermath of the Trojan War. It is considered to be one of his most successful dramas.

A cooling breeze drifts around and the sun is setting. The audience is still arriving and the seats are filling up all around us, many police and uniformed officials wandering around looking important. A mixed lot the audience; mostly Greek in ultra-smart though casual clothes. Two beautiful women, obviously Italian judging by their accents and enviable sports gear and ringleted curls, draw the immediate attention of some of the surrounding men, young couples in scruffy shorts and hiking boots and family groups. I am dressed up after all, it is not every night that one goes to experience a Greek tragedy in the magnificent setting in the ancient amphitheatre of Epidaurus. I have collywobbles in the pit of my stomach as I sense the same expectation of much of the crowd; it will be a night to remember.

The substantial and beautifully produced programme in Greek and English is most informative but I notice quite a few 'typos'. We are to see Karyofyllia Karabeti, one of Greece's finest dramatic actress as Electra in a new production by a young and innovative producer. I read that:

The fifth century tragic poets took the moral of their works most seriously.

The postscript also mentions that children under six years are not allowed and states this rule is strictly enforced yet, to my dismay, immediately in front of us is a harassed looking woman with a toddler with a dummy in its mouth. I hope it sleeps. His fat, unkempt mother looks as if she is incapable of disciplining anyone, least of all, herself. Her equally overweight teenage daughter has a huge head of frizzy hair and she fidgets and shifts around throughout the entire evening, it was she and not the baby who should have been banned, and she is sitting directly in front of me. It is getting darker and spotlights have been turned on, they blaze down lighting the entire theatre; I notice how serious the audience is, most of them are reading the programme or gazing intently down on the circular stage, once known as the 'orchestra'. Speaking of orchestras where is it? The musicians and conductor are listed on the pages but they are not to be seen, my heart sinks, is the music pre-recorded? There is a big black box off centre stage with a panel of flashing red lights that would seem to be more appropriate in Dr Who, is it a gigantic loudspeaker? It turns out that it is a modern-day altar, but the flashing lights and ultra-high-tech idea does not work. Just seems gimmicky. I hope I am wrong.

Three sleek, black cars arrive on the far side of the stage, desultory clapping. A group of dignitaries is ushered to their cushioned seats on the lower level. As the lights are dimmed the entire audience leans forward, concentrating on half a dozen figures in black flowing robes that run around the stage and leave what appear to be their cloaks, on the ground. A polite voice breaks the silence, there are to be no flash photos, no portable telephones. The request is repeated in Italian, English and French but it is ignored, flash photos are taken throughout the play.

And now everything is quiet. Suddenly we are plunged into a Stygian darkness as if we have been consumed by the night. Spooky. The contrast, as blinding white floodlights flood the theatre is a shock and I am recovering my equilibrium when I am almost propelled out of my seat by a tremendous and tumultuous crash of electronic instruments that reverberate and echo around the natural amphitheatre. The effect is riveting. Shafts of penetrating lights seek to illuminate the barrier of pines that flank the edge of the small plateau where the theatre sits. Black-clad women of the chorus run around on silent feet, their flashlights seeking out the audience, the trees, and the night sky. Initially I was disappointed to read that this was an experimental production and would have preferred to have seen the tragedy in its original form—nonetheless, the use of the white light on this pitch-black night is electrifying. It works. The drama is about to unfold.

There is no interval. The performance lasts two hours and Electra is on stage for most of the time. I have never seen an audience so rapt, so intent on hearing every precious word. The most touching scene is when the poor woman, tired, prematurely aged and consumed with bitterness, realises that the ashes in the urn she is holding are not those of her dead brother Orestes after all, and that the man standing before her is he, alive and well and come to take vengeance for the murder of their father. She picks him up and swirls round and round with him in her arms as the audience erupts, clapping and shouting and weeping. I do not believe there is a dry eye in the theatre. The final, brilliant touch is the last scene where Orestes and the chorus chase Aegisthus—their father's murderer—through the backdrop of giant trees with lights from a dozen torches invading every branch and bole and dark corner; the use of the natural surroundings of the theatre is a stroke of genius. As for the acoustics, even when Electra was lying on the ground sobbing and whispering, I could hear every syllable. I was weeping too and quite wrung out by the end. We sat sipping wine as the audience left, streaming down the steep tiers but I wanted to sit there all night and relive the experience; eventually a uniformed man moved me on with a smile. The tragedy was over, and I hoped Sophocles was resting at ease with the electronic sounds echoing around the hills and valleys of the ancient theatre of Epidaurus.

*

I remember my first visit to the site that was initially established as the Sanctuary of Asclepius, the God of Healing, known in modern times as the Lourdes of the Greek World. The ancient world's best-preserved theatre with the finest acoustics seated six thousand and was later increased to thirteen thousand in the second century BC by extending and dividing the rows of seats upwards thus doubling the capacity. Miraculously it survived the two major earthquakes in AD522 and AD551 that destroyed the surrounding sanctuary.

I was with Amanda and Tom a friend, when I recorded this in my diary dated November 1991: It was mid-day.

"Climbing up ancient, worn steps through tall trees I found myself in a clearing which led to the ancient theatre where a vast semicircle of tiered seats followed the natural curve of Mount Kynorton enveloping the circular 'orchestra', stage, which to my surprise was not elevated above ground level. The columns of two monumental gates stood on either side of the stage entrance through which members of the chorus, essential to all Greek tragedies, made their entrance. The theatre was bathed in a clear morning light, that clarity of light which is so peculiar to Greece and I wondered once again what it was that numbed my brain when I visited these early Greek sanctuaries and shrines. Was it just the light or a combination of light, ancient stones and the presence of spirits that had this effect on me? It was as if I had drunk too much red wine on a hot day and was having difficulty focusing on the here and now. It happened every time."

This site has a profound effect on many who go there, and it is worth reading Henry Miller's book, *The Colossus of Maroussi* where he writes of his visit to Epidaurus.

Standing in the very centre of the great theatre scented by its forested slopes of green pines and cypresses, I felt the same spiritual stillness as Henry Miller. And then I heard the nightingales. The surrounding trees echoed with their sparkling notes and it was as if I had been invited to a special concert by the Goddess Euterpe, alone but for the nightingales. I tested the acoustics by dropping a coin onto the ground in the centre of the orchestra. The soft clunk as it landed was barely audible to me, yet the sound flew to the top tier of the seats where Amanda and Tom reacted by jumping up and down in obvious amazement, their excited voices drifting down over the silent stone tiers to tell me that the amplification was astonishing. I whispered—and my voice echoed around me as if in a cave and my words travelled with clarity to my listeners and they repeated them, word for word. I am told by those who should know that no architect or acoustics expert has ever, as yet, been able to duplicate the phenomenal acoustics of this ancient theatre built in the natural curve of the hill. Goat bells in the distant hills; there have always been goat bells.

*

I love the summer when the sea is as smooth as silk, the *tzitzikia* protest even through siesta, spiny acanthus is sporting oyster-pink flowers, lacy golden yarrow sways above an explosion of giant-sized seed heads that filter the sun and the dried seed pods of the asphodel rustle when the *meltemi* finds them—I blow them into the air—he loves me, he loves me not—I know he loves me. This means Greece to me.

*

In search of the caretta-caretta turtles, we have finally met Tzulia, the Gytheio based coordinator of the Sea Turtle Protection Society and I am working on a story about the *caretta-caretta*, loggerhead turtle, an endangered species as its nesting grounds in Greece are being overrun by tavernas and beach bars and tourist-related activities. Last night we joined Stewart, one of the many volunteers at Mavrovouni, one of the laying beaches and sat by two turtle nests for three hours. At about midnight by the light of the torch we saw a tiny round head push through the soft sand, it stopped still for a while, as if checking out the terrain but we could see the sand around it sinking a little and shifting. Then, within seconds a batch of ten 'hatchlings', newly born turtles, suddenly erupted out of the sandy hollow; it was astonishing how quickly they appeared, and Stewart told us that the hatchlings wait until they are all ready and then literally force the first one above the surface. They are only six centimetres long but so strong, their diminutive round heads peer out of their soft carapaces while strong flippers push and pull as they scrabble their way out of the nest and head at great speed towards the sea. They exhibit the most incredible determination, their instinct guiding them into waves. For me it was a sad moment because it is estimated that of every thousand hatchlings that reach the water, only one survives. He answered the million-dollar question. How do hatchlings know where the sea is after they are hatched? They are guided either by reflected starlight on the sea's surface or the light on the horizon between the sea and sky, but they are now easily disorientated by the lights of tavernas and beach bars, thus the Sea Turtle Protection Society monitors the nesting beaches throughout the summer—from the initial egg laying in May to the emergence of the hatchlings that lasts from late July to October. And they seem to be doing a fantastic job. Geoff and I have adopted a hatchling for each of our three grandchildren—I like the idea and it is a unique way for the STPS to earn revenue; they also sell T-shirts, skivvies, postcards and brooches.

*

Funeral in Areopolis, dang-dang, dang-dang, dang-dang. A melancholy bell rings out over the village through the early morning sounds of barking dogs, awakening birds, cockerels, *tzitzikia* getting into gear and the metallic rumble and crunch as Yiannis rolls back the heavy black steel gates. I have never heard the bells tolling for a death before and these solemn, slow, double sounds fill the air with obvious grieving. It is the silence between the tolling bells as much as the sound that sets the mood. Someone of importance has died, a priest I would imagine. We drive past the church later in the morning, and there are a dozen or so solemnly dressed black-clad women sitting along the stone seats outside the church, in the shade of the mulberry trees. Inside I can see people moving around, chattering as they go, holding bunches of flowers while the priest is chanting mournfully; it is obviously a very solemn occasion although I sense the women are not actually taking much notice of the service. Mid-afternoon as we drive past on our way for a swim, I can see the lid of a coffin leaning against the outer wall of the church embraced by wreaths of white flowers; more villagers, including men in ill-fitting suits, are converging for the service. Mid-afternoon the following day and the solemn bells toll once more, dang-dang dang-dang dang-dang competing with the *tzitzikia* that have no respect for either the dead or the sanctity of siesta. I notice the yodelling spaniel does not join in; he is obviously exhausted.

*

We have plenty of time to read and I am enjoying *Palace Walk*, the first book in the Cairo Trilogy by Naguib Mahfouz, it is superbly written in a unique style. Ruth recommended it to me although I have never heard of him; he has won the Nobel Prize for Literature, the first Arab writer to do so and I have already ordered the second and third books from Foyles.

*

We spend the day in search of the fiery spirit raki in Arna, our favourite mountain village high in the Taygetus mountains. The members of my family who have visited and lived in Crete for a while, have told me that if I come back to Australia without a supply I may as well not visit them at all! In autumn, the high country in the Peloponnese is more enchanting than ever; Arna is surrounded by cherry orchards and chestnuts loaded with conkers, shaggy chrysanthemums, late roses and hollyhocks in the gardens. The colossal plane tree in the tiny square is losing its leaves and it is cool in the shade where we have our Greek coffee. On the way to Arna we finally traced the ruins of Beaufort Castle that we had promised ourselves we would find long ago; it is the most handsome of all the ruined Frankish castles and is appropriately named. It sits alone in the mountains next to a village called Agios Nikolaos on a rocky hill with many of the ruined walls, bastions, and archways still intact.

Evening and we have had a delightful and successful outing; we purchased a couple of bottles of raki, chatted to the very friendly villagers, one of whom we had met on our first visit, and now it is not long before we depart for Australia. We are both a bit forlorn at the thought of leaving Areopolis but the prospect of seeing our families and our grandchildren again is exciting. I am absolutely ready to leave.

*

CHAPTER EIGHTEEN

KINDRED SPIRITS

Recently we explored Skopa, the islet near Kotronas, although since our visit I discovered that it is neither an islet nor an island, it is an isthmus, a narrow strip of land that connects Kotronas with the Skopa peninsula; it only becomes an island when the high tide separates it from the mainland. Not that this matters. We swam off its miniature beach of black sand dotted with oval black pebbles of all sizes, some with a curious white stripe encircling the glistening sea-smooth stones; we collected a few but when they are dry, they lose their sheen so I keep them in the bathroom and dampen them occasionally. The beach sits quietly in a hidden spot below high jagged rocks and as we swam around the island, it was high tide so it *was* an island—we discovered a gigantic fissure through the cliffs that ended in a cave; brilliant orange and purple lichen covered the rocks with scores of technicoloured fish feeding—and seemingly undisturbed by us humans.

On the mainland south of Skopa, there is a high rocky headland with an almost hidden cottage perched on the narrow plateau that juts out into the sea. Stately dark cypresses stand guard as olive trees dance around, their silver leaves glistening while uneven steps dig into the sheer rock face that leads down to the water from the plateau. A heavenly spot. We tread water for ages and agree that we covet that place, we want to find out if anyone lives in the small cottage and if it is abandoned, perhaps we can buy it, but we cannot work out how one gets to it as there are no visible access roads. We have been back several times but have never seen anyone around, then the last time we went exploring a small boat came putt-putting round a second promontory, pulled up on a nearby strip of beach, picked up two people with shopping bags and putt-putted around the headland and out of sight. A little later we saw a couple swimming below the sloping black cliffs then standing on a platform of submerged rocks below the dream cottage, so we decided to swim over and investigate more closely. It was a long swim and the underwater world—we were snorkelling—was magnificent; it was as though we were flying over huge mountain ranges with deep gorges and valleys where fish instead of birds were flying. We heard English voices and swam towards them and Geoff, showing none of his usual reserve, greeted the couple and asked if it was their cottage.

"Yes," they said, heads bobbing up and down treading water.

"Would you sell it?" Swimming closer to one another.

"Not likely," said the friendly woman who introduced herself as Lee and invited us to come and have coffee or a drink any day at any time. As we swam away, I thought to myself, she seems to be one of us! And it turned out she certainly was.

A week or so later we found our way there by parking on a road and struggling down a rough six-hundred-metre steep goat track, the smell of thyme filling the cool air to the stone cottage only to discover it was empty. We found it to be an old and small dwelling that had been extended and restored, standing high on the rocky headland known as Nysi, with the sea on three sides and to the south, the headlands and promontories piling up all the way to Cape Matapan. We left our phone number and details and a few days later, a knock on the door announced their arrival at the tower house where we developed an instant rapport and spent an enjoyable afternoon with them. It was so good to meet up with kindred spirits. Chris is a tall, rather quiet pipe-smoking Englishman of about our age and Lee is one of those younger and attractive, entertaining women with an endless supply of stories. We agreed it was too bizarre that we should meet just before we were due to visit our families in Australia. They, like us, were in a fairly new relationship. Chris had inherited the property from a friend while working in the Sudan and he and Lee began to spend their summers there, visiting family in England and the States during the winter months. An ideal lifestyle.

After they left, we were quite elated for the rest of the evening and looked forward to joining them for lunch, which we did the following week. On our arrival we were greeted by a smiling, purring grey tabby cat that followed us around, chatting amicably as we explored the surroundings with shared sensations of envy and admiration. Someone, a lover of gardens who turned out to be Lee, had transformed the narrow rocky space into a charming, semi-cultivated garden between the olives and clumps of indigenous shrubs. She had planted little pockets of nasturtiums and seedlings in the dark earth against winding stone pathways; the narrow borders were flanked by low stone walls that held pots of bright marigolds, wallflowers, purple and mauve daises, shy white cyclamen and violets flowering in secret nooks. Just my sort of garden, so full of surprises and unexpected combinations of cottage garden plants.

Sitting beneath a huge sun umbrella with the sound of crashing waves on all sides at the base of the cliffs, we quaffed heady village wine and whiled away the afternoon hours enjoying Lee's delicious chicken pasta and salad. I felt replete in every sense and delighted to be sitting with new friends sharing their interests and experiences; I felt I never wanted to move ever again. Later, much later, we were persuaded to go for a jaunt in their boat over water so clear it was as though it was not there at all—but for the miraculous shades of turquoise and the fish darting about beneath us. We moored by a sandy half-moon beach where a small herd of goats stood as if paralysed, as we chugged towards them. The little bay at the base of the dominating red cliffs could only be reached by boat and Lee told us she had seen goats drinking from the shallows and assumed they had fallen down the cliff, but when they heard us, they scampered straight up the perpendicular slopes with ease. The seawater was icy cold laced with fresh water fed by springs, the source presumably being from above the cliffs and these intelligent animals were evidently aware of this.

*

I must say being invited into their enticing little hide-away and sharing their lifestyle has fired our desire to buy somewhere in the Deep Mani, but it is going to have to be as close to the sea as their place is. Whether we will or not, is another matter.

Tis all a Chequer-board of Nights and Days
Where Destiny with Men for Pieces plays:
Hither and thither moves, and mates, and slays.
And one by one back in the Closet lays.
(Omar Khayyam from The Rubáiyát)

***

το τέλος